Intimate and Personal Care with People with Learning Disabilities

Intimate and Personal Care with People with Learning Disabilities

*Edited by Steven Carnaby
and Paul Cambridge*

Jessica Kingsley Publishers
London and Philadelphia

First published in 2006
by Jessica Kingsley Publishers
116 Pentonville Road
London N1 9JB, UK
and
400 Market Street, Suite 400
Philadelphia, PA 19106, USA

www.jkp.com

Library of Congress Cataloging in Publication Data
Intimate and personal care with people with learning disabilities / edited by Steven Carnaby and
Paul Cambridge.
    p. cm.
Includes bibliographical references and index.
ISBN-13: 978-1-84310-130-7 (pbk. : alk. paper)
ISBN-10: 1-84310-130-0 (pbk. : alk. paper) 1. Learning disabled--Care. I. Carnaby, Steven.
II. Cambridge, Paul, 1952-
RC394.L37I58 2006
362.196'85889--dc22

                    2006006231

British Library Cataloguing in Publication Data
A CIP catalogue record for this book is available from the British Library

ISBN-13: 978 1 84310 130 7
ISBN-10: 1 84310 130 0

Printed and bound in Great Britain by
Athenaeum Press, Gateshead, Tyne and Wear

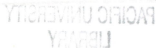

Contents

List of Tables

List of Figures

CHAPTER 1

Introduction

Steven Carnaby and Paul Cambridge

The principle of ordinary living continues to drive the agenda for improving the quality of service provision for people with learning disabilities (Caine, Hatton and Emerson 1998; Ericsson 2005; King's Fund 1980; Mansell 2005), enabling discussion about what constitutes good practice when supporting individuals in many areas of daily living. Much of the research assessing the implementation of service policy uses the Five Service Accomplishments (e.g. Carnaby 2002; Emerson 1992; O'Brien and Tyne 1981) as a framework for analysis, with national policy (Department of Health 2001) using the summary euphemisms of choice and social inclusion as objectives and person centred planning as a policy instrument (see Cambridge and Carnaby 2005; Mansell and Beadle-Brown 2004).

Research has considered in turn the ways in which services are demonstrating a commitment to enabling choice, participation, a presence in the community, and affording people respect. For example, Stalker and Harris (1998) review ways in which people with learning disabilities are being supported to make choices, while Myers *et al.* (1998) review the extent to which those using services can be regarded as being 'present' in their communities.

Such evidence reveals that much more needs to be achieved before people with learning disabilities can be said to be fully integrated into society (Carnaby 1998), particularly those with profound and multiple learning disabilities who remain excluded from many of the most basic and ordinary aspects of decision-making in their lives. In addition, however, a body of research into sexuality and sexual abuse reveals that many more able people with learning disabilities, are vulnerable to abuse or exploitation in their community presence and interactions (Brown, Stein and Turk 1995; Cambridge 1997; McCarthy and Thompson 1997). Many of these experiences reflect how people without learning disabilities stigmatise and perceive people with learning disabilities, but also how people with learning disabilities see themselves negatively as people with disability whom society does not like. For example, important support and service response issues have been recognised in relation to how women with learning disabilities see their bodies and appearance in negative ways (McCarthy 1998) and the role of female staff in relation to men with learning disabilities who have difficult sexual behaviour (Thompson, Clare and Brown 1997). Such considerations impact directly on how intimate and personal care may be provided and experienced.

A central issue emerging from the literature is a general failure to recognise the diversity and heterogeneity of the learning-disabled population (Carnaby 1999; McGill 2005). People able to secure supported employment, travel independently and make informed choices about their sexual relationships will have very different needs and experiences from those requiring significant support in all area of their lives (Lacey 1998). People with learning disabilities at both ends of this continuum may require support for intimate and personal care, for example, the man with a mild learning disability who also happens to have a severe physical disability and the woman with a profound and multiple learning disability who is totally dependent on others for everything. In recognition of such widely varying characteristics and needs, some call for a review of expectations regarding ordinary living principles as they are applied to people with high support needs, which can be complex and often involve additional physical and/or sensory disabilities (Smith 1994). Designing services for a diverse group such as people with learning disabilities aims for inclusive support structures and an equitable, 'ordinary' approach. However, it is likely that a reluctance to acknowledge the extent to which some individuals need particular types of support – in key areas of their lives – where notions of independence and autonomy are essentially inappropriate, puts those individuals at risk of discrimination (Bartlett and Bunning 1997), in that in reality they may not receive support at a level and intensity that they require. Combating discrimination is not only about treating people equally, it is also about providing equitable support, tailored and targeted according to sometimes widely varying needs.

'ORDINARY' LIVING AND INTIMATE SUPPORT

A key area for people with learning disabilities, particularly those with high support needs, is intimate and personal care and yet it is an area of management and practice that remains relatively invisible, being largely ignored in the learning disability literature. It is an aspect of life that is still taboo in many societies, sitting uncomfortably within the 'ordinary living' philosophy. This is partly explained by the difficult territory – it raises issues that confront us as human beings and that may be compounded by a sense of powerlessness to affect change. We are conditioned through medical models to think in terms of curing disability, rather than finding ways to accept and acknowledge disability as difference. Intimate and personal care is consequently often at the sharp end of promoting social models of disability and may indeed be seen as a microcosm of the issues relating to disability politics more widely (Oliver 1990; Shakespeare, Gillespie-Sills and Davies 1996).

Individual care interactions are undoubtedly political. Humanists wishing to provide intimate and personal care in a kind and thoughtful way might seek to better understand how someone with a learning disability receiving intimate and personal care feels about themselves and how they experience particular care interactions, trying to place themselves in such a position. However, this approach imports a non-disabled assumptive world into the lives and experiences of people with learning disabilities. Our perceptions are coloured by a society that tends to devalue differences, usually devalues disability and certainly devalues dependency of the type and level of most people who need support with intimate and personal care.

Shifting from societal and political context to consider individual subjective experience, it can be argued that intimate and personal care for people with learning disabilities lies at the foundation (and perhaps permeates most levels) of what can be described as a 'hierarchy of needs' (Maslow 1970).

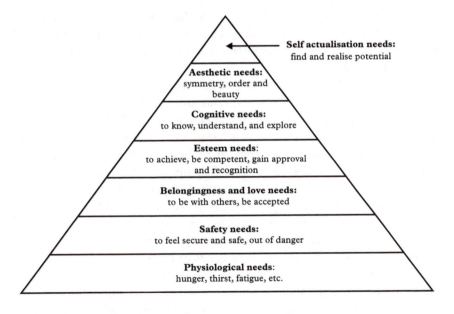

Figure 1.1 Maslow's hierarchy of human needs, adapted from Maslow (1970)

As Maslow suggests, Figure 1.1 indicates that an individual's physiological needs create the basis of a pyramid that progressively builds through other needs relating to safety, belongingness, esteem, understanding and finally self-actualisation. This model is used by a number of health and social care providers to illustrate their commitment to the 'whole' person and their individual potential for development. In this context, meeting intimate and personal care needs can be considered at each and every level of such a hierarchy. The management of continence is a physiological need when thought about in terms of physical comfort and bodily care, but the ways in which it is provided are also likely to impact upon an individual's sense of personal safety and security – particularly if there is exposure to abusive practice. In turn, having one's intimate support needs sensitively acknowledged is an integral part of feeling that one belongs and is accepted by others. It might be argued, therefore, that if we struggle with ensuring that we get intimate care practice 'right', it does not augur well for our practice in supporting other areas of people's lives that are perhaps more visible and readily monitored.

Service providers have often been left to grapple with the issues without clear guidance and where guidance does exist, it often refers to the physical aspects of intimate and personal care. Examples include the use of aids and adaptations, health and hygiene issues such as avoiding cross-infection (Cambridge and Carnaby 2000) or task identification and completion – without guidance on exactly how to undertake tasks. These issues are clearly crucial to fulfilling a duty of care, but limit the scope for viewing intimate and personal care as an opportunity for quality interaction within the context of a consistent and inclusive support model.

Failing to establish competencies in intimate and personal care provision risks the development of inconsistent, value-laden and therefore institutionalised care practices. In addition, the social taboos surrounding intimate care in particular provide a context within which staff are not accustomed to discussing concerns about intimate care practice, and where guidelines and policies are vague and too generalised to serve a specific purpose. Acknowledging diversity of culture and ethnicity also raises issues about competence and the appropriateness of particular intimate and personal care practices (Cambridge and Carnaby 2000). The risks of such fractures in practice and quality are particularly evident when working with service users who need support to participate in their own care or who do not communicate their needs or preferences in standard ways. The former tasks are also arguably the least valued of roles in health and social care, affording the lowest status in the labour market. Currently, services tend to reinforce this view by ignoring the need to train staff effectively and the importance of opening debates at service, team and supervision levels in relation to specific care tasks or individual clients about what constitutes effective, individualised and appropriate practices.

This book explores these issues in a number of ways. Part 1 focuses on the wider context of intimate and personal care provision. First, there is important recognition that those providing intimate support are often not specifically trained in this important area of practice and as crucially, tend not to be offered opportunities to reflect on the necessarily intrusive role that they play in people's lives and the feelings and responses these confront and generate. In Chapter 2, we describe research we carried out with support workers who talked about how they felt in this role, and their need to interpret (and sometimes invent) generic policy and guidance. Our key observation is that in a worse case scenario, untrained, perhaps inexperienced staff are being asked to provide the most intimate of support, sometimes to the most vulnerable members of our society who are unlikely to be able to express their perspective on this situation in standard ways, let alone disclose abuse, mistreatment or neglect. The acknowledgement of this (in our view) unacceptable situation sets the scene for the remainder of the book's more detailed analysis of intimate and personal care practice and provision, in terms of specific key issues and their impact on the ways that care is offered to particular groups of people with learning disabilities.

The first key issue concerns ethnicity and culture, discussed by Robina Shah (Chapter 3), who provides a useful overview of the social construction of race, ethnicity and culture in relation to people from minority ethnic communities with learning disabilities and their carers, focusing in particular on issues of social inequality and disadvantage. Her critique of some of the attempts at recognising cultural and ethnic diversity concludes with an emphasis on intimate and personal care practice, suggesting that developing culturally sensitive provision is likely to be complex and challenging but ultimately feasible.

Michelle McCarthy and Paul Cambridge turn to issues relating to the interface between sexuality and intimate and personal care in Chapter 4. By describing ways in which intimate and personal care practice directly relates to issues concerning sexual parts of the body, sexual expression and the constructed perceptions surrounding sexual behaviour, this chapter reflects on the particular contexts for individuals (both supporters and those being supported) as experienced due to their gender and sexuality. In addition, time is spent outlining response to inappropriate sexual behaviour that might emerge during intimate and personal care, emphasising the importance of thorough assessment and consistent boundary setting that gives everybody clear messages about what is and is not acceptable in intimate environments.

In Chapter 5, Paul Wheeler and Neil James discuss a third important general area for contemplation: health and hygiene. This chapter presents the evidence underpinning the argument that people with learning disabilities are more vulnerable to health inequalities for reasons much broader than those relating simply to impaired cognition. By outlining the 'health' element of health and social care in this way, the authors assert the need for particular attention being paid to the maintenance of personal hygiene in order to enable people with acknowledged vulnerabilities to poor health to live comfortable lives of acceptable quality. In addition, they place intimate and personal care within the legal context in relation to key concepts such as capacity and consent as particularly important given the complexities raised in preceding chapters.

The first section of the book concludes with a discussion of the role played by policies and procedures in the delivery of intimate and personal care. In Chapter 6, Paul Cambridge presents the policy context relating to adult protection in particular and develops a critique of policy implementation, leading to the proposal that learning from this experience needs to directly inform the production of a robust policy framework in order to ensure the delivery of high quality, safe intimate and personal care practice. It is concluded that only by acknowledging the complexities encountered in this important area of service delivery and its interface with emotive issues such as abuse, sexuality and neglect can those responsible for writing policy be sure that they have done all that is possible in safeguarding the vulnerable – service users and workers alike.

Part 2 concentrates more explicitly on practice issues. In Chapter 7 we aim to provide a context for discussion of the nature of provision by taking a critical look at the characteristics of multi-disciplinary working. People with learning disabilities living in the community are likely to receive at least some support from professionals linked with a local community team, and it is argued here that the ways in which these teams are organised and configured is crucial in terms of ensuring quality outcomes for service users. This is even more significant when support is offered around complex areas of daily living such as intimate and personal care. It is suggested that by encouraging people to work across rather than within professional disciplines, a more holistic approach regarding assessment and intervention is likely to result.

Chapters 8 to 11 discuss intimate and personal care needs and practice in relation to particular groups or characteristics of people with learning disabilities, thought to require particular attention. Neil James and Paul Wheeler present an account of how people with mild learning disabilities can be supported with intimate and personal care within the context of teaching independent living skills. They provide practical guidance on how this might be achieved, giving particular examples of teaching programmes. The emphasis here is on the likely relationship between appearance, independence, autonomy and self-esteem, and perhaps focuses on tasks we have described as being 'personal' rather than 'intimate' care. In contrast, Chapter 9 concentrates on people with profound and multiple learning disabilities who are likely to require total assistance in many areas of their lives. This chapter argues the importance of encouraging staff and other supporters to think about 'planned dependence' to some extent. This perhaps removes some of the pressure – implicit in the principle of normalisation – to teach independent living skills to the detriment of both the individual with disabilities and the members of staff supporting them. Within this context, individual needs are reframed and valued as they stand. The chapter offers guidance with regard to good practice, with specific reference to involving service users as much as possible in the process of intimate care, especially when their physical needs determine that others do 'to' them.

Chapters 10 and 11 develop perspectives on intimate and personal care across the lifespan. Steven Carnaby and Angela Mallett report on a training initiative for staff working with children and young people with learning disabilities originally developed from the research reported in Chapter 2. Training participants reported a wide range of concerns and dilemmas, some relating to contrasts between the settings in which children and young people are supported and others relating to the particular boundary issues encountered in working with children in such intimate ways. The chapter concludes with some suggestions for good practice. In Chapter 11, Eleni Hatzidimitriadou and Alisoun Milne outline outline issues for older adults with learning disabilities, calling for the need to raise the profile of a growing and ageing population, which presents unique and specific challenges to service providers, particularly in the area of intimate and personal care. Again, the authors present a range of principles for developing good practice.

Our final chapter reflects on the wide and diverse range of issues, concerns and dilemmas raised by contributors, observing that a number of common themes emerge from these various discussions. In reviewing these themes, we provide a final overview that attempts to address both policy and practice gaps in the delivery of intimate and personal care. In so doing we hope that we will enable readers with interests in promoting the provision of high quality service for people with learning disabilities to develop and build effective local strategies and individual responses.

REFERENCES

Bartlett, C. and Bunning, K.T. (1997) 'The importance of communication partnerships: a study to investigate the communicative exchanges between staff and adults with intellectual disabilities.' *British Journal of Intellectual Disabilities 25*, 148–153.

Brown, H., Stein, J. and Turk, V. (1995) 'The sexual abuse of adults with learning disabilities: report of a second two-year incidence survey.' *Mental Handicap Research 8*, 1, 1–22.

Caine, A., Hatton, C. and Emerson, E. (1998) 'Service provision.' In E. Emerson, C. Hatton, J. Bromley and A. Caine (eds) *Clinical Psychology and People with Intellectual Disabilties.* Chichester: Wiley.

Cambridge, P. (1997) 'How far to gay? The politics of HIV in intellectual disability.' *Disability & Society 12*, 3, 427–453.

Cambridge, P. and Carnaby, S. (2000) *Making it Personal: Providing Intimate and Personal Care for People with Intellectual Disabilities.* Brighton: Pavilion.

Carnaby, S. (1998) 'Reflections on social integration for people with intellectual disability: does interdependence have a role?' *Journal of Intellectual and Developmental Disability 23*, 3, 219–229.

Carnaby, S. (1999) *Designs for Living: A Comparative Approach to Normalisation for the New Millennium.* Aldershot: Ashgate Press.

Carnaby, S. (2002) 'The bigger picture.' In S. Carnaby (ed.) *Learning Disability Today.* Brighton: Pavillion Publishing.

Department of Health (2001) *Valuing People: A New Strategy for Learning Disability for the 21st Century.* London: Department of Health.

Emerson, E. (1992) 'What is normalisation?' In H. Brown and H. Smith (eds) *Normalisation: A Reader for the Nineties.* London: Routledge.

Ericsson, K. (2005) 'The institution of the mind – the final challenge.' *Tizard Learning Disability Review 10*, 1, 57–61.

King's Fund (1980) *An Ordinary Life: Comprehensive Locally Based Residential Services for Mentally Handicapped People.* London: King's Fund Centre.

Lacey, P. (1998) 'Meeting complex needs through collaborative multi-disciplinary teamwork.' In P. Lacey and C. Ouvray (eds) *People with Profound and Multiple Intellectual Disabilities: A Collaborative Approach to Meeting Complex Needs.* London: David Fulton Publishers.

Mansell, J. (2005) 'Deinstitutionalisation and community living: an international perspective.' *Tizard Learning Disability Review 10*, 1, 22–29.

Mansell, J. and Beadle-Brown, J. (2004) 'Person-centred planning or person-centred action? Policy and practive in intellectual disability services.' *Journal of Applied Research in Intellectual Disabilities 17*, 1–10.

Maslow, A. (1970) *Motivation and Personality,* Second Edition. New York: Harper & Row.

McCarthy, M. (1998) 'Whose body is it anyway? Pressures and control for women with intellectual disabilities.' *Disability & Society 13*, 4, 557–574.

McCarthy, M. and Thompson, D. (1997) 'Prevalence study of sexual abuse amongst people with intellectual disabilities referred for sex education.' *Journal of Applied Research in Intellectual Disabilities 10*, 2, 105–124.

McGill, P. (2005) 'Models of community care in the UK: past and present.' *Tizard Learning Disability Review 10*, 1, 46–51.

Myers, F., Ager, A., Kerr, P. and Myles, S. (1998) 'Outside looking in? Studies of the community integration of people with intellectual disabilities.' *Disability & Society 133*, 3, 389–343.

O'Brien, J. and Tyne, A. (1981) *The Principle of Normalisation: A Foundation for Effective Services.* London: The Campaign for Mentally Handicapped People.

Oliver, M. (1990) *The Politics of Disablement.* London: Macmillan.

Shakespeare, T., Gillespie-Sills, L. and Davies, D. (1996) *The Sexual Politics of Disability: Untold Desires.* London: Cassell.

Smith, B. (1994) 'An ordinary life for people with an intellectual disability and sensory impairment?' *British Journal of Intellectual Disabilities 22*, 140–143.

Stalker, K. and Harris, P. (1998) 'The exercise of choice by adults with intellectual disabilities: a literature review.' *Journal of Applied Research in Intellectual Disability 11*, 1, 60–76.

Thompson, D., Clare, I. and Brown, H. (1997) 'Not such an ordinary relationship: the role of women support staff in relation to men with learning disabilities who have difficult sexual behaviour.' *Disability & Society 12*, 4, 573–592.

Part 1

The Context of Intimate and Personal Care Provision

CHAPTER 2

Staff Attitudes and Perspectives

Steven Carnaby and Paul Cambridge

INTRODUCTION

Despite being a major area of support and provision for people with learning disabilities, particularly those with additional sensory or physical disabilities, intimate and personal care has been widely neglected in terms of good practice development. The body of relevant published research is also fairly limited. In the absence of clear guidance and consensus, our starting point in attempting to address this important area was the personal experiences, values, assumptions and expectations of those providing care for people with learning disabilities. In this chapter, we revisit the ground-breaking initial research that set out to review staff attitudes and perspectives in order to assess the ways in which they might impact on practice.

THE WIDER LITERATURE ON INTIMATE AND PERSONAL CARE

Broadly speaking, the intimate and personal care literature falls into one of two main approaches. The social deconstruction of personal care provision tasks such as the bath (Sloane *et al.* 1995; Twigg 1997) leads to interesting commentaries on personal boundaries and an important appraisal of concepts such as 'dependency' and 'intimacy'. Medical perspectives reference, for example, the importance of genital hygiene (e.g. Cantu 2000) but tend to do so outside a consideration of social factors. Studies relating specifically to people with learning disabilities tend to focus on key areas – for example menstruation (e.g. Carlson and Wilson 1996; Epps, Prescott and Horner 1990) – but tend to do so without placing the issues within any wider perspective on intimate and personal care.

RESEARCH AS A TOOL FOR WIDENING DEBATE

Our initial research, leading to the publication of the staff training resource pack *Making it Personal* (Cambridge and Carnaby 2000) set out to open a debate and explore staff experiences and perceptions, rather than provide a comprehensive and detailed analysis of staff behaviour and attitudes. Our key research questions were as follows:

- How do staff define intimate and personal care and what care tasks do staff include under these headings?

- How do staff rate different intimate and personal care tasks in terms of satisfaction and what are the differences in how staff perceive and experience different tasks?

- What evidence is there that personal experience (such as gender, culture and sexuality) or other influences (e.g. views of partners or relatives) affect these perceptions, and in what ways?

- What are the differences in how individual members of staff approach the intimate and personal care needs of particular individuals and what are the explanations for these?

In this first case study, the staff participating in the research were working in a specialist unit within a day centre or a specialist residential service for people with profound and multiple learning disabilities. Both services supported individuals who required total assistance with intimate care. There were two main components to data collection:

1. Interviews with staff, organised into two parts: (a) a short interview aimed at eliciting personal attitudes towards intimate and personal care and (b) a service user-centred interview. The latter aimed to identify the similarities and differences between the ways intimate and personal care was provided by different members of staff provided to the same individual. Both interviews used questionnaires devised by the authors (see Appendices 1–3 at the end of the book).

2. Review and content analysis of service policies, care plans and mission statements.

Throughout the interviews, specific tasks were categorised as either 'intimate care' or 'personal care'. This list was generated during an earlier workshop with practitioners working with people with learning disabilities, from a range of services across Britain (Carnaby 1998). These tasks are listed and categorised in Table 2.1.

In addition, a range of tasks were identified that relate functionally to the provision of intimate and personal care, but that do not necessarily involve direct contact with service users. These include changing soiled laundry and cleaning up various body fluids and body products – vomit, faeces, urine and blood.

Table 2.1 Classification of intimate and personal care tasks

Intimate care tasks	Personal care tasks
Dressing and undressing (underwear)	Shaving
Helping someone use the toilet	Skin care or applying external medication
Changing continence pads soiled with faeces	
	Hair care
Changing continence pads soiled with urine	Help with feeding
	Brushing teeth
Bathing or showering	Applying deodorant
Washing intimate parts of the body, i.e. genitalia	Dressing and undressing (clothing other than underwear)
Menstrual care	Washing non-intimate body parts
Administering enemas	Prompting to go to the toilet or bathroom
Administering rectal medication	

FINDINGS FROM THE CASE STUDY

Views on policy and practice links

All of the day unit staff interviewed were aware of a policy for intimate and personal care, but reported that the policy was general rather than particular and lacked individualised information. Overall it was felt that the policy failed to reference to relevant standards or expectations, other than offering statements such as support 'with dignity and respect' and the requirement for the provision of 'same-gender care' practice. While the team offered same-gender support as much as possible, there were incidences of women offering support to male service users as a result of staff sickness or other circumstances affecting the availability of male staff and the gender distribution within the team. It was also noted however, that male staff never provided intimate support for female service users. Overall, respondents felt the policy document was inadequate, suggesting that more credence was given to individual care plans drafted by the key-workers or individual service users. Such care plans tended to emphasise and state the *kind* of support needed (such as changing continence pads) and its frequency (such as after lunch and before getting on the service transport to go home). However, they also generally failed to make adequate reference to *how* the service user concerned was to be supported during such care tasks and *how* specific tasks should be undertaken.

In contrast, none of the residential service staff interviewed were aware of a general policy for intimate and personal care. They reported that in practice *implicit* guidelines appeared to be in place – for example, closing the door when changing an individual's continence pad, or informing the individual about what is to happen. There was consequently more reliance on 'word of mouth' in terms of following 'accepted practice':

> One [member of staff] teaches the other one…you can't do your own thing, you have to follow everyone else, to change, to move them. It's different for each one of them.

Support worker job descriptions referenced issues such as 'lifting and handling' and suggested that intimate and personal care needs should be 'delivered with dignity'. The staff we spoke to felt that such descriptions were too vague and that more detailed and specific guidance was required, recognising and reflecting the significant time that can be spent by staff engaged with providing intimate care and the central importance of such work in supporting residents with learning disabilities.

Staff also identified some obvious practice risks and gaps – where policy failed to be explicit or was not underpinned by practice guidelines for individuals. One participant talked about personal interpretation:

> the bit about cleaning under the foreskin is not written down anywhere. The care plan says ensure genitals and anus are clean, but this leaves me to interpret [what I need to do] based on my own standards and knowledge of hygiene.

There was also a general recognition by staff that same-gender intimate and personal care policies have in-built shortcomings, being based on sexist and heterosexist assumptions about caring roles and gender. They failed to recognise or respond to the risk of sexual abuse to male service users or neglected the risk of physical abuse more widely. Indeed the latter can become particularly acute when staff are untrained and poorly supported (Cambridge 1999). In particular they tended to ignore the needs of lesbian and gay identified staff who were expected to undertake same-gender care within the blanket policy:

Same-gender intimate care does nothing to protect them [gay men]. As an out lesbian within the team, I also find working intimately with women difficult and sometimes wonder what my colleagues are thinking.

Staff members' previous experience in providing intimate and personal care

In both services, experience of providing intimate and personal care varied greatly – for some their current post was the first experience they had encountered of providing such support and one participant had worked with older adults with dementia for seven years. Other respondents had the experience of bringing up their own children or providing informal care for partners or parents. They commented that such experience has been a valuable asset for informing their approach to and conduct of intimate and personal care work for people with profound and multiple learning disabilities, particularly in the absence of clear policies and guidelines but also in relation to their feelings – although the nature of the caring role to someone outside the family sometimes generated different responses. One person had experience of nursing and referred to the 'routine' nature of intimate and personal care.

Training

One of the day unit staff team had trained as a psychiatric nurse, while other team members had all completed in-service training in topics as diverse as food handling, communication, basic first aid and disability awareness. When asked specifically about intimate and personal care, one participant reported a meeting with a community nurse who had facilitated a discussion about practice issues and attitudes.

Some of the in-house courses and workshops described by respondents are likely to have had clear practice and theoretical links with intimate and personal care practice – for example, lifting and handling, first aid, health and hygiene and communication. However, respondents reported no explicit references to intimate and personal care practice during any of this training. In contrast, it was observed to be a regular component to nurse training, focusing on the effective functioning of intimate care tasks.

All of the permanent residential staff interviewed had considerable experience in providing intimate and personal care for people with learning disabilities, people with physical disabilities and/or older people with dementia, ranging from two-and-a-half to six years. This particular service utilised a relatively high proportion of long-term agency staff in the team and it was noted that some individual agency staff were relatively inexperienced (for example, their second assignment in learning disabilities and their first with people with profound and multiple learning disabilities). Staff availability and turnover are central factors in helping to explain the use of agency staff. Addressing such factors is consequently relevant to striving to provide high quality and consistent support to individuals with complex needs (Cambridge and Carnaby 2000b).

General feelings and attitudes about the work

Some of the staff working in the day unit reported that there had not been many opportunities to discuss or think about intimate and personal care from the perspective of individual service users:

> It depends on the person...their behaviour is difficult sometimes. People need different things. It's not until I'm talking to you that I realised what people need...

Others seemed to find it easier to dissociate themselves from such tasks:

> It's a routine, [I] don't really think about it, it's part of the job – a very important part. There's nothing hard about it.

More inexperienced staff members and service managers were however, able to describe their feelings about providing intimate care and place these into context:

> Initially, [I had] mixed feelings. As you go along, it becomes second nature, the importance of what you're doing, making things more comfortable for people, has more significance. I started off thinking I couldn't do it for any length of time, now I realise I can.

Overall, the staff members interviewed tended to take an empathic approach, reporting that they aimed to provide care in ways that they would want or expect themselves, should they ever need such support. The importance of respect and dignity was recognised, but the only tangible way in which such values seemed able to be translated to practice, was in terms of the conduct of intimate and personal care in appropriate safe and private places and informing service users about what was happening, or about to happen. The latter was also thought to give service users greater 'control' or 'involvement' over the tasks and process of intimate care delivery.

The residential staff team reported that a very significant part of their working lives was spent providing intimate and personal care. Despite this they also felt that it was not a part of their job that was really recognised to be important or that they had been well prepared for:

> It took a while to get used to it...very few people go into this work knowing what it's like. It's having to adapt to things and dealing with stuff that can be unpleasant. But you don't get the same training as if you were a nurse. You get to a point where you do become blasé about it because you

do it so often. I don't think it gets to a point where you *enjoy* doing it – but if you don't do it, nobody else will.

Attitudes and preferences about specific tasks

Overall, staff expressed a more positive attitude towards the personal care tasks they undertook, compared with intimate care. Different intimate care tasks were generally rated higher than personal care tasks in terms of dissatisfaction – reflecting greater dislike and less job satisfaction compared with personal care (Table 2.2). This is also evident in the aggregate average ratings for intimate and personal care tasks. There were some tasks in intimate care (such as dressing and undressing of underclothes) which were rated less negatively, but these were more akin to personal care and were similar in their ratings to personal care tasks. Some intimate care tasks were particularly disliked and highly rated negatively (such as bathing and showering and washing genitalia and menstrual care [for the day service] and the administration of enemas [for the residential service].

Personal care tasks most disliked were shaving and brushing teeth for the residential service, although ratings only approached the average for intimate care tasks. Most interesting, was the consistently high ratings (dislike) for the tasks associated with intimate and personal care that are to do with cleaning up body products without personal contact with service users. Task-specific and average aggregate ratings were highest for the residential service in this category. The findings are summarised in Table 2.2.

The basic dichotomy emerging between care categorised here as 'personal' versus care categorised as 'intimate' arguably mirrors wider negative social constructs about dependency and dependency relationships in society. This is reflected in some of the wider observations made by staff about their work. Intimate care tasks have certain things in common – associations with bodily functions, body products or personal hygiene that require direct or indirect contact with or exposure of the sexual parts of the body. All such factors carry social taboos:

> Intimate care is about hands-on work, which invades accepted personal and social space.

In contrast, personal care, although often involving touching another person, relates to touch that is more socially acceptable. It also generally has the purpose of helping with personal presentation and hence social functioning. By comparison with intimate care, such tasks are more socially valued.

However, intimate care tasks could also be differentiated in their task-specific ratings. In this category, tasks associated with basic bodily functions, such as continence management, or those tasks needing more intrusive action

Table 2.2 Summary of average participant ratings of job satisfaction from intimate care tasks, personal care tasks and tasks associated with intimate and personal care

Intimate care task	Average rating		Personal care task	Average rating		Associated tasks	Average rating	
	Day unit N = 6	Residential service N = 9		Day unit	Residential service		Day unit	Residential service
Dressing/undressing (underclothes)	2.6	3.0	Shaving	1.5	3.3	Changing soiled laundry	3.2	3.8
Helping someone use the toilet	2.6	2.8	Skin care	2.5	2.3	Cleaning up vomit	3.4	4.5
Changing continence pads (faeces)	3.0	3.8	Feeding	2.5	2.3	Cleaning up faeces	3.2	4.0
Changing continence pads (urine)	3.0	3.3	Hair care	2.2	1.8	Cleaning up urine	3.2	3.5
Bathing and showering	4.0	2.0	Brushing teeth	2.3	3.0	Cleaning up blood	3.2	3.8
Washing genitalia	3.8	3.5	Administering deodorant	2.0	2.0	Associated tasks domain (all tasks)	3.2	4.4
Menstrual care	4.3	3.5	Dressing/undressing (outer clothing)	2.8	2.0			
Administering enemas	N/A	5.0	Washing (e.g. face/hands)	2.8	2.5			
Administering rectal medication	N/A	3.0	Prompting to use the toilet	2.6	2.8			
Intimate care domain (all tasks)	3.3	3.3	Personal care domain (all tasks)	2.4	2.5			

Rating: 1 = like very much/high job satisfaction and 5 = dislike very much/very little job satisfaction

from the supporter, such as the use of suppositories, enemas or pessaries, were consistently rated as more negative by staff and were said to be more difficult or uncomfortable to carry out than tasks such as washing or bathing, where the person is effectively cleansed. As one participant suggested:

> Try giving someone rectal diazepam in the High Road…We are at a real disadvantage. Nursing uniforms allow you to put your fingers up someone's bottom… We are never given that sort of permission by society or the person concerned.

Figure 2.1 conceptualises the location of intimate and personal care tasks along a continuum from physical dysfunction to the support of positive social functioning. There was also a parallel continuum of staff values and attitudes concerning the conduct of intimate and personal care, ranging from relative dislike to relative like for the associated tasks.

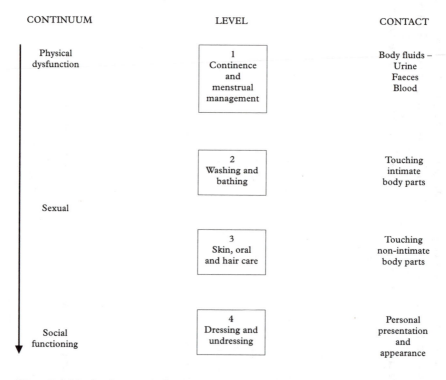

Figure 2.1 Moving between intimate and personal care

Staff stories about the views other people hold about intimate and personal care

Day unit

Respondents were clear about how they thought others perceived their role, with some relating conversations that described them as 'martyrs', providing an essential service that many in the community would feel unable to provide themselves. Significantly, participants also constructed links between attitudes in the community towards their role in providing intimate care, with attitudes towards people with learning disabilities in general:

> The odd person says, 'I don't know how you can do it', but that's not really about personal care, it's about the service user group we work with in general...' I think work should be done on improving people's views and attitudes.

Specialist residential service

The residential team reported similar experiences to their day unit colleagues. In particular, friends and relatives were said to have shown either disbelief:

> the majority think I must be bonkers – why did I take a degree to clean up [other people's bottoms]? Some think I should have a pat on the back, but most think 'I couldn't do that'.

Or admiration:

> they think I'm better than this – I'm an angel for doing it; I shouldn't waste my time on people like this. They don't try and find out what the job's about and why I like it.

Respondents considered that such views about their role were related to wider societal views about the relatively low social status attached to providing intimate care, also reflected in their relatively low economic status of care work in the labour market. Moreover, other professionals within social care and learning disability were also seen to perpetuate such attitudes, some seemingly not recognising the centrality of intimate care to their work and to the lives of many people with learning disabilities. These included senior managers within commissioning and providing services as well as key professionals:

> The GP sees our users as expensive and undeserving consumers. When we talked with him about a service user defecating everywhere, he didn't believe it.

Some respondents consequently reference status hierarchies within disability more widely and learning disability in particular, voicing the view that people with learning disabilities and those requiring intimate support were at the bottom of such hierarchies.

Staff views on training

There was no complacency from either service in relation to respondents' views on their own training needs or performance in delivering intimate and personal care. The majority of those interviewed felt that they were 'doing well given the circumstances', referring to their perception of a lack of support for their work and a reluctance by management to recognise the significance of intimate and personal care. This underlines the reliance of staff on their own strategies and other members of the team for introducing criteria for good practice in this area.

When asked to list the qualities needed by staff who were expected or required to provide intimate and personal care, respondents included common sense, empathy (namely 'treating people with respect and dignity; to be able to think about people's needs and not just see the [day centre] as a toilet'); sensitivity and patience. However, many staff were also in a position to reference specific skills deficits and specify areas where more help and guidance was required in relation to enabling more effective and productive intimate and personal care practice. Communication, in particular, emerged as a critical area of concern:

> I want help to work out the messages I'm getting from vocalisation, eye contact, body language, and what look like signs of some sort.

SERVICE USER-CENTRED INTERVIEWS WITH STAFF

The service user-centred interviews aimed to gain a sense and understanding of the degree of consistency between how different staff members provided intimate support to the same service user. In both settings, it was observed that while responses relating to the *type* of task required to meet an individual's intimate care needs largely concurred, there was significant variation between different accounts of *how* the tasks were usually conducted. These differences can be described in terms of the following:

- *The language used to inform individuals about what is happening or about to happen to them.* Staff members used different phrases to describe the same care task or interaction – for example: 'I'm going to freshen you up' and 'I'm using the wash cream now' were used by different staff members to inform the same individual that her genitals were being cleaned.

- *The order in which tasks were carried out.* Staff used different approaches and processes for undertaking the same task – for example, one member of staff might remove a pad and dispose of it before applying wash cream, whilst another might lift the person's legs while washing them with the pad only partly removed.

- *The pace at which tasks were completed.* Some staff members felt it important to leave individuals for a few moments to become aware that they were on a changing bench, whilst others felt it best to complete the work as quickly as possible so that the individual could return to their previous activity.

A key similarity between the two services, revealed from the service user-centred interviews, was the absence of formal assessments of an individual's communication skills. The only approach observed in both services was the focus on informing people, where informing was equated with user 'control' or 'involvement' in the care task – an example presented by staff during the interviews was the 'running commentary' for service users who do not communicate using language:

> OK John, let's see now... I'm just going to pull your trousers down now, and see if your pad needs changing. That's it, right, now your underpants. OK John? Now, I think you need freshening up a bit... I'll just get some wash cream on the glove...that's it...this might be a bit cold, John...that's it...OK?... Right, I'll just move your leg this way...

While such an approach is likely to assist in generating a warm atmosphere between the staff member and the service user, and may help put the staff member at ease, it cannot be assumed that such a commentary is meeting its intended goal of 'involving' or indeed 'informing' the service user about what is happening or about to happen.

The absence of assessment of communication skills also meant that no adaptations or augmentative tools were being used to increase service users' awareness of their intimate care environments. The residential service in particular did not seem to view the intimate care setting as a potentially interactive environment within which staff could develop positive, quality relationships with the individuals they were supporting. Similarly, in both services, no tangible measures had been taken to increase the extent to which service users could have an element of control over the proceedings.

At a more theoretical level, relatively abstract concepts such as dignity and respect were referenced to simple and tangible devices, such as intimate care delivery in private places, outside clear operational guidance for their translation into practice. This often raised new dilemmas for staff and services, with tensions emerging between privacy and safety in relation to the demands of adult protection or the monitoring of quality (Cambridge and Carnaby 2000a). Tensions relating to issues of race, religion and culture also surfaced, with staff tending to feel unease about the cultural appropriateness of some intimate care practices based on White European norms for all service users (Cambridge and Carnaby 2000b).

DISCUSSION

This small-scale, exploratory study has raised some initial questions about the ways in which people with high support needs are helped with intimate care in perhaps the most vulnerable areas of their lives. The staff interviewed in both services reported feeling unsupported and devalued by service managers but also by their friends and family. Guidance tended only to be provided in the form of generic policies that largely failed to take account of the diversity and range of tasks required to adequately meet what are often very complex and pervasive needs They also did not adequately address adult protection beyond sexual abuse, the reality of caring across gender from women workers to male service users, the use of agency staff or considerations of cultural diversity.

The authors are still working on the results of a study of intimate and personal care provided to children and young people with learning disabilities in school and residential and respite settings, which shows similar findings. Here however, child protection concerns surfaced at a level adult protection concerns did not in adult services:

> I feel it can be an intrusive act and worry about child protection.

> I don't worry about doing it, only about someone saying I have abused someone whilst doing it.

Although it was observed that the older the young person was the easier it was to work out what the person would like or not like, such as having the door closed or a male or female providing the care, most staff voiced concerns about providing intimate and personal care during puberty – while it was observed as normal to wipe a young child's bottom as part of the nurturing process, it proved difficult for staff to relate this to older children. Female staff also referenced fears about providing intimate and personal care to older boys and male staff fears about comforting when the child was upset or distressed.

Overall, while staff attitudes towards the work appear to vary, the trend is that people find more intrusive, intimate tasks more challenging to carry out than those that are less intrusive and more to do with personal care. This is probably intuitive, in that society is often accepting of support required to enable individuals to look presentable. However, the provision of intimate tasks involving continence and other aspects of health are hidden from the mainstream of society, and unless staff entering the field of social and health care have been informal carers, they are less likely to have encountered the issues relating to the care of adults in this way before.

Acknowledging and then addressing this potential for inexperience must be on the agenda for those developing good practice in intimate and personal care. Without doing so, services run a higher risk of authorising support that is provided by people who have not had the opportunity to reflect on how they will be carrying out the work or how the work in turn might be affecting them personally. In both instances, the end result may well be a poorer standard of insistent provision and a workforce left open and vulnerable to a range of complex and challenging situations. The starting point is to make intimate and personal care more visible in job and person specifications and recruitment processes and ongoing support, training and staff development. Laying this foundation will then enable the development of person-centred quality intimate and personal care interactions.

ACKNOWLEDGEMENTS

This chapter is based on research first published in Carnaby and Cambridge (2002).

REFERENCES

Cambridge, P. (1999) 'The first hit: a case study of the physical abuse of people with intellectual disabilities and challenging behaviours in a residential service.' *Disability & Society 14*, 3, 285–308.

Cambridge, P. and Carnaby, S. (2000a) 'A personal touch? Managing the risks of abuse in intimate and personal care for people with intellectual disabilities.' *Journal of Adult Protection 4*, 2, 4–16.

Cambridge, P. and Carnaby, S. (2000b) *Making it Personal: Providing Intimate and Personal Care for People with Intellectual Disabilities.* Brighton: Pavilion.

Cantu, S. (2000) 'Phimosis and paraphimosis.' www.emedicine.com/emerg/topic423.htm

Carlson, G. and Wilson, J. (1996) 'Menstrual management and women who have intellectual disabilities: service providers and decision-making.' *Journal of Intellectual and Developmental Disabilities 21*, 1, 39–57.

Carnaby, S. (1998) 'Workshop presentation: issues in intimate and personal care for people with intellectual disabilities.' Second Tizard Intellectual Disability Summer School, University of Kent at Canterbury.

Carnaby, S. (2000) 'Workshop presentation: individual planning in intimate and personal care for people with intellectual disabilities.' Making it Personal national conference, ORT House, London. 13 June.

Carnaby, S. and Cambridge, P. (2002) 'Getting personal: a case study of intimate and personal care practice in services for people with profound and multiple learning disabilities.' *Journal of Intellectual Disability Research 26*, 2, 120–132.

Epps, S., Prescott, A. and Horner, R. (1990) 'Social acceptability of menstrual-care training methods for young women with developmental disabilities.' *Education and Training in Mental Retardation*, March, 33–44.

Sloane, P., Rader, J., Barrick, A., Hoeffer, B., Dwyer, S., McKenzie, D., Lavelle, M., Buckwater, K., Arrington, L. and Pruitt, T. (1995) 'Bathing persons with dementia.' *The Gerontologist 35*, 5, 672–678.

Twigg, J. (1997) 'Deconstructing the "social bath": help with bathing at home for older and disabled people.' *Journal of Social Policy 26*, 2, 211–232.

CHAPTER 3

Race, Ethnicity and Culture – Providing Intimate and Personal Care within a 'Person-Centred Approach'

Robina Shah

INTRODUCTION

The NHS and social care landscape is changing to become more inclusive and 'person-centred'. The recent agenda of modernisation and reform is regarded to be the most radical in years to deliver equity and equality in how both services are planned and provided to the local community. Within this dynamic process, inequalities and how to address them remains a high priority and yet there remain many tensions between learning disability services and the overall plan of service change. In other words, progress is slow for people with learning disabilities and their families and as the current DH *Valuing People* report shows (Greig 2005) it is even slower for those who are from a minority ethnic community.

To understand why this may be the case and why it is important to ensure that services are committed to providing intimate and personal care within a person-centred approach, the following discussion will describe the past, present and current circumstances of people with learning disabilities from minority ethnic communities, in particular the South Asian community.

THE WIDER CONTEXT

The 2001 Census (Office for National Statistics 2003) reported that South Asian communities made up 4.0 per cent of the UK population (1.8% Indian, 1.3% Pakistani, 0.5% Bangladeshi, 0.4% Asian other, according to Census categories), adding up to approximately 2.3 million people. As South Asian communities have proportionately more young people than White communities, the number of people from South Asian communities is rising and will continue to do so. They face substantial inequalities, discrimination and disadvantage. They are more likely to live in inner city areas in substandard housing and to suffer discrimination in employment, education, health and social services (Azmi *et al.* 1996; Baxter 1990; Chamba *et al.* 1999; Hatton *et al.* 2000; Shah 1995, 1998). There are also ethnic variations in health and this is linked to higher rates of chronic illness in the most disadvantaged minority ethnic communities in the UK: the Bangladeshi and Pakistani communities (Modood *et al.* 1998).

Research into disability and ethnicity have highlighted a number of key areas in relation to the experiences of carers from minority ethnic communities – for example, low service receipt and poor access to services and formal support structures; a lack of information and knowledge about services and available resources; high levels of unmet needs; reduced or lower levels of receipt of benefits and financial exclusion compared with White carers with similar circumstances; poor standards of communication often related to delay in understanding diagnoses and service entitlement and receipt; isolation, lack of support and high levels of carer stress (Azmi *et al.* 1997; Baxter 1998; Beresford 1995; Chamba *et al.* 1999; Hatton *et al.* 2000; Hatton *et al.* 2004, Shah 1995).

There is increasing concern among health and social care providers of the need to understand and interpret appropriately the terms, 'race, ethnicity and culture'. This is mainly due to the fact that in spite of health and social care legislation, national policy and guidance, there seems to be little change in improving the quality of life for people from minority ethnic communities. Recognising the inequalities that people from minority ethnic communities face is an important objective of the report *Valuing People* (Department of Health 2001), which explicitly states that race, culture and ethnicity are fundamental factors in developing and improving services for people with learning disabilities from minority ethnic communities. However, to fully appreciate the value that these themes bring in shaping and constructing our perception of their relevance to improving services to people from minority ethnic communities and to 'person-centred care', the terms need to be defined and understood.

RACE, ETHNICITY AND CULTURE

A number of factors emerge from research that aims to address the impact of ethnicity on the experience of caring in South Asian communities. It is evident from the way in which race, ethnicity and culture are used within research that there is often confusion about their interpretation in relation to research findings. In discussions of research and service practice these terms have been confused or used interchangeably resulting in reduced positive service outcomes for the carers themselves. It is important therefore that these terms need to be clearly defined especially if they are being used as explanatory variables determining the circumstances or life experiences of carers in South Asian communities. Assumptions about the importance of race, ethnicity and culture will lead to very different outcomes about the planning and provision of appropriate services, staff development and professional practice.

What is race?

Race can be defined as a population distinguished as a discrete group on the basis of genetically transmitted physical features, such as skin colour (Betancourt and Lopez 1995). As the genetic characteristics used to distinguish racial groups are comparatively small and arbitrary (relating to a small number of physical characteristics), the concept of race has very little validity as an explanatory construct (Emerson and Hatton 1999). Similarly the eugenic political use of racist explanations of behaviour (Herrnstein and Murray 1994) illustrate the negative consequences of using race as an explanatory construct for many people with severe learning disabilities (Smith 1995).

A major issue in the racialisation of health research is that it is assumed that the population can be meaningfully divided into 'ethnic' or 'racial' groups, taking these as primary categories and using these categories for explanatory purposes. Stratification by class, income and so on is then seen as unimportant; issues of institutional and individual racism as determinants of health status or health care become peripheral at best (Ahmad 1993).

What is ethnicity?

Ethnicity too is often used interchangeably with race although the construct of ethnicity is essentially socio-political rather than biological. Ethnicity can be defined as a set of individuals who share a common and distinctive heritage, and who have a sense of identity as a group. However, ethnicity is not necessarily a monolithic construct. For example, Mink (1997) suggests that behavioural ethnicity (distinctive beliefs, values, norms and languages underpinning social behaviour) and ideological ethnicity (customs and beliefs that are observed but are not central to the person's life) may be quite different.

Thus, as Emerson and Hatton (1999) note, identification with an ethnic group may be associated with diverse beliefs and behaviours, which are subject to change over time as different ethnic groups interact with each other. Although there appears to be overlap between the constructs of ethnicity and culture, there are some distinctive differences between them in relation to ethnic identification, perceived discrimination and bi-lingualism. Therefore, when considering ethnicity as an explanatory variable, it is important to identify which aspects of ethnicity are important and how they influence the overall outcome of the debate.

What is culture?

As with ethnicity, culture is of little value as an explanatory construct without specifying which aspects of it are perceived to be important and how they influence behaviour. Most definitions of culture emphasise aspects of individuals' physical and social environments, which are shared by a group, and are learned or transmitted across generations (Betancourt and Lopez 1995). Of particular focus here is subjective culture, collective beliefs, values and social norms identified by individuals as shared.

However, the important point to emphasise in relation to understanding how people perceive health and illness is to recognise that culture is a dynamic entity that changes to incorporate fresh ideas and perspectives as people develop new ways of responding to their environment. Those who oppose the use of the categories of culture and ethnicity, and the exploration of difference, are often described as anti-racists (Smaje 1995). They suggest that cultural analysis is a diversion from the more important issue of showing how racism is a common experience of all Black (non-White) people. This then becomes the major factor involving them in social disadvantage and often a higher rate of illness from a range of diseases and conditions (Ahmad 1993).

Cultural needs are also defined largely as independent of other social experiences centred on class, gender, racism or sexuality. This means that a group identified as culturally different is assumed to be initially homogeneous (Shah 1995). Anti-racists also argue that culturally based research using ethnicity as the independent variable has not led to much improvement of services for Black people or to an improvement in their health status.

In this way cultural awareness training may contribute to the reinforcement of stereotypes, unless the cultural awareness itself avoids stereotyping and shows the complexity of identity formation (Shah 1995). Therefore, the culture of a group does influence, but does not necessarily determine, the way that people live. Detailing such differences and the beliefs that they are based on can help to break down crude stereotypical views of ethnic minority groups, indicating that the behaviours that health professionals and others find hard to understand are based on their values and beliefs (Shah 1995).

The tendency to form judgements about others solely on the basis of racial, ethnic or religious identity lies at the heart of the processes examined in many studies (Chamba et al. 1999; Hatton et al. 2004; Shah 1995; Shah and Hatton 1999), that is, prejudice/stereotypes and discrimination.

Ahmad (1993) has argued that discourses built around the concept of culture and cultural difference play an important part within the strategies of control of people from minority ethnic communities through state systems of immigration control, education, professional ideologies and practices. The effect of an emphasis entirely on cultural difference to explain inequalities and differences in health and social care services is to pathologise culture, making it the cause of as well as the solution to inequalities in social care services. Many studies openly challenge this school of thought by comparing the needs of Asian families to their White peers and arguing that culture is not rigid but changing for all people (Chamba et al. 1999; Hatton et al. 2004; Mir et al. 2001). These studies suggest that inequalities in provision of social care services are related to racism, where it is the difference between racial and cultural groups that are seen to be deviating from 'White cultural norms' and how this is socially and structurally reinforced.

The discussion so far demonstrates a general pattern of disadvantage experienced by people with learning disabilities from minority ethnic communities. There is consistency between their socio-economic position, unemployment trends, poor health status, reduced access to health and social care services.

It is also important to acknowledge the distinct differences between families from minority ethnic communities with a person with severe learning disabilities. For example, there is variation between specific ethnic groups, particularly in relation to languages spoken (Chamba et al. 1999; Hatton et al. 2004; Shah 1995). There is also variation within ethnic groups, for example, in terms of identified needs (Hatton et al. 2000).

INTIMATE AND PERSONAL CARE

The intimate and personal care arrangements for people with learning disabilities from minority ethnic communities have now been recognised in the policy and practice guidance associated with the NHS and Community Care Act. Here, the 'particular care needs' of Britain's ethnic minority populations have been noted and have prompted services in health and social care to respond to the statement proactively. There is no doubt that government policy on health and social care creates important opportunities for Black and other minority ethnic communities by presenting the opportunity of needs-led care planning.

The opening of consultation and planning processes to direct local influence, a new awareness of carers' needs and a recognition of the particular circumstances of Black and ethnic minorities (Hatton et al. 2004; Mir et al. 2001; Shah 1995). These opportunities, however, arise in the context of existing demands, particularly the long-standing challenges of providing appropriate community care services to Black and Asian communities. Empirical evidence suggests considerable differences in the experiences of community care provision in relation to recognising and responding to the intimate and personal care needs of people from Black and other ethnic minorities (Hatton 1999; Hatton *et al.* 2004; Shah 1995; Shah and Hatton 1999).

Service organisations frequently ignore the personal and intimate care needs of people with learning disabilities from minority ethnic communities by assuming that their policies, procedures and practices are equally appropriate for everyone by default, organised according to a 'White norm'. Straightforward examples include the inability of health and social services to provide support for people who do not speak English (Hatton *et al.* 2004; Shah 1995) or the unavailability of vegetarian food or halal meat in day care and domiciliary services. Other examples include the lack of availability of washing facilities such as running water through a shower rather than a bath and arrangements for removing unwanted hair. Essentially, informed choices about how to accommodate intimate and personal care needs in culturally appropriate ways are not provided.

Such practices legitimise the non-recognition of the community care needs of minority ethnic communities. Other common problems faced in personal and intimate care services include the use of cultural stereotypes in explaining the experiences of users, as well as the racist attitudes held by frontline practitioners (Ahmad 1993; Chamba *et al.*1999; Hatton *et al.* 1998, 2000; Hatton *et al.* 2004; Mir *et al.* 2001; Shah 1995).

Studies of South Asian children with learning disabilities, deafness and haemoglobin disorders have demonstrated how racist attitudes can affect service delivery and personal care support to carers from minority ethnic communities. For example, misinformation and bias concerning consanguineous marriages as a cause of impairment may affect professional practice adversely and alienate families and people with learning disabilities, leading to the low take up of genetic counselling services (Chamba *et al.* 1998; Shah 1995). Other studies of parents with thalassaemia found that health care professionals often relate the condition explicitly to consanguineous marriages and are consequently unsympathetic to parents as they consider the condition to be self-inflicted (Atkin and Ahmad 2000). This has sometimes influenced the personal and intimate care management of people with learning disabilities being disengaged from the decision-making process completely and replaced by the carer's voice only (Hatton *et al.* 2003).

The colour-blind approach can be shown to reinforce often-negative stereotypes and racist attitudes towards people with learning disabilities from minority ethnic communities. This in turn can exacerbate the invisibility of minority ethnic carers and reinforce the neglect they experience from service planners (Shah 1995). Understanding the intimate and personal care needs of people with learning disabilities from minority ethnic communities is much more about the process than just the physical management of care. Questions asked about personal care and intimate care issues are often not described or discussed in a sensitive manner (Hatton *et al.* 2004).

Similarly, specialist services set up to respond to the needs of these communities can have an adverse affect by retaining the structural disadvantage and power relationship of White norms over others. For example, by emphasising culture while ignoring obscuring differences of power between different groups (Ahmad 1993).

There is evidence to suggest that religion and culture are important components in the lives of families and people with learning disabilities from minority ethnic communities. Beliefs and values shape and inform the self-concept and willingness of carers and users to take up services and continue to use services (Azmi *et al.* 1997; Baxter 1990; Hatton *et al.* 2000; Mir 2001; Shah 1995). However, at the same time, stereotyped assumptions may be working to disadvantage carers and individuals with learning disabilities by failing to acknowledge individual and personal choice (Beresford 1995; Chamba *et al.* 1999; Hatton *et al.* 2000; Shah 1995).

This is particularly true in the context of personal and intimate care. Services need to think out of the box and provide opportunities for people with learning disabilities from minority ethnic communities to exercise choice and control over their personal care plans. Health and social care services need to deconstruct the definitions of ethnicity and culture in a way that uniquely seeks to represent the individual rather than the group norm.

This systemic cultural service-based approach devalues the identity of the individual who, though perceived to be from a specific cultural group has actually no real identity with it. While people with disabilities and carers from minority ethnic communities face considerable difficulties in accessing relevant health and social care services there has been increasing recognition of the need to legislate for improved services to meet their needs (Shah 1995). This has come in the shape of various pieces of legislation in the last decade including: the Children Act 1989; the NHS and Community Care Act 1990; the Carers' (Recognition and Services) Act 1995; the Carers and Disabled Children Act 2000; and the National Service Frameworks for Learning Disabilities: 'Valuing People'. The real challenge facing service planners is how they demonstrate a change in their practice using the new powers afforded to them through the legislation and how best to provide an all inclusive approach to families, adults, and children with learning disabilities from minority ethnic communities.

The white paper *Valuing People* (Department of Health 2001) outlines a strategy that enables services and care management to think differently. Through person centred planning there is an opportunity to produce a truly individualised service, which routinely takes in to account the ethnic, cultural and religious needs of *all* people with learning disabilities. This approach challenges the notion of not assuming any 'norm' of a typical service user and can influence the way in which true partnership between all people with learning disabilities can acknowledge individual need within an individual's definition of what that need constitutes. To elicit a response the question must be asked about cultural or religious needs, and personal preferences and priorities of having those needs met sensitively. Personal and intimate care plans will inform the components of the person-centred approach. A successful measure of this will be the extent to which people with learning disabilities themselves feel included in this process.

Within the *Valuing People* framework, there is recognition that disabled people as a group and people from minority ethnic communities are also less likely to enjoy life according to these principles than other people. *Valuing People* as a whole is designed to improve the lives of disabled people in terms of rights, independence, choice and inclusion. Regarding people from minority ethnic communities, *Valuing People* states that:

> the Government expects all agencies to improve their practice to fulfil the
> ...legal obligations set out in the Race Relations Amendment Act 2000.
> This means that health and social services are subject to the new duty to
> promote race equality in the performance of their functions, and should ensure that local services are culturally competent and can meet all the cultural needs of their communities.

In this way the person centred planning framework needs to demonstrate how it is compliant with the Race Relations (Amendment) Act 2000.

The Race Relations Act 1976 as amended gives public authorities a new statutory duty to promote race equality. The aim is to help public authorities to provide fair and accessible services, and to improve equal opportunities in employment. The general duty also expects public authorities to take the lead in promoting equality of opportunity and good race relations, and eliminating unlawful discrimination. The aim of the duty is to make the promotion of racial equality central to the work of public authorities. In practice, this means that public authorities must take account of racial equality in the day-to-day work of policy-making, service delivery, employment practice and other functions. Since public authorities must meet all three parts of the duty – eliminating unlawful discrimination, promoting equal opportunities and promoting good race relations – they must make sure they know how all their policies and services affect race equality. For example, a new person-centred policy may help to promote equal opportunities, but if it is badly introduced, it may actually damage race relations.

The legislation will help ensure public services become more accountable to the people they serve and allow everyone the opportunity to give their views about the services that affect them. Thus it will help provide the kind of public functions and services that disabled people from minority ethnic communities need, want and deserve – as well as helping to further equality of opportunity and promote better race relations.

THE ROLE OF PERSON CENTRED PLANNING

In the context of person centred planning the legislation should help social services and health to transform their performance on race and disability equality. For example, in five years' time one would expect to see year-on-year improvements in:

- representative staff profiles that reflect the diversity of their local community not just in numbers but also in philosophy
- equitable and accessible services for disabled people from minority ethnic communities, which underpin their social inclusion in all areas of life
- increasing numbers of disabled people and their families participating fully as equal citizens
- improved understanding of the diverse health and social care needs of disabled people from minority ethnic communities, and a commitment to addressing these diverse needs
- service design and service planning that reflect the rights of all disabled people to choice, independence and inclusion
- a workforce skilled in meeting the needs of all disabled people in the local population, including people from minority ethnic communities
- improved opportunities for disabled people from minority ethnic communities to participate in employment, public life and service delivery
- more disabled people and their families being able to talk to relevant professionals in the language of their choice
- action to address other likely inequalities, such as inequalities according to gender
- reliable evidence base of data categorised by ethnicity and learning disability.

The guiding principles of *Valuing People* and the general duties of both the Race Relations Act (RRA) and Disability Discrimination Act (DDA) are entirely compatible and reinforce each other. Rather than looking at compliance with *Valuing People*, the RRA and the DDA separately, it makes sense for services to reflect strategically on where they are going with regard to both disability and race equality as part of a single, integrated framework. This guidance suggests that health and social service providers should establish an equality scheme that accommodates both race and disability and in so doing present a person centred planning approach and framework that is inclusive.

It will take time, resources and commitment to get these systems in place. Different services will move at different rates. For this reason, it is important that progress is monitored regularly and audited in a way that measures achievement realistically. Successful implementation will depend on how a service will be able to provide leadership and support, ensure resources are available, engage with the disabled people in a person-centred manner, provide a scrutiny role, organise and participate in training on race equality and disability equality, challenge existing cultures and traditions and work with the equality planning process to extend knowledge of the disability and race equality standard within the service care framework.

Similarly, improving life chances for disabled people complements this person-centred philosophy. The report *Improving Life Chances for Disabled People* (Department of Health 2005) marks a key landmark in cross-government policies for disabled people. This report makes recommendations across four key areas:

1. *Independent living* – increasing disabled people's ability to live independently at home, at work and in the community with support based on personal need, choice and empowerment through a major expansion of Direct Payments in the form of individual budgets.

2. *Early years and family support* – family-focused support, childcare and early education that enables families with young disabled children to achieve 'ordinary lives' and remain economically and socially included.

3. *Transition to adulthood* – planning focused on the individual needs of disabled young people, based on smooth provision of support and services during transition and leading to appropriate opportunities and choices in adulthood.

4. *Employment* – early intervention supporting disabled people to stay in touch with the labour market; improving the employment prospects of disabled people through ongoing personalised support, with employers supported in a key role, while providing security for those unable to work.

The concept of person centred planning is not revolutionary – the request for individual need assessments have been with us for a long time. What is unusual is the alignment of an individual approach through person centred planning that integrates culture and ethnicity as an integral part of the intimate and personal care planning process. The advantages and benefits this will bring in the provision and planning of support services in the context of care management will be manifest in the development of mainstream services with the range of skills and resources needed to meet the full range of needs demanded of them.

MOVING FORWARD

Good professional practice is therefore about how we develop our skills and knowledge to be more responsive to the personal and intimate care needs of people with learning disabilities from minority ethnic communities. The social construction of ethnicity and culture can be helpful as well as a hindrance in enabling personal and intimate care plans to reflect culturally diverse backgrounds.

It is important to accept that positive as well as negative feelings will be present when changes are implemented that involve a whole new method of working. It is always important to note that sometimes there will be resistance, which may mean a greater form of support for some staff members who may be feeling de-skilled and lack confidence to find different ways of working.

More than often it is the lack of understanding about ethnicity and how it impacts on professional practice that can lead to hostility towards its implementation. Some organisations are far too hasty in implementing change in this area resulting in the process being ignored or not thought through.

The important message to remember is the commitment to provide equality in all personal care services – a commitment measured by improving access, communication and active engagement with parents, children and people with learning disabilities from minority ethnic communities. The real challenge is identifying the starting point, thinking through the issues and setting clear targets with achievable goals.

The discussion and debate around planning and improving services to minority ethnic communities is important. There has to be a safe environment to discuss it, one that is free from the negative influence of political correctness – one that allows people to say how they really feel and to deconstruct definitions of ethnicity in relative rather than absolutist terms. Allowing the individual themselves to interpret and describe what their cultural identity and ethnicity is and how much of the values, beliefs and attitudes they hold actually bear an influence on how personal and intimate care plans should be written for them, with them, and not without them.

Everyone's contribution is valuable. Organisations need to establish their definitions on equality of care in the context of recent race and disability legislation; they should be clear, purposeful and understood by everyone. Only then can the process move forward and lead to good qualitative services that truly deliver person-centred care pathways for all.

REFERENCES

Ahmad, W. (1993) 'Making Black people sick: 'race', ideology and health research.' In W. Ahmad (ed.) *'Race' and Health in Contemporary Britain*. Buckingham: Open University Press.

Atkin, K. and Ahmad, W. (2000) 'Family care-giving and chronic illness: how parents cope with a child with a sickle cell disorder or thalassaemia.' *Health and Social Care in the Community 8*, 1639–1651.

Atkin, K. and Rollings, J. (1996) 'Looking after their own? Family care-giving among Asian and Afro-Caribbean communities.' In W.I.U. Ahmed and K. Atkin (eds) *Race and Community Care*. Buckingham: Open University Press, pp.73–87.

Azmi, S., Hatton, C., Emerson, E. and Caine, A. (1997) 'Listening to adolescents and adults with intellectual disabilities from South Asian communities.' *Journal of Applied Research in Intellectual Disabilities 10*, 3, 250–263.

Azmi. S., Hatton, C., Emerson, E. and Caine, A. (1998) 'Informal carers of adolescents and adults with learning difficulties from the South Asian Communities: family circumstances, service support and carer stress.' British Journal of Social Work 28, 6, 821–837.

Baxter, C., Poonia, K., Ward, L. and Nadirshaw, Z. (1990) *Double Discrimination: Issues and Services for People with Learning Difficulties from Black and Minority Ethnic Communities*. London: King's Fund Centre.

Beresford, B. (1995) *Expert Opinions: A National Survey of Parents Caring for a Severely Disabled Child*. Bristol: The Policy Press.

Betancourt, H. and Lopez, S. (1995) 'The study of culture, ethnicity and race in American psychology.' In N.R. Goldberger and J.B. Veroff (eds) *The Culture and Psychology Reader*, pp.87–107. New York: New York University Press.

Chamba, R., Ahmed, W., Hirst, M., Lawton, D. and Beresford, B. (1999) *On the Edge: Minority Ethnic Families Caring for a Severely Disabled Child*. Bristol: Policy Press.

Department of Health (2001) *Valuing People: A New Strategy for Learning Disability for the 21st Century*. London: The Stationery Office. www.valuingpeople.gov.uk/documents/ValuingPeople.pdf

Department of Health (2005) *Improving Life Chances for Disabled People*. London: Department of Health.

Emerson, E. and Hatton, C. (1999) 'Future trends in the ethnic composition of British society and among British citizens with learning disabilities.' *Tizard Learning Disability Review 4*, 28–32.

Greig, R. (2005) *The Story So Far…* London: Department of Health.

Hatton, C., Akram, Y., Shah, R., Robertson, J. and Emerson, E. (2003) 'The disclosure process and its impact on South Asian families with a child with severe intellectual disabilities.' *Journal of Applied Research in Intellectual Disabilities 16*, 177–188.

Hatton, C., Akram, Y., Shah, R., Robertson, J. and Emerson, E. (2004) *Supporting South Asian Families with a Child with Severe Disabilities*. London: Jessica Kingsley Publishers.

Hatton, C., Azmi, S., Caine, A. and Emerson, E. (1998) 'Informal carers of adolescents with learning difficulties from the South Asian communities: family circumstances, service support and carer stress.' *British Journal of Social Work 28*, 821–837.

Hatton, C., Akram, Y., Shah, R., Robertson, J. and Emerson, E. (2000) *South Asian families with a child with severe disabilities: circumstances, support and outcomes.* (Report to the English Department of Health.) Manchester: Hester Adrian Research Centre, University of Manchester.

Herrnstein, R. and Murray, C. (1994) *The Bell Curve: Intelligence and Class Structure in American Life.* New York: Free Press.

Mink, I. (1997) 'Studying culturally diverse families of children with mental retardation.' In N. Bray (ed.) *International Review on Research in Mental Retardation, Vol. 20*, pp.75–98. San Diego: Academic Press.

Mir, G., Nocon, A. and Ahmad, W. with Jones, L. (2001) *Learning Difficulties and Ethnicity.* London: Department of Health.

Modood, T., Berthoud, R., Lakey, J., Nazaroo, J., Smith, P., Verdes, S. and Beishon, S. (1998) *Ethnic Minorities in Britain: Difference and Diversity.* London: Policy Studies Institute.

Race Relations (Amendment) Act (2000) London: The Stationery Office.

Shah, R. (1995) *The Silent Minority. Children with Disabilities in Asian Families.* The National Children's Bureau.

Shah, R. (1998) *Sharing the News with Asian Parents.* London: Mental Health Foundation.

Shah, R. and Hatton, C. (1999) *Caring Alone – Young Carers from South Asian Communities.* Ilford: Barnardos.

Smaje, C. (1995) *Health, Race and Ethnicity.* London: King's Fund Institute.

Smith, J.D. (1995) 'For whom the bell curve tolls: old texts, mental retardation and the persistant argument'. *Mental Retardation 33*, 199–200.

CHAPTER 4

Sexuality and Intimate and Personal Care

Michelle McCarthy and Paul Cambridge

INTRODUCTION

Intimate care relates to the sexuality of people with learning disabilities primarily because it involves the exposure of private areas of the body and the sometimes difficult feelings associated with having these parts seen and touched by others or, indeed, seeing or touching other people's private areas of the body. More directly, these are also the sexual parts of the body – the breasts, vagina, penis, testicles and anus. They therefore take on an added status and relate directly to the sexuality of service users and to the feelings of staff undertaking such intimate care. In addition, however, there are also secondary aspects to sexuality that relate to a whole collection of activities associated with personal care that are relevant. Helping someone dress and look good or simply advising or supporting a person make their own choices about what to wear and how they look is relevant to self-image and the sexual self. The intimacy and closeness of personal care can also generate feelings on the part of staff and service users, both positive and negative, about how we feel about allowing our private and personal space to be occupied by someone else or how it feels to be in someone else's private and personal space and what this means.

For many people with learning disabilities, especially those with severe and profound disabilities, the only times they may have their bodies seen and touched by others will be during intimate and personal care (or medical examination or treatment). It is often assumed that people in such situations do not understand the significance of what is happening to them or their bodies. However, not only will they pick up messages from carers but they will also have sexual and physical feelings and sensations that may not be placed in an appropriate social context or be understood for what they represent to self or others.

They may of course have an explicit individual sexuality, and in some cases a sexual self or sexual life. We need to remember that not everyone receiving intimate care will have a severe learning disability, because there may be reasons related to physical disability why someone needs help with washing or bathing the sexual parts of their bodies. Even if they do have a severe learning disability, this does not mean that they will not have sexual aspects to their experiences. It is therefore very important to carry out personal care tasks in a way that is as respectful as possible to the person's sexuality and adult status.

Many people with learning disabilities will have experience of not having their privacy and dignity respected during personal care. They will not have been in a position to do very much about this and yet will still be dependent on others carrying out those care tasks for them. They may have had to 'harden' themselves to this emotionally and psychologically. They may therefore not appear to show any reactions or preference about how their care tasks are carried out, nor who helps them in this way. The challenge for service providers is, however, to make up for the mistakes of the past (McCarthy and Thompson 1998) and develop intimate care support that acknowledges their individuality as people with physical and sexual feelings, as adults and as individuals. Choice and positive interactions during intimate care are difficult to develop for people with more severe learning disabilities, but communication and other techniques are available for helping develop quality outcomes for both staff and service users (Cambridge and Carnaby 2000a). Unfortunately this is a hard task, as hard-pressed staff tend to want to complete the more unpleasant intimate care tasks as quickly as possible for the person and with minimal interaction (Carnaby and Cambridge 2002).

In some cases where people may have a less severe learning disability but possibly additional physical disabilities they will have a sexual life and a sexual identity, although this may not have been acknowledged by service providers or helped to become externalised. They may masturbate, they may have contacts and friendships with other people with learning disabilities, some possibly sexual and they may have experienced sex or sexual touching from someone without a learning disability. The latter is most likely to have been of a form that would be defined as sexual abuse, due to the probable lack of understanding or consent involved. It is therefore important not to assume that anyone receiving intimate care will not know, perceive, care, feel or understand or misunderstand something about what might be happening to them during intimate care.

MANAGING SEXUAL AROUSAL, MASTURBATION AND SELF-STIMULATION

Staff and family carers need to be helped to understand why it is that a person with a learning disability might become sexually aroused during intimate and personal care and to respond to sexual arousal in appropriate ways. First, we need to realise that this is not a behaviour peculiar to them – the experience of having the sexual parts of your body seen and touched, even if it is in the course of an otherwise intrusive or unpleasant medical procedure, or within a professional context, can be sexually arousing or exciting for some people. Conversely, other feelings and emotions may also be aroused, such as embarrassment, distress, fear or shame. These emotions may be confused with sexual arousal, by the individual themselves or by carers or others close to the individual.

Second, people whose avenues for any kind of sexual expression may be extremely limited may find that they have to take what opportunities they can to feel and be sexual. For some people with severe and profound disabilities, especially those who are totally dependent on others for all their care and who usually wear incontinence pads, the only time they may have access to their own genitals or provide themselves with or experience sexual stimulation, even unintended on the part of the carer, may be during intimate and personal care. In these circumstances, it is neither surprising nor unreasonable, that some people will seek to use the opportunity to sexually stimulate themselves, or indeed try to get the other person to do it for them. However, the fact that this behaviour is to be expected does not necessarily make it any easier for staff and carers to accept it or respond appropriately to it.

It is therefore important to consider in advance how to respond if such behaviour surfaces during intimate care and there are several suggested courses of action.

First and foremost, staff should not go along with any physical prompts or verbal requests to provide sexual stimulation from people they are providing intimate care to. Staff are in a formal and professional relationship with the person they are providing intimate care to, unlike for example, helping a sexual partner during an illness or recuperating from hospital care when there may already be an established consenting sexual repertoire and understanding between the two people. Adult protection, intimate care and sexual abuse policies in services for people with learning disabilities, and more widely, all make clear that any direct sexual touching or stimulation is inappropriate. Indeed, it is an offence under the 2003 Sexual Offences Act for a member of staff or anyone else in services for people with learning disabilities to have sex (which includes touching intended as sexual) with a service user. To do this would indeed risk allegations and/or suspicions of sexual abuse and would likely be a criminal offence. If, for example, the individual tries to push a staff member's hand towards their genital area, the staff member should gently but firmly resist any such movement and explain why they are doing so (for example, 'No, I'm sorry, that's a private thing', 'I'm not going to do that', 'I don't want to' or 'It's not allowed'). Even if people have very limited receptive communication skills, and won't understand the meaning of some or any of the words, it is possible they may pick up on the tone of voice and overall meaning.

If the individual is able to understand what is said to them, then the staff member should explain that what they seem to want (i.e. sexual stimulation) is a private activity, that they are not allowed to do it for them and that it should be attempted later when the person is alone. This possibility may of course only be realistically available to some individuals when they are in bed and others may not, for various reasons, be able to touch and stimulate the sexual parts of their own bodies themselves, and such limitations will need to be acknowledged in any response. If the individual is not able to, or doesn't respond to such reasoning, then if it is safe to do so, the member of staff could always withdraw from the immediate care interaction and leave the individual alone for a while. Clearly, if the individual is at any significant risk if left alone in particular circumstances, such as drowning if left unsupervised in the bath, this is not an option, but in many other circumstances it will be.

Under both of the above circumstances it is of course very important to record what has happened and discuss this with the manager or staff team. There may be a personal file, incident report book or changeover meeting at which such situations can be reported and discussed. Any concerns should also be discussed with the line manager in a way that respects the individual's dignity, that is, during a private conversation such as supervision, and not informally over coffee in the presence of other staff or other service users. As with other areas of sexuality, confidentiality, rights and need-to-know criteria will be important to consider.

A principle governing personal care is that it should be an aim for all people with learning disabilities to learn, as far as is possible, that their bodies belong to them and that no one may see or touch the private parts of their bodies unless they wish to engage in sexual contact with them (subject to legal considerations about who this is and the person being able to give informed consent) or when it is necessary for their personal or medical care. In order to put this principle into practice, individuals must therefore be given as much privacy as possible, for example, when they bathe, wash or use the toilet and be informed and consulted about personal care before and during such interactions. They can also be supported to do some things for themselves in some cases, which may take more time but will reinforce important messages about their body and who it belongs to. Carers being present on a routine basis, when this is not strictly necessary for safety or to help with hygiene, is not appropriate. When individuals do attempt to use such opportunities for sexual arousal (e.g. masturbating while in the bath or when having an incontinence pad changed) it is especially important that they be given the maximum privacy possible for this. Generally speaking, it is never appropriate for a staff member or family carer to be present when an individual is masturbating. The individual with learning disabilities needs to be clear about this as much as anybody else. In other words, in order for individuals to learn that other people can only have access to (i.e. see or touch) the private parts of their bodies in strictly limited circumstances, it is necessary to, in fact, limit those circumstances. In this way, it maximises the chances of individuals developing the ability to recognise when something untoward might be happening and thus serves a protective purpose with regard to sexual abuse.

RESPONDING TO INAPPROPRIATE SEXUAL BEHAVIOUR

Masturbation or sexual self-stimulation are the most commonly reported inappropriate sexual behaviours experienced and reported by staff during intimate and personal care. Indeed, this is the case more widely in sexuality work, particularly for men but also less frequently, women with learning disabilities (McCarthy 1996), so we should not be surprised when such behaviours surface. Concerns primarily centre on four key and sometimes inter-related themes (Cambridge, Carnaby and McCarthy 2003):

1.   The person is considered to be unable to masturbate properly, usually meaning that it is thought they are unable to reach orgasm/ejaculate.

2.   The person does not know how to masturbate, usually meaning that they have been observed rubbing their penis or vagina, generally when exposed during intimate care.

3.   The person is doing it too much, usually meaning that the duration or frequency of the masturbation is such that staff consider that it interferes with intimate or personal care.

4.   The person is using inappropriate objects or means to help them masturbate, usually meaning that they are using objects not intended to aid masturbation or which could hurt them, such as soap or flannels or shampoo containers.

Of course, if masturbation happens at all during intimate care this is itself an inappropriate sexual behaviour, causing difficulties for carers or staff.

The understanding of such behaviours is often complicated when they are also associated with other challenging behaviours. Staff may relate hypotheses they have developed to help them understand or explain the behaviours they have observed during intimate care. An example is linking unsuccessful masturbation with sexual or other frustration, leading to challenging behaviour (e.g. Sheppard 1991). Causal links may therefore be constructed between masturbation, as it presents itself or is perceived to be a problem, and challenging behaviour.

Often underlying such considerations are issues of gender and sexuality. Masturbation is generally reported to be much more of an issue for men with learning disabilities than with women (McCarthy 2002). More widely it has been observed that the sexuality of men with learning disabilities is seen as relatively pathological, with a range of sexual behaviours reinforcing such perceptions (Cambridge 1997; Cambridge and Mellan 2000). Conversely, it has been observed that the sexuality and sexual experiences of women with learning disabilities has remained relatively hidden (McCarthy 1999; McCarthy and Thompson 1998). Such basic observations are mirrored in discussions in staff training in sexuality and learning disability (Cambridge and McCarthy 1997). This is one of the reasons why sexuality and gender need to be considered together in designing intimate care and responding to any sexuality issues that arise whether in relation to service users or the feelings of staff. The other is the known incidence of sexual abuse and the vulnerability of both men, and particularly, women with learning disabilities from sexual abuse during private care interactions from men.

What contributes to perceived problem behaviours, such as masturbation or self-stimulation during intimate care is the way services construct space and organise support, with communal and collective spaces such as living rooms, bathrooms and toilets, often merging along the public–private continuum with shared or individual spaces such as bedrooms (Parkin 1989). By and large, private space is at a premium in services for people with learning disabilities. In residential services someone may have their own bedroom, but its use may be discouraged during the day, there may be no locks on bedroom doors and staff and other service users may not respect privacy. This is why simple messages such as a right to privacy and respect have received prominence in some educational materials (e.g. Cambridge 1996; McCarthy and Cambridge 1996). Private spaces in day services or services for people with profound and multiple learning disabilities are even scarcer, and the only places available for someone to masturbate may be the toilets or during intimate care.

In addition to the tendency to disrespect or disregard privacy in services for people with learning disabilities, there is also a tendency to desexualise and to de-individualise people with learning disabilities (Carnaby 1997 and 1999). This can mean that ordinary sexual behaviours, when they do surface, are interpreted as inappropriate. Masturbation is, for example, crudely referenced as a behaviour problem on the Adaptive Behaviour Scale (Nihira *et al.* 1974, referenced and discussed in Felce, Lowe and De Pavia 1994).

The first step in responding is to clarify and accurately describe what is happening. Six key sets of questions (McCarthy and Thompson 1998) that can be asked about the actual behaviour, evidence and context are:

1. What is the actual behaviour? For example, is the person touching themselves sexually, what part of the body are they touching, how are they touching it, are they actually masturbating, are they trying to get the carer to touch them sexually during intimate care and so on?

2. How do staff respond to the situation? For example, is this consistent and do some staff or responses seem to be more effective than others?

3. Does the behaviour (for example, masturbation) vary between places or settings (such as home, day care or residential service) and what might explain this variation?

4. Is there a daily or temporal pattern to the person's masturbation and are there times when this is not a problem? For example, does it only happen during intimate and personal care?

5. Is this a new behaviour or has it been going on for some time and if the latter, what has been tried?

6. Does the nature or provision of intimate care vary between places, settings or people and does there seem to be a relationship to the inappropriate sexual behaviour reported during intimate care?

Depending on the individual situation or behaviour, more detailed questions are likely to need to be answered, for example:

- For a woman, does she directly stimulate her clitoris, vagina or breasts and is this done with her hands or with an object such as a sponge or flannel? Does she seem to achieve satisfaction, whether through orgasm or not?

- For a man, does he get an erection, does he stimulate his penis (or anus), does he use his hand or an object such as a flannel and does he ever ejaculate?

It should also be asked whether there is any suspicion or evidence that the person may have experienced sexual abuse. If so, and especially for people with very limited verbal communication, touching their genital area may be their only way of drawing attention to something having happened to that part of their body.

Answers to the above questions will help place the behaviour on a continuum between sexual arousal, self-stimulation and masturbation, which will inform the response. They will also help develop and test the hypothesis about the link between masturbation and other stimuli such as warm water or indirect contact through washing or hand over hand or indeed other challenging behaviours. In some cases, it may be necessary to collect information to help decide on the function of the masturbation and clarify the attribution if it is a challenging behaviour. This can be done using a simple but widely recognised ABC

(Antecedent, Behaviour, Consequence) approach to understanding setting conditions and triggers as part of behaviour analysis (e.g. Murphy 1994).

In many cases it will also be important to check out some even more basic, but often overlooked possibilities, particularly in relation to situations where the woman or man is considered to be unable to masturbate effectively. For example, does the person have a vaginal, penile or urinary tract infection? Are there any signs of a skin irritation or condition, such as thrush or eczema? Could having an erection cause pain for the man, as with a very tight foreskin? Is the person on any form of medication that could reduce their ability to masturbate or reduce their libido, such as anti-psychotic medication? All such possibilities are generally more easily checked out during intimate care than any other care situation.

In trying to understand a person's sexual behaviour, staff need to be encouraged to reflect on their own beliefs and values about sexuality. We draw on a range of models and sources for this, including our cultural backgrounds, subjective feelings ('gut reactions'), beliefs about how common or uncommon a certain type of sexual behaviour is, our understanding of the law, and so on. The models of 'normality' people hold can be influential in determining our responses and staff need to be helped to recognise that many of us make distinctions about what we think is 'normal' or 'abnormal' on an instinctive and subconscious level, rather than as a result of considered reflection.

Finding out more about a person's motivations and purposes will obviously require careful and respectful observation. Intimate and personal care or help with washing or bathing can sometimes provide the only such opportunities (Cambridge and Carnaby 2000a). If a person is able to discuss such matters, then private and respectful conversations can help. However, in many cases, if staff already consider that someone is unable to masturbate effectively, then they are likely to hold similar information or observations to support their concerns or will have collected evidence indirectly. It will remain important to check such evidence at staff meetings or case reviews in order to validate any assumptions or interpretations as a first step to planning responses or deciding on what additional information may be needed to inform any intervention or response. Considerations likely to surface from such work include links with activities and levels of meaningful engagement. If people lack meaning in most of their daily lives, which is often the case for people with profound and multiple learning disabilities requiring intimate care, they are more likely to engage in self-involved behaviours that serve the purpose of relieving boredom or frustration.

The need for structured sex education is likely to emerge for many people with learning disabilities, but again it is the more severely disabled people who are likely to have been excluded from sex education. Most will not have had their sexuality or sexual needs addressed directly at all in their lives and consequently have not been given basic messages about masturbation being a normal and enjoyable activity, either on your own or with a consenting partner or about the importance of privacy. At least a discourse on sexuality has been initiated (Downs and Craft 1997) for people with severe learning disabilities and techniques are available to give people a positive response verbally or through other forms of communication (Ware 1996), that the behaviour is allowed and valued in certain places.

If a man is deemed to be masturbating too much or ineffectively, it is sometimes suggested that chemical responses using medication designed to suppress the male sex drive (such as Androcur) will help the situation. However, without the person's informed consent, which in the case of someone with a profound or severe learning disability would be very unlikely, this is not a realistic or ethical option to consider. In addition to the ethical problems, there is the question of effectiveness, as experience suggests that men who take this medication may still experience sexual feelings and attempt sexual activity but are unable to reach orgasm. This can then exacerbate the problem it was trying to solve. Rather, support staff need to be asking whether the individual concerned is having enough 'private' time. For example, if appropriate and safe, is he being given time to relax alone in the bath or shower, or have time to rest in bed when not actually sleeping, without wearing pads or restrictive clothing?

GENDER AND SEXUALITY

Most services today acknowledge that intimate and personal care is best carried out by staff members of the same-gender as the individual with learning disabilities. Indeed, many have guidelines and policies that stipulate that this should be the case. Providing a staff member of the same-gender as the individual receiving care is a concrete way of respecting the person's dignity and adult status. Given the predominance of women in direct care roles, there should always (except in highly unusual circumstances) be sufficient women staff to assist women with learning disabilities. Providing personal care to men with learning disabilities is more complex. The under-representation of men in direct care roles means that often there may not be enough male staff available to assist men. Moreover, there are gendered roles for caring that make it rightly or wrongly more socially acceptable for women, rather than men, to provide intimate care (Bradley 1993; Orme 2001; Williams 1993) and conversely for men, rather than women, to respond to challenging behaviour (Clements et al. 1995). Many men with learning disabilities will, for example, be used to women, whether mothers or sisters, providing intimate care for them.

The importance and complexity of gender, particularly when related to sexuality and sexual identity of staff, is something that managers and commissioners need to consider at a service-wide level and bear in mind when seeking to recruit, train and retain staff. It must always be remembered that receiving personal care puts people with learning disabilities at an increased risk of sexual abuse, as it is conducted in private and largely outside scrutiny and can involve touch (Cambridge and Carnaby 2000b) and all available evidence suggests that male staff are far more likely than female staff to sexually abuse both women and men with learning disabilities. Clearly same-gender care rationales largely protect women with learning disabilities from the risk of sexual abuse but fail to protect men with learning disabilities from such risks, just as they fail to address issues of physical abuse or neglect (Cambridge and Carnaby 2000b).

Some lesbian and gay staff may feel anxious about providing same-gender personal care, because of the homophobic prejudices of others. Interviews with staff (Cambridge and Carnaby 2000b) have highlighted such issues (see Chapter 2). Any prejudices that surface will need to be vigorously challenged in services, to avoid reinforcing such barriers and the outcome of lesbian and gay staff not engaging positively and safely in intimate and personal care in the same way as other staff. Gay identified men risk particular vulnerability when providing intimate care to men in a similar way that heterosexual men might feel if expected to provide intimate care to women, when referencing the evidence on sexual abuse.

PARTICULAR ISSUES FOR WOMEN

Menstrual care

Helping women with learning disabilities understand and manage their periods is a task that should only be undertaken by women staff and carers, except at the request of an individual woman or where, in an extreme situation, there is no other choice. This assertion is based on the fact that when asked, women with learning disabilities consistently report an overwhelming preference for other women to assist them in their menstrual care (McCarthy 2002; Rodgers 2001). Women with learning disabilities reflect a generally held view in most, if not all known societies, that menstruation is 'women's business' and something that is generally kept private from men (Laws 1990).

Where women need direct assistance with menstrual care, then almost always they will be assisted to use sanitary towels. The use of tampons is an issue that is rarely discussed in services or indeed the literature, although occasionally staff and carers do ask for guidance on this and it is referenced in some training materials on intimate and personal care (Cambridge and Carnaby 2000a). Unless women can be taught to use tampons independently, then their use is not appropriate. Staff or family carers inserting tampons for a woman with learning disabilities is not an acceptable part of personal care. It is too intrusive a procedure and is not comparable to placing a sanitary towel or incontinence pad into a person's underwear. Inserting tampons is more comparable with inserting vaginal pessaries or anal suppositories and these are procedures that staff would only be expected to undertake if medically necessary. Clearly, use of tampons is not medically necessary, although obviously many women find them convenient and preferable to sanitary towels.

How women with learning disabilities feel about their bodies and appearance

Traditionally it has been believed that one of the 'advantages' of having a learning disability was freedom from many of the pressures society places on individuals to conform to its standards. This may be true in some aspects of life, but evidence suggests that women with mild and moderate learning disabilities feel the same pressures around their appearance and body image as other women do (McCarthy 1998). This means that many often feel themselves to be unattractive, as measured by the unrealistic and impossibly high standards of eternal youth and beauty that society sets for women. Just like their non-disabled counterparts, many women with learning disabilities focus their dissatisfaction with their bodies upon their weight and express a desire for weight loss. However, unlike their non-disabled counterparts, women with learning disabilities often find that staff or family carers take decisions about weight loss out of their hands and make decisions for them: 'They say "You can't have this, you can't have that"'; 'They won't let me have ice cream' (quotes taken from McCarthy 1998, p.561).

Evidence also suggests that even during life stages such as the menopause, where weight gain is expected and normal for women (though not inevitable), women with learning disabilities still find themselves under pressure from staff to maintain or lose weight (McCarthy 2002). Services also contribute to women's dissatisfaction about their weight in other ways, that is, prescribing and administering medication that causes (sometimes considerable) weight gain.

The suggestion here is not that the weight of women (or indeed men) with learning disabilities should never be of concern to staff or family carers. This is not the case, especially where individuals are clearly under- or over-weight or where they have conditions that predispose them to difficulties about controlling their eating, such as Prader-Willi Syndrome. Helping individuals to lose weight if that is what they personally want or where it is medically beneficial is an appropriate course of action. However, helping them to resist pressures to lose weight, because this meets arbitrary and unrealistic standards set by society is also appropriate.

With regards to other aspects of their appearance, such as the way they dress or do their hair, these can also be problematic areas for some women with learning disabilities. It is an under-researched area, but evidence from women with mild and moderate disabilities suggests that some women resent the comments and control that others (staff and family carers) have over them: 'I like choosing my own clothes, but they never let me choose my own'; 'The staff didn't like it when I had blond highlights, they said I look like a tart' (quotes taken from McCarthy 1998, p.567).

Once again, it may, in some circumstances, be perfectly appropriate for staff and family carers to offer advice, guidance and indeed take some decisions on behalf of individuals if they cannot do so for themselves. Not to do so would mean the person's dignity and adult status could be seriously compromised. Nevertheless, when people can make their own choices and are denied the right to express their individuality through their appearance, this is an equal affront to their dignity and status.

PARTICULAR ISSUES FOR MEN

A potential reason why men with learning disabilities should ideally receive intimate and personal care from men is the general absence of positive male role models in services for people with learning disabilities. In many cases, male support staff are simply absent or occupy managerial or specialist posts. If men are not seen to be providing intimate care for male service users then this will reinforce negative stereotypes about gendered roles and caring and expectations about male behaviour. There is certainly enough evidence from sex education at one-to-one and group levels that men with learning disabilities hold relatively rigid stereotypical images about gender, based on names, dress codes, hair length and segregation (Cambridge and McCarthy 1997). This is mirrored in sexual identity, with most men with learning difficulties who have sex with men identifying as heterosexual rather than gay (Cambridge 1997).

At a practical level, however, there are clearly intimate and personal care tasks male support staff or carers will be potentially more competent at doing for and with men with learning disabilities, based on a knowledge of their own bodies, experience and perceptions. These are also likely to be tasks that it would be more appropriate for men to do and the most inappropriate for women carers to undertake for men with learning disabilities, either in relation to their own feelings or to how the man with learning disabilities might experience or interpret them. The most obvious example is genital hygiene. Cambridge and Carnaby (2000a) reference the comments of a male care worker who had no detailed individual guidelines to help him decide how to wash a male service user's penis during intimate care:

> The care plan says something like 'ensure genitals and anus are clean'. This leaves it up to me to interpret inputs based on my own standards and knowledge. (Cambridge and Carnaby 2000a, p.4)

Issues such as genital hygiene have until recently been largely neglected for men with learning disabilities, despite medical evidence that such neglect can have serious health consequences. Conditions such as phimosis and paraphimosis (where the foreskin cannot be retracted over the glans of the penis or where a history of repetitive forceful retraction causes the formation of a fibrotic ring of tissue that restricts the penis) can result from incorrect circumcision or can be congenital, affecting around one per cent of men. They can cause problems such as urinary obstruction, hematuria and preputial pain and in acquired phimosis, there is likely to be a history of poor hygiene.

At the other end of the continuum, tasks such as dressing and shaving are also arguably better conducted by men. Men will have directly experienced the feeling of wearing different types of clothes or underwear, be able to make suggestions about positive aspects of male dress or appearance based on masculine self-image and have a first-hand understanding of the sensations and results of different approaches to shaving, to name a few examples.

What can potentially compromise positive interaction between male carers and male service users are differences and similarities in sexuality. For example, if a male carer is out as a gay man at work and the service user knows this, then there is the potential for this to be used either positively or negatively – refusing personal care from a gay man or, if they have homosexual feelings themselves, possibly using personal care as a way to receive sexual gratification. This is simply the reverse side of the heterosexual coin, as we know only too well how some men with learning disabilities sexually harass female staff during intimate and personal care.

Men with learning disabilities who have sex with men would benefit from the understanding and advice a gay identified staff member might be able to offer during one-to-one personal care situations, for example, on assertiveness, HIV risk or simply giving positive messages that it's OK to feel a certain way about another man. Positive gay role models could be hugely beneficial to men with learning disabilities who have sex with men and who are largely excluded socially or economically from developing a gay identity. Similarly heterosexual male carers could provide the same support to heterosexual service users, but generally without the risk that they would be compromising their status as a carer. Such problems and potentials need to be acknowledged when organising same-gender intimate and personal care between men.

Conversely, same-gender intimate care can be an excellent opportunity for male carers to give relatively 'informal' but structured and considered sex education and advice to service users, through an agreed care plan and in response to assessed needs or requests for information on the part of the service user. It may be more ordinary and natural for men to talk about the male body and sexual parts in a comfortable and ordinary fashion when 'allowed for' by the circumstances and opportunities presented during regular personal or intimate care interactions. Personal care situations, one-to-one and private, are also likely to be a more appropriate and productive place to offer advice about personal appearance and personal relationships.

CONCLUSION

Sexuality and considerations of sexuality and gender clearly have a central role to play in designing and delivering intimate and personal care, both in terms of staff and service users. Intimate care sometimes provides a stark focus on the sexuality of service users, whereas it is more easily ignored in many other care situations or interactions. Personal care also provides hidden opportunities to work productively with individuals on issues of sexuality in its widest sense. Often individual care guidelines avoid being explicit about how particular care tasks should be conducted, developing a generic language around the sexual body parts and therefore risking inconsistent approaches and the neglect of health and hygiene.

Adult protection and sexuality policies clearly need to reference intimate and personal care and conversely, intimate and personal care policies need to recognise issues relating to sexuality of staff and service users. They also need to begin to unpack the restrictions as well as safeguards that same-gender intimate and personal care policies impose. Services need to initiate an intelligent debate about how service users' needs can be best met during intimate and personal care, not simply those related to the design and conduct of particular care tasks, but more holistic needs relating to self-image, identity, sexuality and so on. Whilst gender is clearly a very important consideration, it is not the only one, and users and carers need to be matched when considering a whole collection of attributes including sexuality and culture.

REFERENCES

Bradley, H. (1993) 'Across the great divide.' In C.Williams (ed.) *Doing 'Women's Work'*. London: Sage.

Cambridge, P. (1996) *The Sexuality and Sexual Rights of People with Learning Disabilities: Considerations for Staff and Carers*. Kidderminster: British Institute of Learning Disabilities, p.34.

Cambridge, P. (1997) 'How far to Gay? The politics of HIV in learning disability.' *Disability & Society 12*, 3, 427–453.

Cambridge, P. and Carnaby, S. (2000a) *Making it Personal: Practice and Policy in Personal and Intimate Care and People with Learning Disabilities*. Brighton: Pavilion Publishing.

Cambridge, P. and Carnaby, S. (2000b) 'A personal touch: managing the risks of abuse during intimate and personal care for people with learning disabilities.' *Journal of Adult Protection 2*, 4, 4–16.

Cambridge, P., Carnaby, S. and McCarthy, M. (2003) 'Responding to masturbation in supporting sexuality and challenging behaviour in services for people with learning disabilities.' *Journal of Learning Disabilities 7*, 3, 251–265.

Cambridge, P. and McCarthy, M. (1997) 'Developing and implementing sexuality policy for a learning disability provider service.' *Health and Social Care in the Community 5*, 4, 227–236.

Cambridge, P. and Mellan, B. (2000) 'Reconstructing the sexuality of men with learning disabilities: empirical evidence and theoretical interpretations of need.' *Disability & Society 15*, 2, 293–311.

Carnaby, S. (1997) 'What do you think? A qualitative approach to evaluating individual planning services.' *Journal of Intellectual Disability Research 41*, 225–231.

Carnaby, S. (1999) 'Individual programme planning: where is the individual?' *Tizard Learning Disability Review 4*, 3, 4–9.

Carnaby, S. and Cambridge, P. (2002) 'Getting personal: an exploratory study of intimate and personal care provision for people with profound and multiple learning disabilities.' *Journal of Intellectual Disability Research 46*, 2, 120–132.

Clements, J. *et al.* (1995) 'Real men, real women, real lives? Gender issues in learning disabilities and challenging behaviour.' *Disability & Society 10*, 4, 425–435.

Downs, C. and Craft, A. (1997) *Sex in Context: A Personal and Social Development Programme for Children and Adults with Profound and Multiple Impairments.* Brighton: Pavilion Publishing.

Felce, D., Lowe, K. and De Pavia, S. (1994) 'Ordinary housing for people with severe learning disabilities and challenging behaviours.' In E. Emerson, P. McGill and J. Mansell (eds) *Severe Learning Disabilities and Challenging Behaviours: Designing High Quality Services.* London: Chapman & Hall.

Laws, S. (1990) *Issues of Blood: The Politics of Menstruation.* Basingstoke: Macmillan.

McCarthy, M. (1996) 'The sexual support needs of people with learning disabilities: a profile of those referred for sex education.' *Sexuality and Disability 14*, 4, 265–279.

McCarthy, M. (1998) 'Whose body is it anyway? Pressures and control for women with learning disabilities.' *Disability & Society 13*, 4, 557–574.

McCarthy, M. (1999) *Sexuality and Women with Learning Disabilities.* London: Jessica Kingsley Publishers.

McCarthy, M. (2002) 'Going through the menopause: perceptions and experiences of women with intellectual disability.' *Journal of Intellectual and Developmental Disability 27*, 4, 281–295.

McCarthy, M. and Cambridge, P. (1996) *Your Rights about Sex: A Booklet for People with Learning Disabilities.* Kidderminster: British Institute of Learning Disabilities, p.20.

McCarthy, M. and Thompson, D. (1998) *Sex and the 3R's.* Brighton: Pavilion Publishing.

Murphy, G. (1994) 'Understanding challenging behaviour.' In E. Emerson, P. McGill and J.Mansell (eds) *Severe Learning Disabilities and Challenging Behaviours: Designing High Quality Services.* London: Chapman & Hall.

Orme, J. (2001) *Gender and Community Care.* Basingstoke: Palgrave.

Parkin, W. (1989) 'Private experiences in the public domain: sexuality and residential care organisations.' In J. Hearn *et al.* (eds) *The Sexuality of Organisations.* London: Sage Publications.

Rodgers, J. (2001) 'The experience and management of menstruation for women with learning disabilities.' *Tizard Learning Disability Review* 6, 1, 36–44.

Sheppard, R. (1991) 'Sex therapy and people with learning difficulties.' *Sexual and Marital Therapy* 6, 3, 307–316.

Ware, J. (1996) *Creating a Responsive Environment for People with Profound and Multiple Learning Difficulties.* London: David Fulton.

Williams, C. (1993) 'Introduction.' In C.Williams (ed.) *Doing 'Women's Work'.* London: Sage.

CHAPTER 5

Health and Hygiene

Paul Wheeler and Neil James

INTRODUCTION

In the past, a considerable amount of health care was provided by long-stay learning disability institutions (Morgan, Ahmed and Kerr 2000). However, since the passage of the 1959 Mental Health Act, the introduction of normalisation/social role valorisation and the white paper *Better Services for the Mentally Handicapped* (Department of Health and Social Services and the Welsh Office 1971), there has been a developing policy aimed at integrating people with learning disabilities into the wider community and providing access to appropriate occupational and recreational activities (Sowney and Barr 2004). This movement towards integration has culminated in legislation such as the 1990 National Health Service and Community Care Act and the publication of more recent policy documents such as *Valuing People* (Department of Health 2001b), *Fulfilling the Promises* (National Assembly for Wales 2001) and *Same As You* (Scottish Executive 2000).

Although we have seen a move away from large-scale residential care there remains, and always will remain, a need for residential care, and this will be for a variety of reasons. For example, Jenkins (2005) highlights that as a result of advances in medical technology, children with profound and multiple disabilities who previously might have died in childhood are surviving to adulthood. Likewise, the life expectancy of adults with intellectual disability is increasing. Such changes undoubtedly have implications for the care planning process to meet the particular needs of these and other individuals who may experience epilepsy, cerebral palsy, challenging behaviour, autism, profound and multiple learning disabilities and poor mental health.

This chapter briefly considers some of the health needs of people with learning disabilities and issues of access to health care. It also discusses issues relating to infection control and intimate and personal hygiene prior to discussing two areas of intimate and personal care about which concern is often expressed by carers, namely, skin care and menstrual management.

HEALTH INEQUALITIES AND PEOPLE WITH LEARNING DISABILITIES

People with a learning disability are likely to experience similar health needs as the general population. However, in addition to common illnesses and disorders, a number of studies demonstrate that people with a learning disability are more likely to experience health problems than the general population (Welsh Office 1995). In relation to older people with a learning disability, their health needs are likely to be similar to those of older people without a learning disability. However, the health needs of young and middle-aged people with a learning disability are dissimilar to those of members of the general population of a similar age. This may be due to what Beange (2002) refers to as the 'healthy survivors' effect'. That is to say that because people with severe and profound learning disabilities have a reduced life expectancy, the limited number who do survive to older age are likely to be healthier.

Some of the health problems that people with a learning disability experience are the direct result of the syndrome that has resulted in their having a learning disability. For example, people with Down's Syndrome are more likely to experience respiratory difficulties or dementia. Likewise, people with Fragile X have a much higher incidence of epilepsy than the general population. However, many of the health problems experienced by people with a learning disability are not directly due to their learning disability but are the result of lifestyle factors and the indirect consequences of having a learning disability (Jansen et al. 2004). Such factors include social, economic and employment restrictions. The three most widely recognised such factors are nutrition, lack of exercise and medication.

Nutrition

People with a learning disability may be at risk of both over- and under-nutrition. Obesity is a particular risk for people with Down's and Prader-Willi Syndromes. However, there are also high rates of obesity reported amongst people with mild to moderate learning disabilities living in the community who do not have either syndrome. Under-nutrition is mainly prevalent amongst people with severe and multiple disabilities and this may be attributed to such things as dysphaghia (difficulty in swallowing). Unless adequate nutrition is provided through artificial means such as PEG feeding (percutaneous endoscopic gastrostomy), poor nutrition may be a cause of increased mortality.

Lack of exercise

Many people with a learning disability are physically less active than the majority population. This may be due to clinical issues such as quadriplegia, but equally it may be due to their leading sedentary lifestyles. Reasons may lie in the individual being unwilling to undertake physical activity. Alternatively, it may be due to their being reliant on others to support them in undertaking such activity or barriers such as lack of staffing, finances or transport. Physical activity is not only important for positive physical health, but it has also been demonstrated to produce benefits in behaviour, self-concept and mental health issues such as depression.

Medication

Although medication may be necessary for the well-being of individuals if, for example, they experience epilepsy, side-effects may have considerable negative effects on an individual's life. This is particularly the case in relation to psychotropic medication, which may cause extra pyramidal side-effects (movement disorders) and other effects such as weight gain and dental caries. Polypharmacy (the treatment of a person with more than one medication) is common among people with learning disabilities and this may increase the risk of side-effects. A further risk of side-effects arises from the reliance on third-party reports, a lack of regular medication reviews and the inappropriate prescribing of psychotropic medication in order to control behaviours.

These lifestyle factors cause substantial health issues for people with a learning disability. It is therefore important not only that service providers are aware of such issues but that they are addressed in individuals' care plans.

PARTICULAR HEALTH NEEDS OF PEOPLE WITH A LEARNING DISABILITY

In addition to the need for services to be aware of the risk factors outlined above, it is also important that they are aware of particular health needs associated with people with a learning disability. These include cancer, cardiovascular disease, constipation, epilepsy (Kerr *et al.* 2003), thyroid disease (Phillips, Morrison and Davis 2004), gastroesophageal reflux disease, *Helicobacter pylori* and other infections (Turner 2001), osteoporosis and fractures, obesity, poor dental health (Rawlinson 2001), sensory problems (Kerr *et al.* 2003; Woodhouse, Adler and Duignan 2004), and poor mental health (Chaplin 2004). Additionally, they are more prone to accidental injury than the majority population (Sherrard, Ozanne-Smith and Staines 2004).

ACCESS TO HEALTH CARE

Despite the fact that people with a learning disability may have greater health needs than the majority population, research suggests that they are less likely to receive appropriate health care than the non-learning disabled population (Lindsey 1998). In fact, the concern is such that the Disability Rights Commission (DRC), which was created in order to enforce the Disability Discrimination Act 1995 and reduce discrimination on the grounds of disability has recently launched an investigation into the health inequalities experienced by people with a learning disability. Although the findings of the DRC's investigation will not be available for some time, there is a body of literature that provides possible reasons for this phenomenon, some of which will be briefly considered.

First, many generic primary health and social care workers lack information about the additional health care needs of people with a learning disability and in particular, the potential health complications arising from conditions causing learning disability (Cassidy *et al.* 2002). For example, people with Down's Syndrome are more likely to have unstable neck joints and hearing and vision deficits than the general population.

Second, access to health care generally relies on self-reporting (Kerr *et al.* 2003). Given the communication difficulties of some clients this is not always possible. As a result of this, health issues are only addressed if noted by carers, many of whom have little knowledge about the health needs of people with a learning disability. Even where issues are noted by carers, GPs and other generic health care workers may not have the appropriate skills to communicate with a person with a learning disability. This means that they have to rely predominantly on the reports provided by the carer attending the consultation with the individual with the learning disability. As a result of such things as high staff turnover and the frequent use of bank and agency staff, it may be the case that the carer will lack a detailed knowledge of the client and their health needs (Martin 2003). Such factors make it difficult for health care professionals to obtain an accurate history of an individual's health care difficulties. Additionally, GPs and other health care workers are unlikely to be able to undertake an adequate consultation with a person with a learning disability in the consultation periods generally offered. However, they may be unwilling to offer extended appointments due to the payment systems in place. Such issues may lead to poor diagnosis and treatment.

Health surveillance

A third issue relating to access to health care is that of health surveillance. Many people with learning disabilities are not offered appropriate screening. For example, studies have suggested that primary health care workers do not see the relevance of women with learning disabilities receiving breast or cervical screening (Nightingale 2000). Similarly, despite the recognition of health needs over and above those of the general population, appropriate assessments are often not offered on a regular basis.

Government policy, as found in documents such as *Valuing People*, recommends the introduction of 'health action plans'. This implies some form of health needs assessment. Additionally, the National Minimum Standards Directive issued under the Care Standards Act 2000 (Department of Health 2001) states that adults with learning disabilities should be offered health checks on a minimum of an annual basis. This policy is supported by a number of recent research studies that demonstrate the value of the regular health screening of people with a learning disability (e.g., Hunt, Wakefield and Hunt 2001; Martin *et al.* 2004). Such screening often appears to pick up health issues that would have otherwise gone unnoticed. For example, in the study undertaken by Martin *et al.* of 53 clients, 46 (87 per cent) of those attending a health check required one or more health interventions. Such health assessments are generally undertaken by GPs and nurses. However, some assessments such as the OK Health Check (Matthews 1997), are suitable for use by carers to identify health needs prior to clients being seen by a health professional.

Other issues that may increase the level of inequality of health care experienced by people with a learning disability include a lack of compliance with health professionals' management plans; poor or non-existent follow up; transport problems; behavioural problems; low expectations of their health; a possible inability to read and make appointments; poor understanding of time; and a lack of understanding of the process of consultation.

INFECTIONS AND INFECTION CONTROL

As noted above, one area of concern is that people with a learning disability appear at greater risk of infections than the general population. This appears to be the case whether or not the person lives in an institution or group setting (Turner 2001).

Common infections include infection of the eyes and eyelids (Woodhouse, Adler and Duignan 2004), infection of the ears (Cassidy *et al.* 2002) infection of the mouth (Rawlinson 2001), and food-borne infections (Beumer and Kusumaningrum 2003). One of the most common infections experienced by people with a learning disability is *Helicobacter pylori*. This may result in gastritis, peptic ulcer, stomach cancer, dyspepsia and pain. The pain arising from this infection may be a cause of the person exhibiting behaviours such as aggression to self and others and withdrawal. Treatment with antibiotics is possible. However, a recent study by Wallace, Schluter and Webb (2004) suggests that treatment is not as effective in people with a learning disability as in the general population. Moreover, they found that people with a learning disability are likely to experience more side-effects from the treatment than the general population. One possible reason for this is drug interactions between the treatment and other medication the person may be taking.

Given the fact that infections may cause pain and suffering, that treatment of infections may not always be successful and that it may lead the individual to experience side-effects that are likely to impact on their quality of life, it is important that prevention of infection is given greater consideration.

It is generally accepted that a frequent cause of infection is the fact that personal care and hygiene is often inadequate. This may be for a variety of reasons including a lack of understanding of the importance of hygiene on the part of the client or care staff, a dislike of touch by clients, especially those with autistic spectrum disorder, or because of the belief that people should have the right to decline intimate and personal care. This latter issue will be discussed in a little more length in the next section.

Infection control, although sometimes interpreted as a 'health issue' is as applicable in a social care setting or domestic setting as in a health care setting. Although the basic principles of infection control have been long recognised, there has been a recent resurgence of interest in this subject as a result of concerns about the terrorists releasing biological agents, severe acute respiratory syndrome (SARS) and the increasing number of persons becoming infected whilst in-patients in hospitals (Madeo 2004).

One of the most important practices in preventing infection is adherence to what are generally referred to as 'universal precautions'. These relate to three main practices: hand hygiene, the use of personal protective equipment and the safe use and disposal of sharps. Of these three principles, the most important is probably adequate hand washing as this prevents human to human transmission of infective materials which is considered to be the most common method of transmission of pathogens (Curtis, Cairncross and Yonli 2000). This requires that people wash their hands with ordinary soap, ensuring that all areas of the hand are cleaned including the finger tips, between the fingers and the back of the hands. Drying the hands, preferably with a paper towel, is an equally important part of this process as damp hands more readily transmit pathogens (Gould *et al.* 2000). Additionally, failure to dry the hands may result in chapped hands, which create more crevices in the skin, which can harbour pathogens that then contribute to cross-infection.

The use of antibacterial agents in such things as liquid soaps, washing up sponges, and impregnated chopping boards, does not necessarily reduce pathogenic organisms, and therefore they should not be relied on (Beumer and Kusumaningrum 2003). Likewise, alcohol rubs, whilst they are effective at killing bacteria on clean hands, are not effective if used on dirty hands. However, there is a growing body of evidence that suggests that the routine use of an antiseptic hand cream after hand washing and drying is beneficial in the prevention of cross-infection (Gould *et al.* 2000). Hands should be washed frequently throughout the day, and in particular after toileting (self or others) and before and after providing other personal and/or intimate care, as contact with human excretion is one of the main causes of the transmission of infectious disease (Curtis and Biran 2003).

The use of personal protective equipment such as gloves and aprons is also important in the prevention of transmission of infection. However, the wearing of gloves does not remove the need for adequate hand washing, and it is important that they are changed prior to care staff providing intimate or personal care to a different client. Likewise, personal protective equipment should be changed between different activities such as handling dirty laundry and aiding a client with personal hygiene activities (Bennett and Mansell 2004).

Although at first consideration the last of these three principles, safe use and disposal of sharps, may be thought to be irrelevant to non-medical professionals, this is not the case, as support staff may be required to shave clients or may have to dispose of broken items such as crockery.

INTIMATE AND PERSONAL HYGIENE

Given the increased likelihood of people with a learning disability experiencing infections it is important that their intimate and personal hygiene needs are adequately attended to. Where possible, clients should be encouraged to attend to these needs themselves. In many cases this may require that clients are taught new skills (see Chapter 9), are provided with relevant aids such as walk-in baths, or are provided with support in a variety of forms. In other cases, despite such interventions, the client may be unable to attend to their intimate and personal hygiene needs. Where this is the case, clients are reliant upon their carers to ensure that their hygiene needs are adequately met.

Despite the importance of the adequate provision of such care the possible implications arising from either its performance or non-performance for both client and carer are rarely considered (Carnaby and Cambridge 2002). Yet there are numerous important issues that should be considered in relation to such care. For example, what constitutes personal care? How is it different to intimate care? What are the legal and ethical issues relating to the provision of such care?

Who should perform such care? How should such care be undertaken? This section will seek briefly to address some of these issues.

WHAT CONSTITUTES PERSONAL CARE?

In Carnaby and Cambridge's study (2002), carers were asked to categorise particular care activities as either 'intimate care' or 'personal care'. Staff tended to display a preference for carrying out those activities regarded as 'personal care' over those regarded as 'intimate care'. It is not wholly clear from the study why this is the case, but some suggestions relating to such issues as social taboos and societal attitudes towards people with learning disabilities and the value of such care emerge (see Chapter 2). A further reason may be carers' concerns with ethical and legal issues.

ETHICAL AND LEGAL ISSUES

Generally speaking, it is recognised that care should be provided in a manner that is ethical. In other words, prior to commencing care activities, consideration should be given to four ethical principles, namely: 'non-maleficence' (not causing harm), 'beneficence' (doing good), 'autonomy' (treating people with respect and giving them information so as to make their own choices) and 'justice' (considering who will be advantaged/disadvantaged by performance or non-performance of the act).

At times these principles may appear to lead to oppositional or contradictory views. For example, imagine a client who spits at carers every time they approach him to clean his teeth and then hits out until they leave him alone. One carer, following the principle of autonomy, may argue that the client is expressing choice and that the client's teeth should not be cleaned against their will. Another carer may argue along the principle of beneficence that although cleaning the client's teeth may not be enjoyable for the client, it is preferable that the client has their teeth cleaned than they develop dental caries and experience the pain associated with this and the possible long-term need for more invasive interventions such as dental surgery.

In such a situation, carers may turn to the law and ask, 'Which action is lawful?' However, because the law relating to this issue is not to be found in one place and has developed over a period of time, people are often unsure of how they should act in order to comply with the law. For example, the carer who expressed concern in relation to the autonomy of the client may argue that by spitting and hitting out at staff, the client is dissenting to the care offered. They may also believe that if they then go ahead and clean the client's teeth, they are committing an assault on the person. The other carer, however, may be concerned that if they do not provide oral hygiene and the client develops dental caries they will be deemed to have failed to provide adequate care for the client and will be found to be negligent.

In deciding which carer is correct, two questions must be considered. First, does the client have sufficient capacity to consent? Second, if they do have sufficient capacity, have they in fact consented? On a practical level, deciding whether a person has capacity is not a simple issue, as there is no single legally recognised way of ascertaining this, and a court will not necessarily accept the view of an expert such as a psychologist (*R. v. Robbins* [1988] Crim. LR 744). However, there are a number of principles that should be followed. First, there is a rebuttable presumption that all adults have capacity to consent. Second, the law recognises that some decisions are more complex than others and that as a result of this, a person's capacity to consent or otherwise should be assessed in relation to the particular decision that needs to be made. The leading case on the issue of capacity to consent to treatment is *Re C* (Re C (Adult: Refusal of Treatment) [1994] 1 All ER 819). The judge in this case, Thorpe J., reformulated the common law test of capacity to consent to treatment as a three-part test:

- First, the person must comprehend and retain the information given them about the treatment.

- Second, the person must believe the information given them.

- Third, the person must be able to weigh the information in the balance in order to arrive at their choice.

This test recognises that while a person may understand and retain information given to them about a proposed act, as a result of disability they may not believe that information. It also recognises that their decision need not be rational as in *Re T* (Re T (Adult: Refusal of Treatment) [1992] 4 All ER 649) where Lord Donaldson stated that 'the patient's right of choice exists whether the reasons for making that choice are rational, irrational, unknown or even non-existent'. If a person is found to lack capacity in relation to a particular decision, they can neither consent nor withhold their consent (an issue that will be discussed below). If, however, it is ascertained that a person does have the capacity to consent, the next question is 'Has the person in fact consented?' As with the question of capacity, the question of whether the person has in fact consented is answered by reference to other questions, namely:

- Has the person sufficient information about the proposed act?

- Is there an absence of coercion, inducement or fraud?

If both of these questions can be answered positively, then the person's consent or refusal to consent is valid and must be honoured.

If it is found that the client lacks capacity to consent to care and treatment, then no one, not even a parent or advocate, can currently consent on their behalf.[1] In such a case, care and treatment may only be given if it is in the client's best interests. Unfortunately, there is no single test for 'best interests'. However, the courts have stated that best interests are 'not limited to medical best interests' (Re MB (Medical Treatment) [1997] 2 FLR 426). Rather, they encompass such things as 'the invasiveness of treatment, potential benefits and risks and the indignity of the patient' (*Airdale NHS Trust* v. *Bland* [1993] AC 789). They also include 'emotional issues' (Re A (Male Sterilisation) (CA) [2000] 1 FLR 549) and are 'related to quality of life and ... incorporate broader ethical, social, moral and welfare decisions' (*SL* (By Her Litigation Friend, the Official Solicitor) v. *SL* (Her Mother) [2000] EWCA civ. 162). In short, best interests are akin to a welfare appraisal and a balance sheet should be drawn up (*A Hospital NHS Trust* v. *S and others* [2003] EWHC 365). Figure 5.1 demonstrates the complexity of consent and capacity issues:

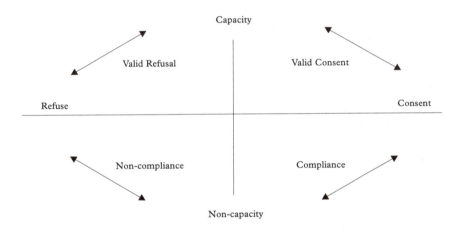

Figure 5.1 Schematic diagram of the complex nature of valid consent and capacity

Given the above issues and the frequent complexity of striking a balance between promoting autonomy and fulfilling one's duty of care, it is extremely important that people do not simply administer intimate and personal care on an ad hoc basis. Rather, services should provide clear policy guidelines that relate to other relevant policy documents such as adult and/or child protection policies, health and safety policies and whistle-blowing policies. However good a policy is, however, it is unlikely to be wholly appropriate to the needs of every individual given the heterogeneity of people with a learning disability. In recognition of this fact, care should be planned around an individual's identified needs following an appropriate assessment and consideration of such matters (where possible) by a multi-disciplinary team. Such assessment and consideration should then be carefully documented. Documenting planned care benefits both clients and carers alike. For example, it goes some way to ensuring that clients receive individualised intimate and personal care in a consistent and appropriate manner, even when such care is being provided by staff who do not know the client such as bank or agency staff. It also reduces the likelihood of litigation or criminal prosecution being brought against staff in relation to such issues as negligence or assault (Wheeler 2003).

Having considered broader issues relating to the provision of intimate and personal care, the following sections of this chapter consider two issues that give particular rise to concern for carers, namely skin care and menstrual management.

SKIN CARE

Recent policy documents stipulate that people with a learning disability should have annual screening of their health needs that include epilepsy, challenging behaviour, mental health, skin and physical health (Department of Health 2001a, 2001b; Martin 2003). This is because there is a higher incidence of specific health problems amongst people with a learning disability (such as epilepsy, challenging behaviour, ill health due to lack of exercise, and sensory impairments). Such health issues may result in them being more susceptible to problems with their skin (Jansen et al. 2004). Studies have also shown (see Jansen et al. 2004) an increased rate of skin disorders of two to three times that of the general population. Given these factors it is important that people with a learning disability receive adequate skin care and monitoring.

The skin is the largest organ of the body and is the most exposed and therefore its care needs to be adequate in order for it to remain healthy and fulfil its many functions (Brown, Wimpenny and Maughan 2004; Penzer and Finch 2001). The functions of the skin include physical protection, regulation of temperature, synthesis of vitamin D and sensory perception (Penzer and Finch 2001). The importance of maintaining healthy skin can also serve to promote positive physiological, psychological and social well-being, as having a skin disorder such as acne, psoriasis or pruritis can lead to loss of self-esteem, self-confidence, social withdrawal, anxiety, depression and stigmatisation along with emotional and physical scars (Jackson 2002; Callender 2004; Brown, Wimpenny and Maughan 2004).

Extra care and special consideration is required for people who have specific behaviours that can result in damage to the skin. These may include self-injurious behaviour, skin picking and compulsive behaviours, which may be the result of particular behavioural phenotypes or mental health problems (Holland et al.

2003). Also, those from ethnic minorities may have further skin care considerations and needs as highlighted by Callender (2004). As we age the skin condition also changes in that it becomes less elastic and the overall healing process from wounds and skin damage can take longer (Penzer and Finch 2001). For those who have limited mobility the risk of breakdown, skin trauma and loss of sensation in the skin is significantly increased especially if there is constant pressure to the same areas of skin (such as the buttocks and hips). Knowledge of the side-effects of psychotropic medication is also important as it may make some people susceptible to skin damage due to increased photosensitivity and therefore the use of sun block may be appropriate.

Promotion of healthy skin therefore may have a number of facets and is incumbent within health promotion activities. To promote healthy skin it is important that the person has an adequate fluid and dietary intake and this may be monitored by use of appropriate charts. If the person has reduced mobility they may need to be given regular verbal prompts and encouragement to change position or may require physical support and appropriate aides obtainable from the local occupational therapy service (for example, hoist, slide sheet or lifting belts). It is also possible to acquire specialist pressure-relieving materials such as mattresses and cushions that are an aid to protection of the skin. For those who need support regarding continence it is important that regular continence checks, the renewing of continence materials and the use of barrier creams is incorporated into the management plan. Penzer and Finch (2001) suggest that water and emollient therapy should be used for skin care in people who are incontinent, as over-washing can be a problem in maintaining skin health (Ersser and Penzer 2000; Penzer and Finch 2001). Other health-promoting activities for the skin include the use of barrier creams such as zinc and castor oil, ensuring that finger nails and toe nails are cared for and kept short, ensuring that the person is dried properly after washing, good coordination of care and the promotion and maintenance of good hygiene.

If necessary, daily monitoring and recording of skin condition should be undertaken with the assistance of tools such as the Waterlow Scale (Waterlow 1992, 1997). When undertaking a skin assessment Penzer and Finch (2001) consider the use of four senses to collect information. These are observation, touch, smell and listening. Note should be made of any unusual markings or changes in the shape or size of blemishes/moles. Guidance should be sought about appropriate creams from the GP or practice nurse.

MENSTRUAL MANAGEMENT

According to the World Health Organization (2000) most women with a learning disability will have regular menstrual cycles commencing around the same time as other women within the general population. Like young women without a learning disability, young women with a learning disability should be informed about menstruation prior to their first menstrual period in order to help reduce not only the impact of this event, but also their anxiety over the physiological changes that they will experience (Fegan, Rauch and McCarthy 1993; Schwier and Hingsburger 2000). They should be assured that what they are experiencing is normal and happens to other women. It may be beneficial and empowering to support the woman in using a chart to keep a record of when she has had a period and when the next one is due.

In explaining menstruation and its management, information should be given by an appropriate person in an understandable format using terminology and vocabulary that the person themselves may use. Where necessary this should be supplemented with the use of augmentative communication strategies, such as visual cues, pictures and story books. Time should be spent discussing a variety of issues including the different types of sanitary products, what they are, how to use them, changing, disposal into a bin and not down the toilet and reminding them of the need for personal hygiene such as washing hands. Again, to support this process it may be necessary to use pictures showing the process from start to finish (for example, see Fanstone and Katrak 2003) or use teaching methods such as chaining or prompting (see Zarkowska and Clements 1994 and Chapter 9 of this volume). There are also a number of training packs that have been developed that can assist in teaching and these are listed in the further reading/resources section in the reference list found at the end of this chapter.

Women with learning disability are also prone to non-sexually transmitted infections such as candida, cystitis and urinary tract infections. Susceptibility to these infections may be the result of a number of factors including being run down, using the contraceptive pill or antibiotics. Symptoms that should be discussed with the person and monitored include itchiness, soreness, frequent urination or abnormal discharge. Pre-menstrual tension may also be experienced and this has a number of physiological symptoms such as headaches, tender breasts, physical tiredness, and change in bowel habits (Fegan, Rauch and McCarthy 1993; Mayo 1999). Women may also experience psychological symptoms such as irritability, depression, anxiety, mood swings, confusion and aggression (Mayo 1999). One of the most frequently reported symptoms reported by women is migraine headaches (Kaunitz 2000). Any of these symptoms can have a detrimental effect on the emotional or behavioural well-being of the person (Connolly 2001). Dependent on the person's ability to communicate there may be a change in behaviour that reflects their discomfort/pain. To help identify causes of any change in physical, emotional or behavioural well-being a thorough assessment should be undertaken that includes detailed history taking, functional behavioural assessment, review of any daily records and the elimination of any physical health needs or psychiatric disorders (Connolly 2001). In order to assess the severity and impact that menstruation may be having on the quality of life of the woman, psychological assessment may also be undertaken using appropriate rating scales to assess for anxiety and depression.

If the person has epilepsy and there is found to be an increase in seizure activity around the time of the menses this may be due to catamenial seizures. Catamenial seizures are related to a reduction in progesterone levels and if this is the case then progesterone supplements may be prescribed during particular times of the menstrual cycle (Smith and Wallace 2001). Also, the use of anti-psychotic and anti-epileptic drugs (AEDs) can have an affect on hormonal and metabolic functions, which may possibly result in the early onset of age-related health issues, memory and cognitive changes (World Health Organization 2000). There may also be problems with drug interactions, particularly with oral contraceptives and enzyme-inducing AEDs (such as phenytoin, carbamazepine and topiramate) that may result in both contraceptive failure and breakthrough bleeding (Smith and Wallace 2001). Consultation with the appropriate specialist may result in a reviewed intervention that reduces problems and concerns (for example, the prescription of an alternative AED that is not enzyme-inducing). A change in the menstrual cycle may also be due to the person's weight as being under- or overweight can affect not only the menstrual cycle (Knox 1999) but also the ratio of oestrogen/progesterone levels that can impact on premenstrual symptoms (Mayo 1999).

Management of menstrual symptoms may be supported by interventions based on behavioural and psychological interventions such as relaxation training and cognitive behavioural therapy (Connolly 2001). Evidence also suggests that the use of exercise can benefit mood symptoms and premenstrual complaints (Connolly 2001). Mayo (1999) reports that recent research findings indicate that nutritional supplements may be effective in controlling symptoms of PMS. The management of menstruation in women with learning disability is not that dissimilar to that of women without learning disability and many women with learning disabilities can, with appropriate training, gain the skills necessary to manage their menstrual care (Grover 2002).

CONCLUSION

Despite the wholesale move from health to social care, this chapter has clearly highlighted the importance of non-health care workers such as parents and social care workers being aware of the health and hygiene needs of the people they support. It is recognised that some of these issues may be considered sensitive by those being asked to assist clients in their personal hygiene. However, such questions can not be avoided if services are to provide holistic, effective and good quality care. In order to enjoy a good quality of life and community participation, positive health outcomes are required, including physiological and psychological well-being. It is therefore imperative that intimate and personal care is planned on an individual client basis using a multi-professional process in accordance with appropriate policies and the law.

NOTE

1   Should the Mental Capacity Bill 2004 be enacted, this situation will change.

REFERENCES

Beange, H. (2002) 'Epidemiological Issues.' In V.P. Prasher and M.P. Janicki, *Physical Health of Adults with Intellectual Disabilities*. London: Blackwell Publishing, pp.1–20.

Bennett, G. and Mansell, I. (2004) 'Universal precautions: a survey of community nurses' experience and practice.' *Journal of Clinical Nursing 13*, 413–421.

Beumer, R.R. and H. Kusumaningrum (2003) 'Kitchen hygiene in daily life.' *International Biodeterioration and Biodegradation 51*, 299–302.

Brown, J., Wimpenny, P. and Maughan, H. (2004) 'Skin problems in people with obesity.' *Nursing Standard 18*, 35, 38–42.

Callender, V.D. (2004) 'Acne in ethnic skin: special considerations for therapy.' *Dermatologic Therapy 17*, 184–195.

Carnaby, S. and Cambridge, P. (2002) 'Getting personal: an exploratory study of intimate and personal care for people with profound and multiple intellectual disabilities.' *Journal of Intellectual Disability Research 46*, 2, 120–132.

Cassidy, G., Martin, D.M., Martin, G.H.B. and Roy, A. (2002) 'Health checks for people with learning disabilities.' *Journal of Learning Disabilities 6*, 2, 123–136.

Chaplin, R. (2004) 'General psychiatric services for adults with intellectual disability and mental illness.' *Journal of Intellectual Disability Research 48*, 1, 1–10.

Connolly, M. (2001) 'Premenstrual syndrome: an update on definitions, diagnosis and management.' *Advances in Psychiatric Treatment 7*, 469–477.

Curtis, V. and Biran, A. (2003) 'Hygiene in the home: relating bugs and behaviour.' *Social Science and Medicine 57*, 657–672.

Curtis, V., Cairncross, S. and Yonli, R. (2000) 'Domestic hygiene and diarrhoea – pinpointing the problem.' *Tropical Medicine and International Health 5*, 1, 22–32.

Department of Health (2001a) *National Minimum Standards for Care Homes for Younger Adults*. Published by the Secretary of State under Section 23(1) of the Care Standards Act 2000, London.

Department of Health (2001b) *Valuing People: A New Strategy for Learning Disability for the 21st Century*. London: HMSO.

Department of Health and Social Services and the Welsh Office (1971) *Better Services for the Mentally Handicapped*. Cmnd 4683. London: HMSO.

Ersser, S.J. and Penzer, R. (2000) 'Meeting patients' skin care needs: harnessing nursing expertise at an international level.' *International Nursing Review 47*, 167–173.

Fanstone, C. and Katrak, Z. (2003) *Sexuality and Learning Disability – A Resource for Staff*. London: fpa.

Fegan, L., Rauch, A. and McCarthy, W. (1993) *Sexuality and People with Intellectual Disability.* Artarmon: MacLennan and Petty Pty Limited.

Gould, D., Gammon, J., Donnelly, M., Batiste, L., Ball, E., De Melo, A.M., *et al.* (2000) 'Improving hand hygiene in community health care settings: the impact of research and clinical collaboration.' *Journal of Clinical Nursing 9,* 95–102.

Grover, S.R. (2002) 'Menstrual and contraceptive management in women with an intellectual disability.' *Medicine and the Community 176,* 108–110.

Holland, A.J., Whittington, J.E., Butler, J., Webb, T., Boer, H. and Clarke, D. (2003) 'Behavioural phenotypes associated with specific genetic disorders: evidence from a population-based study of people with Prader-Willi syndrome.' *Psychological Medicine 33,* 141–153.

Hunt, C., Wakefield, S. and Hunt, G. (2001) 'Community nurse learning disabilities: a case study of the use of an evidence-based screening tool to identify and meet the health needs of people with learning disabilities.' *Journal of Learning Disabilities 5,* 1, 9–18.

Jackson, K. (2002) 'Chronic plaque psoriasis: an overview.' *Nursing Standard 16,* 51, 45–52.

Jansen, D.E.M.C., Krol, B., Groothoff, J.W. and Post, D. (2004) 'People with intellectual disability and their health problems: a review of comparative studies.' *Journal of Intellectual Disability Research 48,* 2, 93–102.

Jenkins, R. (2005) 'Older people with learning disabilities. Part 1: Individuals, ageing and health.' *Nursing Older People 16,* 10, 30–33.

Kaunitz, A.M. (2000) 'Menstruation: Choosing whether...and when.' *Contraception 62,* 277–284.

Kerr, A.M., McCulloch, D., Oliver, K., McLean, B., Coleman, E., Law, T. *et al.* (2003) 'Medical needs of people with an intellectual disability require regular assessment, and the provision of client- and carer-held reports.' *Journal of Intellectual Disability Research 47,* 2, 134–145.

Knox, H. (1999) *SEXplained 2... For Young People.* Chiswick: Knox Publishing.

Lindsey, M. (1998) *Signposts for Success in Commissioning and Providing Health Services for People with Learning Disabilities.* London: Department of Health.

Madeo, M. (2004) 'Commentary on Bennett, G. and Mansell, I. (2004) Universal precautions: a survey of community nurses' experience and practice'. *Journal of Clinical Nursing 13,* 413–421. *Journal of Clinical Nursing 13,* 1017–1019.

Martin, G. (2003) 'Annual health reviews for patients with severe learning disabilities.' *Journal of Learning Disabilities 7,* 1, 9–21.

Martin, G., Philip, L., Bates, L. and Warwick, J. (2004) 'Evaluation of a nurse led annual review of patients with severe intellectual disabilities, needs identified and needs met, in a large group practice.' *Journal of Learning Disabilities 8,* 3, 235–246.

Matthews, D. (1997) 'The OK Health Check: a health assessment checklist for people with learning disabilities.' *British Journal of Learning Disabilities 25,* 4, 138–143.

Mayo, J.L. (1999) 'Premenstrual Syndrome: a natural approach to management.' *Applied Nutritional Science Reports 5,* 6.

Morgan, C.L., Ahmed, Z. and Kerr, M. (2000) 'Health care provision for people with a learning disability: record-linkage study of epidemiology factors contributing to hospital care uptake.' *British Journal of Psychiatry 176,* 37–41.

National Assembly for Wales (2001) 'Fulfilling the promises: proposals for a framework for services for people with learning disabilities.' Cardiff: Learning Disability Advisory Group, National Assembly for Wales.

Nightingale, C. (2000) 'Barriers to health access: a study of cervical cancer screening for women with learning disabilities.' *Clinical Psychology Forum 137*, 26–30.

Penzer, R. and Finch, M. (2001) 'Promoting healthy skin in older people.' *Nursing Standard 15*, 34, 46–52, 54–55.

Phillips, A., Morrison, J. and Davis, R.W. (2004) 'General practitioners' educational needs in intellectual disability health.' *Journal of Intellectual Disability Research 48*, 2, 142–149.

Rawlinson, S.R. (2001) 'The dental and oral needs of adults with a learning disability living in a rural community.' *Journal of Learning Disabilities 5*, 2, 133–156.

Scottish Executive (2000) *Same as You.* Edinburgh: Scottish Executive Health Department.

Schwier, K. and Hingsburger, D. (2000) *Sexuality – Your Sons and Daughters with Intellectual Disabilities.* Baltimore: Paul H. Brookes Publishing Co.

Sherrard, J., Ozanne-Smith, J. and Staines, C. (2004) 'Prevention of unintentional injury to people with intellectual disability: a review of the evidence.' *Journal of Intellectual Disability Research 48*, 7, 639–645.

Smith, P.E.M. and Wallace, S.J. (2001) *Clinician's Guide to Epilepsy.* London: Arnold.

Sowney, M. and Barr, O. (2004) 'Equity of access to health care for people with learning disabilities.' *Journal of Learning Disabilities 8*, 3, 247–265.

Turner, S. (2001) 'Health needs of people who have a learning disability.' In J. Thompson and S. Pickering (eds) *Meeting the Health Needs of People Who Have a Learning Disability*, pp.63–88. Edinburgh: Bailliere Tindall.

Wallace, R.A., Schluter, P.J. and Webb, P.M. (2004) 'Effects of *Helicobacter pylori* eradication among adults with intellectual disability.' *Journal of Intellectual Disability Research 48*, 7, 646–654.

Waterlow, J. (1992) *The Waterlow Scale.* Taunton, Somerset: Newtons, Curland.

Waterlow, J. (1997) 'Practical use of the Waterlow tool in the community.' *British Journal of Community Health Nursing 2*, 2, 83–86.

Welsh Office (1995) *The Welsh Health and Community Care Survey.* Cardiff: Welsh Office.

Wheeler, P. (2003) 'Patients' rights: consent to treatment for men and women with a learning disability or who are otherwise mentally incapacitated.' *Learning Disability Practice 6*, 5, 29–37.

Woodhouse, J.M., Adler, P. and Duignan, A. (2004) 'Vision in athletes with intellectual disabilities: the need for improved eyecare.' *Journal of Intellectual Disability Research 48*, 8, 736–745.

World Health Organization (2000) *Healthy Ageing – Adults with Intellectual Disabilities: Summative Report.* Geneva: WHO.

Zarkowska, E. and Clements, J. (1994) *Problem Behaviour and People with Severe Learning Disabilities – The STAR Approach* (Second Edition). Cheltenham: Stanley Thornes (Publishers) Ltd.

FURTHER READING/RESOURCES

Books

Cooper, C. (1999) *Becoming a Woman. A Teaching Pack on Menstruation for People with Learning Disabilities.* Brighton: Pavilion Publishing.

Hollins, S. and Downer, J. (2000) *Keeping Healthy 'Down Below'.* London: Royal College of Psychiatrists.

NHS (2000) *Good Practice in Breast and Cervical Screening for Women with Learning Disabilities.* Sheffield: NHSBSP/CSP Publications.

Website

www.drc-gb.org
This is the home page of the Disability Rights Commission. You can download from this site their review of the literature appertaining to health inequalities along with information on the progress of their ongoing investigation into health inequalities.

CHAPTER 6

Developing Policies, Procedures and Guidelines for Intimate and Personal Care in Services for People with Learning Disabilities

Paul Cambridge

INTRODUCTION

Social care services seem increasingly inundated with various policies and procedures for just about every aspect of management and practice: sexuality, adult protection, risk management, the use of physical interventions, infection control, and so on. It is hoped that the provision of intimate and personal care will also be included as policy and that it will be effective. It is, however, easy to perceive of such policies as protecting agencies and sometimes staff, at the expense of what we might claim to be intuitive best practice. Although policies tend to set floors to practice in the hope of eliminating bad practices while raising expectations and standards, they may sometimes unwittingly also set ceilings and stifle innovation and best practice. They can be defensive in as much as they place boundaries on management and support in services for people with learning disabilities, but should also be empowering and enabling, in as much as they should promote best practice. Policies and procedures are also caught in a conceptual dilemma in relation to 'whose' best practices and best interests dominate – much work in social care is based on experience, judgement and responding appropriately to the unexpected as much as it is on reflective management and practice, learning from past experience and being grounded in an interpretative consensus.

Policies therefore clearly have their limits as well as their advantages. The limits are perhaps most obvious when policies relate to the often 'invisible' aspects of social care, such as how to manage risk such as abuse (Lee-Treweek 1994), as opposed to how we execute physical interventions, for example. Even in the latter, where there are tangible things happening that can be observed, there has been a difficult and long-running discourse and debate about the pros and cons of different approaches and the rights, wrongs and moralities of different interventions (Harris 2002).

Less 'visible' policy realms include sexuality and adult protection. Arguably, intimate and personal care is relatively visible as it concerns physical aspects of care and physical tasks. However, it also includes invisible aspects such as the feelings and responses of those providing and receiving intimate and personal care, which is often where things go wrong, or staff develop a perspective skewed towards task completion at the expense of the quality of care provided (Carnaby and Cambridge 2002). Moreover, while it may be visible to the carer, there may be a gap between how it is intended and how it is experienced by the care receiver. Further, although it may be visible to those involved in the actual care interaction, it may be invisible to other carers, staff and service users for reasons of privacy. Intimate and personal care is consequently closer to policy areas such as sexuality, where policy helps identify rights and responsibilities and important principles and values in guiding management and practice.

In adult protection, policy has become important because of national priorities (Department of Health 2001). However, it remains the task of local managers and practitioners to articulate the process of investigations and decision-making in adult protection (Cambridge and Parkes 2004), addressing issues of risk in the degree of autonomy in decision-making. The same demands are present in other policy areas such as intimate and personal care. Indeed, risk management has itself become an important policy domain impacting on management and practice across health and social care services (Alaszewski *et al.* 1998, 1999, 2000; Cambridge 2002).

In areas of policy and practice such as sexuality and intimate and personal care, decision-making and monitoring of effectiveness get more difficult because most situations are unique, varying according to those involved in the care interaction and the nature of their relationship, the particular care task involved and where and when the interaction takes place. Rules and guidelines might not always be informative or very helpful, but are needed to inform the interaction or the decision-making surrounding it. The nature of caring relationships and care interventions also compound policy and guidelines as the phenomenological nature of practice becomes even more evident and stark, exacerbating the challenges for policy formulation and implementation. Here the gap between policy and practice is potentially widened further by the physical isolation of those involved in the care interaction as well as its invisibility – rules surrounding best practice suggest this should be conducted in private to respect the dignity of the person receiving the care. How then, we might ask, can policy in this area ever be properly implemented and monitored for its effectiveness?

This difficulty can be responded to in a number of ways. For example, Kent Social Services Department has led the development of multi-agency policies, procedures and protocols in adult protection (Kent Social Services Department 2000). Each 'policy' level has a function. The broad policy provides a framework in which more detailed procedures and protocols help guide staff action, responses and decision-making. In intimate and personal care we can similarly differentiate across a number of policy levels. For example, the intimate and personal care policy can set expectations such as same-gender care and the circumstances under which cross-gender care is allowed. It can stipulate how care relationships are decided upon and how person-centred decisions about intimate and personal care are made. What it cannot do is specify individual intimate and personal care responsibilities of particular staff for particular service users and how particular intimate and personal care tasks are conducted. In short, policy cannot particularise to individuals from the general level.

Individual intimate and personal care guidelines, on the other hand, can help construct care interactions, based on policy, around the needs of individuals, but again limits are evident. Experience suggests that the ways particular care tasks are conducted between the care giver and care receiver are often the most difficult to define and articulate (Cambridge and Carnaby 2000a; Carnaby and Cambridge 2002).

DEVELOPING AND IMPLEMENTING INTIMATE AND PERSONAL CARE POLICY

The reasons policies often fail have been identified (Brown and Cambridge 1997). These include poor dissemination, being too vague or long winded, containing contradictions between rights and responsibilities (of staff as well as between staff and service users), and the absence of supportive individual planning. The last factor is a particularly important consideration for policies on intimate and personal care, where person-centred approaches are essential for helping ensure good quality and productive care interactions. Other reasons cited for the failure of policies include lack of skills or support on the part of staff and a failure to implement thorough training, which is why priority needs to be given to developing staff training and support materials in intimate and personal care (Cambridge and Carnaby 2000a).

Policies are unlikely to succeed if they do not help resolve the problems faced by staff in their day-to-day work, which is why policy implementation needs to go hand in hand with needs assessment as well as staff training, and why policies should be reviewed and updated in the light of experience.

Experience of policy implementation in adult protection (Brown and Stein 1998) suggests complex organisational, management and practice considerations, supporting some level of policy coordination. This could be achieved by having a manager or practitioner leading in organisations providing intimate and personal care – someone to bounce ideas off or with whom to share concerns, or to take responsibility for developing the policy in light of experience. In some policy areas such as adult protection, the importance of specialist coordinators has been demonstrated (Cambridge and Parkes 2004). Experience in intimate and personal care (Cambridge and Carnaby 2000a) also suggests the need for lead responsibilities and that time will need to be protected to discuss and reflect effectively on practice in intimate and personal care and to feed this through to the development and review of policies and individual guidelines. Often, regular discussion or information-exchange mechanisms such as staff meetings, peer review or supervision do not have the capacity in time or space required to discuss intimate and personal care practice adequately. Having a dedicated lead person can help close this policy–practice gap.

Policies cannot answer all questions or provide guidance on every individual case or difficulty that is likely to arise in providing intimate and personal care. They can, however, provide a framework for establishing general principles, setting out how and by whom decisions should be made and defining associated responsibilities. However, under-prescriptive policies lose practice relevance and can lead to ambiguity, so it is important to achieve a balance between general principles and specific guidance. Having case studies of particular situations or dilemmas and how these might be resolved satisfactorily can help close the policy–practice implementation gap.

A model for policy implementation exists from work in sexuality policy development that could be used to help develop and review intimate and personal care policy in services for people with learning disabilities (Cambridge and McCarthy 1997). Policy development and implementation should not be an abstract exercise, divorced from the experiences of staff, service users or managers. In their case study of sexuality policy development, Cambridge and McCarthy initiated preliminary staff training, men's and women's sex education groups and meetings with relatives in order to include the views of different stakeholders and identify the range of issues which policy needed to acknowledge and respond to as well as potential conflicts.

The policy was then implemented through a consultation and training process with staff and relatives. User consultation groups also proved a helpful mechanism for identifying what was important to service users in best value reviews (Cambridge and McCarthy 2001); although people with profound and multiple disabilities are likely to be unable to participate in such mechanisms, some people with learning disabilities receiving intimate care are able to be consulted. Indeed, insights and transferable lessons can also be provided by discussions with others receiving intimate and personal care, such as people with physical disabilities. More directly, for those individuals receiving intimate and personal care, a working group (Cambridge and Carnaby 2000a) could be constructed, comprising family members, staff or advocates who know the individual well and who could help develop individual care guidelines and advise on the provision of intimate and personal care. Similar consultation groups could be developed at the policy level.

OPERATIONAL POLICIES FOR INTIMATE AND PERSONAL CARE

Figure 6.1 illustrates how policies on intimate and personal care in services for people with learning disabilities are open to influence from a range of sources within and outside services. Similarly the issues covered by policy will be wide, applying not only to how intimate and personal care is organised and delivered and the values that underpin the provision of intimate and personal care, but also how intimate and personal care fits with other policies. These include policies on sexuality, adult protection, risk management and infection control, as well as government policy on social inclusion and the development of learning disability services as articulated in *Valuing People* (Department of Health 2001).

Choice and inclusion at the social policy level will need to be translated to choice in such matters as the provision of intimate and personal care and how this fits with initiatives such as person centred planning. Policies will also need to address how intimate and personal care fits with practice issues such as key-working arrangements, supervision, the use of communication, support of people with profound and multiple learning disabilities and other complex needs, person centred planning, and so on. Policies, procedures and guidelines on intimate and personal care, like those in other areas of practice, will consequently need to work on a number of issues.

The following sections of this chapter examine the main issues that have an impact on how intimate and personal care is provided and that policy will likely need to address.

Abuse and neglect

There are a number of areas where the law should potentially inform the planning and delivery of intimate and personal care for people with learning disabilities. If intimate and personal care is conducted in careless or thoughtless ways that physically hurt the person receiving it, or results in injury, then this

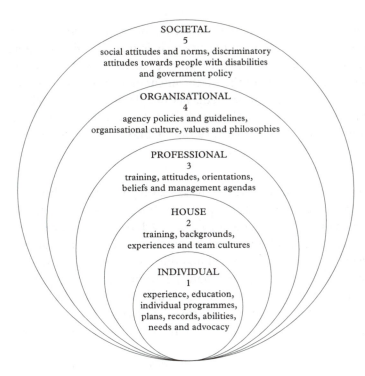

Figure 6.1 Influences on policy and practice

would not only be seen as reckless but, under adult protection policy, would be defined as physical abuse. It might also be seen as assault under criminal law.

Similarly, if a person's intimate care needs, such as those recognised in individual guidelines or through service planning meetings or care plans, are neglected, then this would also constitute abuse under adult protection policy. However, it might also be seen as a failure in duty of care, which might have common law or criminal consequences. Even aspects of care not referenced in guidelines would potentially apply. If someone clearly needed help to use the toilet, or if their continence pad required changing and nothing was done, then this would be irresponsible and could result in pain, injury or other health consequences. Neglect is not doing a care task appropriately with due regard to the person's welfare, as well as not doing it when it would be reasonable to expect it to be done. Leaving someone on the toilet or in a bath unattended, resulting in injury, suffering or distress to the person, are examples of how this might happen.

Policies on intimate and personal care clearly need to spell out that a failure to provide intimate and personal care according to agreed procedures outlined in individual guidelines or according to general policy principles could, depending on the circumstances, be experienced by the person receiving care or be judged by others as abusive, neglectful or even constituting a criminal offence. Most vulnerable adult policies include neglect and mistreatment and, more centrally for intimate and personal care, failure to keep to care guidelines, as categories of abuse, according to the intention of *No Secrets* (Department of Health 2000). Indeed, there are frequent examples where the breaching of care guidelines has been the main characteristic of abusive cultures in residential care (Buckinghamshire County Council 1998; Cambridge 1999a; Macintyre 1999).

Sexuality

Sexuality is another area where the law as well as good practice drivers influence how intimate and personal care is provided. It is in intimate care provision that the sexual parts of people's bodies are exposed during washing and drying or the application of medication, and it is such interactions that can potentially create legal as well as social or cultural dilemmas. Clearly touching someone else's sexual parts such as penis, vagina, anus or breasts during intimate and personal care can be justified when this is part of the care plan and there is a specific reason for this, such as personal hygiene. However, even in such circumstances, other considerations apply, such as whether and how towels, cleaning pads, flannels or gloves are used by the person providing the care.

First, there is usually no necessity for direct contact between the person's fingers and the sexual parts of the other person's body. Second, the task should be done in the least invasive way possible, minimising the use of touch or rubbing which could be experienced as sexually stimulating by the person receiving the care. Clearly there may be instances where this happens but is unintended, such as cleaning under a man's foreskin (Cambridge and Carnaby, 2000b), but the justification for such care interactions needs to be transparent. Third, insertion of fingers or objects should specifically be avoided, as this is potentially a more direct and invasive form of touch or sexual stimulation. The exception would be agreed administering of medication such as pessaries or suppositories. Fourth, if the person reacts sexually, then the carer should have a strategy for withdrawing or closing the care interaction to indicate to the person that it is not of a sexual nature.

Clearly, therefore, any direct or indirect sexual stimulation on the part of the carer would be totally inappropriate and would be defined as sexual abuse under adult protection policy (Department of Health 2000). Moreover, the 2003 Sexual Offences Act makes it an offence for a care worker or anyone else working in services for people with learning disabilities to have sex with a service user, which includes any form of sexual contact such as touching (Wheeler 2004). If a person indicates a wish to masturbate then this should be accommodated through sex education or enabling strategies rather than direct masturbation during tasks of intimate care (Cambridge and McCarthy 1997; Cambridge, Carnaby and McCarthy 2003).

Consent to touch

In many cases we are unable to assess consent to touch on the part of the person receiving intimate and personal care and consequently fall back on 'best interests' or 'duty of care' considerations. However, policy needs to work through these difficult questions. Capacity to consent can be assessed, and comparisons with how people do or don't make decisions in other aspects of their lives can be used to help assess whether someone might be able to give consent to sex (Murphy 2003; Murphy and O'Callaghan 2004) or related aspects such as consent to touch during intimate care. Clearly someone with a profound and multiple learning disability and little or no expressive communication is unlikely to be able to consent in the same way as someone with a moderate learning disability. Indicators may consequently have to be used to help determine their experiences of intimate care, weigh any negative factors against what is in the person's best interests, and what else might need to be done to minimise any negative experiences on their part.

Policies should stipulate the principles for responding to such dilemmas. Nind and Hewett (1994) identify a set of guiding principles to help justify touch: physical contact should only be with the consent of the service user, it needs to have a purpose and it should itself be an important mode of communication. This can be developed into a considered process of checks:

1. Work slowly with the individual.
2. Think carefully about the movements that you make and your body language generally.
3. Sensitivity leads to participation rather than compliance.
4. Use the one-to-one interaction of personal and intimate care as an opportunity for spending time and communicating with the person.

Policies should underline that any negative communication or response on the part of the service user during intimate and personal care, such as facial expression, vocalisation related to distress or pushing the carer away, should always be reported and discussed.

Planning and reviewing intimate and personal care

Policies will need to map out for managers and staff good practice procedures for planning and reviewing the organisation and delivery of intimate and personal care to individuals. This should follow a basic assessment process identifying someone's support needs, what should be in place to effectively meet them and who will ensure that this happens. Everyone receiving intimate and personal care should have individual guidelines, and policy should encourage these to be more than a list of care tasks required and when they should be undertaken – which is often the case (Carnaby and Cambridge 2002). They should ideally record how different care tasks are conducted in ways that have been identified to be least intrusive for the person or preferred by the person themselves, such as the particular materials used and, where possible, who should be providing the care. Policy will therefore need to stipulate how such guidelines are developed, where they are held and how they are used and updated.

As such policies will clearly need to tie in with other aspects of micro-organisation in services for people with learning disabilities. Person centred planning (Department of Health 2001) will need to include the person's preferences and wishes for intimate and personal care with individual service planning, including information on how resources at team level will be used and allocated to ensure intimate and personal care is delivered according to these individualised plans and guidelines. As care planning and care management for people with learning disabilities varies widely between services and local authorities (Cambridge 1999b), it will be important for policies to map such responsibilities and relationships in relation to intimate and personal care.

Key-workers, and care managers where available, will have important roles to play. The key-worker might be the main person responsible for ensuring that intimate and personal care is delivered according to the guidelines and plans and is reviewed through the planning system as well as informally. They may also be the main person directly providing intimate and personal care to the client. The care manager or service manager will be best placed to ensure that individual plans and guidelines are in place in services, that they are consistent between different services and carers, such as those in residential and day services and family carers, and that they are properly reviewed, not only through person centred planning but that the necessary care providers come together to regularly review intimate and personal care. This will be important within residential care itself, where the service manager may need to ensure that members of the team have protected time to review and discuss intimate and personal care provision for individuals.

Same-gender intimate and personal care

Same-gender care principles will undoubtedly need to receive prominence in policy as they underpin most practices. However, policies will need to be clear about the reasons for same-gender care and its inherent limitations. In particular, policy discussion should pay much more attention to the circumstances under which cross-gender care might be appropriate, not only from female staff to male service users, but from men to women where there is a clear rationale for this. This might include circumstances where the care receiver has expressed a preference or where male to female care is justified for other reasons, such as scarcity of other staff or the availability of agency staff. In any case, the risks to the worker and client will need to be addressed, just as they should be in same-gender care.

One of the primary rationales for same-gender intimate and personal care is that it helps protect vulnerable female service users from sexual abuse by male staff. This is rational in so much as intelligence on sexual abuse (e.g. Brown, Stein and Turk 1995; Buchanan and Wilkins 1991; Dunne and Power 1990; Hard and Plumb 1987; McCarthy and Thompson 1996; Sobsey and Varnhagen 1989) demonstrates that almost all known cases of sexual abuse of people with learning disabilities are perpetrated by men. However, the largest group of perpetrators are other service users (Bergh, Hoekman and Ploeg 1997; Brown *et al.* 1995; McCarthy and Thompson 1996; Turk and Brown 1993), although it is important to acknowledge that male staff generally form the second largest group in those studies which examine this. Regardless of the mixed messages in such evidence, it is irrational to use information on sexual abuse to wholly inform the gender of intimate and personal care relationship and interactions from a number of angles.

First, it fails to protect male service users from sexual abuse from male staff during intimate and personal care. Intelligence on sexual abuse informs us that up to half of the victims of sexual abuse are men with learning disabilities (e.g. Brown *et al.* 1995). Second, it fails to protect both women and men with learning disabilities from physical abuse or neglect during intimate and personal care. Neglect is itself a recognised category of abuse (Department of Health 2000). In hidden and private care situations, such risks increase (Lee-Treweek 1994). Intimate and personal care is generally hidden or invisible as it is conducted in private and is where neglect or physical or sexual abuse could happen with a low chance of being witnessed, although some circumstantial or forensic evidence might be available if abuse was suspected. Third, it fails to protect vulnerable women or men with learning disabilities from sexual abuse from male staff or carers in other care situations and settings.

The bottom line of the argument is surely that our skills in recognising and reporting adult protection concerns should not be so weak that we are incapable of putting supervision, monitoring and review systems in place for intimate and personal care that not only ensure the quality of the care we provide but also help protect the recipients of intimate and personal care from abuse, be this sexual, psychological or physical. Moreover, our general competence in adult protection should be such that we should not need to fall back on assumed 'safeguards' such as same-gender intimate care policies.

At one level it could be argued that same-gender policies screen out potential sexual abusers, which is the argument for police checks and POVA.[1]

However, such devices have operational and conceptual holes and cannot and should not replace broader recognition skills and competence in adult protection. They definitely should not deny quality care opportunities for people with learning disabilities or quality care experiences for male staff. Sometimes they achieve the opposite to their intention. For example, they increase risk by allowing or encouraging agency staff, who may be unvetted or unknown to the regular staff team or more importantly to service users, to provide intimate care.

The idea of cross-gender care is embedded in cultural and social norms and expectations. As a society we encourage specific gendered roles in caring as we value caring from women to men and other women. At one level, therefore, same-gender intimate and personal care policies deny the broad cultural appropriateness of caring from women to men, regardless of learning disability. But it is in this area that policies interestingly become elastic and open to pragmatic and resource factors. Men are scarce within and outside social care services, so it is often simply essential for women to provide intimate care to some men with learning disabilities. Moreover, a number of difficulties are associated with the pragmatic interpretation of policies to allow cross-gender care from women to men and the arguable over-zealous interpretation of policies to deny cross-gender care from men to women.

First, such policies often fail to protect women staff from sexual harassment from men with learning disabilities themselves and do not take account of how negatively some women may feel about providing intimate care to men. Second, they inhibit the development of caring roles and caring cultures by men with the implementation of rigid boundaries in one direction excluding men from an important area of care and inhibiting conventional boundaries about the socialisation of gendered roles to be challenged. In the process potentially important resources for providing quality and sensitive intimate and personal care may be denied.

Third, such policies deny choice on the part of people with learning disabilities themselves, which is itself a central policy objective (Department of Health 2001). Although some men with learning disabilities may prefer intimate and personal care from women for inappropriate reasons – for example, they gain sexual gratification from the care interaction – some women may prefer intimate and personal care from a male carer for positive reasons, for example they have a good relationship and level of trust and empathy with the male worker and feel that this should be extended into intimate care relationships.

Fourth, and perhaps most worryingly from the viewpoint of equal opportunities and diversity policies, such policies represent heterosexist assumptions. Technically, of course, they leave both men and women with learning disabilities at risk of sexual abuse from homosexual male and female staff. However, this reduces to an invisible risk from homosexual female staff, given the evidence about gender and sexual abuse. In relation to the assumed risk of abuse from homosexual men, interpretation of this same evidence would suggest that it is not so much the gender of the victim that is significant to the abuser, rather the exercise of power and control over someone who is vulnerable and relatively powerless.

Those receiving intimate and personal care are indeed the most powerless given their high levels of dependency on others, their likely lack of access to sex education and understanding of what is and is not appropriate in relation to sex and their bodies, and their relative lack of voice, either through poor expressive communication or through exclusion from participation and decision-making more widely in services. Policies on intimate and personal care and individual guidelines for care therefore have to give as much consideration to how power-lessness can be addressed as to gender in the care relationship or interaction. When considering gender, formulations need to be based more on the nature and quality of the caring relationship rather than on simple dogma about same-gender care.

Equal opportunities and anti-discriminatory practice

Equal opportunities polices and principles, along with non-oppressive and anti-discriminatory practice, are as important for guiding the provision of intimate and personal care as any other area of practice, as religion and culture have the potential to impact on how intimate and personal care is provided and by whom. Stark evidence points to discrimination in both access to and the quality of health social care services on the basis of race and ethnicity (Ahmad and Atkin 1996; Skellington 1992), underlining the importance of addressing race and culture in policy. This is also important in services for people with learning disabilities because demographic trends are pointing to increasing representation of minority ethnic groups (Emerson and Hatton 1999). This is important both for the support provided to individuals working on staff teams and for service users themselves. Teams have a particular cultural identity, experience or reality, and this may or may not mesh with those of individuals working on teams or those using their services.

In services where most people are unable to speak for themselves, staff cul-ture is likely to be most dominant. This can result in intimate and personal care being delivered in uniform ways, reflecting the social norm rather than any diversity present in the user group. Gender, age and culture are all relevant to ensuring appropriate and respectful intimate and personal care interactions. Pol-icy should state the ways in which such characteristics might inform intimate and personal care relationships, how cultural identity is to be assessed for a per-son with a learning disability (Newland 1999) and how processes of cultural assimilation may need to be countered.

Other considerations include how the culture or religion of staff influences their capacity to provide intimate and personal care and how the culture and religion of service users affects their capacity to receive intimate and personal care. In addition to gender and age matching where appropriate – for example, it might be disrespectful to have a young woman provide intimate care to an older man – policies also need to recommend priorities for matching care giver with care receiver on the basis of culture and race to help develop culturally appropriate care interactions. This will include examples of how intimate care can be provided across and within different cultures and religions, and there are unlikely to be rigid prescriptions. Everyone is part of a culture that operates at different levels – family, friends, local communities, wider communities of interest, religious and ethnic identities and sexual and gender identities – affecting the rituals of daily living (Hannah 1994).

Specific examples of good practice should be provided in policies, but also suggestions for the process by which staff and managers design culturally appropriate intimate and personal care. Individual arrangements can be agreed, for example, through discussions between team members or with team members from a particular culture or religion, both with regard to provision of care from their cultural perspective but also the receipt of culturally appropriate care. Rarely will generalisations apply, and often in the past some minority ethnic identities have been overgeneralised in ways disrespectful to religious, language and cultural groups and sub-groups, typified in the use of terms such as 'Asian culture'. Other ways individual arrangements can be mapped out include consultation with family or relatives, religious or cultural leaders and representatives or local community groups.

Staff sexuality

Same-gender policies also tend to make invisible the needs and feelings of lesbian and gay identified staff who provide intimate and personal care. This risks denying their feelings about providing same-gender intimate care and perhaps the concerns of their heterosexual colleagues about the appropriateness of such practices for homosexual staff. In such situations sexuality intersects with gender to compound the rigidity of such policies. Lesbian and gay staff interviewed in studies about intimate and personal care (Cambridge and Carnaby 2000b; Carnaby and Cambridge 2002) have indeed expressed their concern about what effectively amounts to heterosexist assumptions on the part of policy.

Policies should consequently examine the position and experience of lesbian and gay staff in the provision of intimate and personal care. They should, for example, acknowledge that homosexual staff should not automatically be expected to provide same-gender care, that in some circumstances it might be appropriate for gay men to provide intimate and personal care to women and that it might or might not be appropriate for lesbian or gay identified staff to provide intimate and personal care respectively to lesbian and gay identified service users, depending on how useful such a support relationship might be for reinforcing positive lesbian and gay identities and positive self-image on the part of the service user.

Staff selection, recruitment and supervision

Policies should help to ensure that intimate and personal care is adequately addressed in a range of staffing and personnel processes. This is important to ensure adequate visibility is given to an aspect of social care work that has traditionally been hidden and unspoken about. How many advertisements for jobs in services for people with profound and multiple learning disabilities mention intimate and personal care and in how many interviews is this referenced as perhaps one of the most significant physical aspects of social care work? How many job and person specifications outline expectations or responsibilities for intimate and personal care?

Policies need to work systemically in increasing recognition of the importance of intimate and personal care through all aspects of staff recruitment and retention, underlining how it is a critical aspect of care for many people with learning disabilities – as well as many other groups. But policies need also to stress how it can become a positive aspect of a job and a quality aspect of the support provided to people with learning disabilities, helping move it from the hidden and unspoken realm of 'dirty work' to the visible and empowering realm of 'quality support'.

Part of the job of policies is therefore also to help determine and deliver appropriate staff development. Research on staff values and attitudes (Carnaby and Cambridge 2002) indicates relatively high ratings of dissatisfaction with intimate care tasks such as continence management compared to less intrusive personal care tasks such as hair care, which staff generally report as more satisfying. Such experiences mirror a society that devalues and stigmatises disability and dependency and that values ability, independence and the status of the individual. Training and staff support needs to be targeted at moving intimate and personal care from negative aspects of task completion to the positive aspects of quality interaction.

Training in intimate and personal care also needs to tie together the different policy domains relevant to working with high support needs, including adult protection, sexuality, infection control, equal opportunities and risk management. It needs to be grounded in the real issues that confront support staff and managers on a day-to-day basis in the provision of intimate and personal care and enable and empower them to develop management and practice competence.

Working with agency and bank staff

Due to resource constraints and difficulties in recruiting and retaining staff and regular demands such as sickness and staff leave, most staff teams will be faced with the necessity to use staff from outside the team. Policies can provide important safeguards for ensuring that agency and bank staff are used appropriately and in a considered way in areas of support such as intimate and personal care where the risks of neglect, mistreatment and abuse are highest. Such risks may be heightened because agency staff may not be familiar with working with people with complex needs, may not be accountable in the same way as staff on the regular team and may not be as committed or experienced as the permanent staff.

Policy could stipulate that the use of agency staff is a last resort and that a bank team of workers known to regular staff and service users is employed under such circumstances, aiming to ensure that most gaps in rotas can be filled at short notice. If it proves necessary as a last resort to use agency staff, then they can be employed outside the provision of intimate and personal care. This frees time for regular staff to conduct more sensitive and individual work and care interactions. In either case, policy should stipulate the principles under which agency staff provide intimate and personal care should this ever become necessary (Cambridge and Carnaby 2000a). These stipulations might include:

- always asking the agency regularly employed by the service to send members of staff who have worked with the team on previous occasions

- not allowing agency workers to deliver intimate or personal care on their initial shifts if at all possible

- providing a thorough introduction to the service and the people using it

- explicit reference to the expectations and standards required for the conduct of intimate and personal care

- support, review and feedback, with discussion and information exchange.

In addition, control over the use of agency staff can be gained by taking a more proactive approach, such as visiting the agencies and talking to them about their values and approach, asking about training in areas such as empathic handling or intimate care or about their supervision and support arrangements, and assessing their general competencies for working with people with learning disabilities and complex needs.

Integrating health and social care

Policy and practice in intimate and personal care for people with learning disabilities retains stark contrasts across services, agencies and professional settings. In my experience, different approaches tend to be taken between services in heath and social care settings to providing intimate and personal care. In the former it tends to be a routine expectation and all staff are expected to provide or assist with care tasks, while in the latter it tends to be more socially constructed and regulated. This mirrors the differences between medical and health models on the one hand and social models of disability on the other. However, policies provide an important opportunity to bring together the health and social care aspects of providing intimate and personal care. For example, policies should encourage all staff involved in intimate and personal care to be alert to the illnesses and conditions which might only be identified at an early stage during such care interactions. Examples include oral hygiene and the presence of bleeding gums, sexually transmitted infections or urinary tract infections signified by vaginal or penile discharge, skin conditions such as fungal infections or eczema, signs of self-injury or self-harm such as skin picking or biting, lumps on breasts or testicles, ingrowing toenails or corns, thrombosis or swelling of legs or ankles, high temperatures and wounds such as cuts or pressure sores not healing, unusual body odours or bad smells in urine or faeces. These are only the key signs to look for, but a host of health issues are more likely to be spotted during intimate and personal care, helping develop a preventive approach that enables early intervention. Policies should alert staff to these and clearly articulate what to do if particular health concerns are recognised.

CONCLUSION

As argued, policies are not a panacea to providing good quality intimate and personal care for people with learning disabilities. However, if properly designed and implemented, they have the potential to help services develop competence in this important area of practice. I have come across situations such as an all-male team where men automatically provide intimate care to women with learning disabilities and challenging behaviour, assuming that this is acceptable. I have organised workshops where women participants have expressed a preference for intimate and personal care in a health care context to be provided by men, on the grounds that men are more considerate than other women when providing cross-gender care. Some cultures demand that women provide intimate and personal care and others do not. There seem to be no hard and fast rules about what should or what does happen in the provision of intimate and personal care, but policies have the role and function of helping frame decision-making and guiding action.

Risk assessment and risk management are now central to much health and social care practice, and intimate and personal care is one of the highest risk situations in services for people with learning disabilities, with risks evident for both service users and staff. A risk management approach may be helpful in intimate and personal care in that it can help articulate responses and decision-making for difficult care tasks or for intimate and personal interactions in which difficult issues arise. High-risk situations include the presentation of sexual behaviour by service users during intimate care, balancing the rights of dignity and privacy with the risks of abuse in closed care settings and identifying situations where the risk of neglect is most likely.

Services and practitioners that fail to acknowledge and notify risk are more open to allegations of abuse, neglect or simply bad practice. On the other hand, it also needs to be acknowledged that an unhealthy obsession with defensive practice will itself risk staff and services entering into a mindset of the lowest common denominator of practice, with innovation and creativity stifled. But this is also why policy is so important in an area such as intimate and personal care, where consent to touch may be impossible to gauge, professional judgements may need to take precedence over legal considerations and effective practice uncovered through lateral approaches to care and interaction.

Ultimately, this reduces to the task of identifying what a policy on intimate and personal care might look like and need to cover. The following outlines have been developed to provide a model from which policy and guidelines can be developed. Policies will need to be tailored to the provision of good quality intimate and personal care in specific services and organisational contexts and individual guidelines will need to reflect the intimate and personal care needs of individual service users in the context of such policies. Both policies and guidelines will need regular review in light of experience and changing circumstances.

Policies

1. Introduction
    - Statement as to why intimate and personal care is important.
    - Statement of aims and intent of policy.
    - Links with other policies and procedures, such as risk management, adult protection, sexuality and infection control.

2. Definitions and context

    - Defining and differentiating intimate and personal care.
    - Clarifying the range of care interactions and the different considerations for delivery.
    - Acknowledging how these might be experienced by staff and service users.

3. Key principles

    - Discussion of how key principles can be promoted during intimate and personal care.
    - Choice, respect, dignity, privacy, confidentiality, independence and culturally appropriate support.
    - Why these are important and the conflicts these might bring.

4. Key issues

    - Identification and review of key management and practice issues.
    - Care planning, same-gender care, sexuality, adult protection and the law.
    - Examples and case studies of best practices in these areas.

5. Operational issues

    - Rules for the use of agency staff and newly recruited staff.
    - Support through supervision and line management.
    - Key-working and management responsibilities.

6. Decision-making and responsibilities

    - Use of individual guidelines and autonomy in decision-making.
    - Where to get advice and support when needed.
    - Need to know criteria and information sharing.

What might policy statements look like? The following provide simple examples.

Staff carrying out intimate care tasks will be provided with protective clothing such as disposable aprons and latex gloves. All staff should be aware of the safe methods for the disposal of soiled incontinence pads and other items soiled with body fluids and of used protective clothing. All such soiled items to be placed in the yellow medical waste bin.

Areas where intimate and personal care tasks are carried out should be private with a suitable amount of space available for completing the task with the equipment required. As a last resort a screen should be used if there is no suitable space.

Involve the user in all aspects of the care task using their own individual form of communication. Keep them informed of what is going to happen and what is happening, such as any transfers you need to make such as from a wheelchair to the toilet (all transfers should be supported by two members of staff). Where possible ask the person to indicate any preferences and let them know when you will be touching them and why. Be observant of any physical signs of discomfort or stress and reassure the person if this happens. Report any pressure marks, bruising or possible health issues.

Individual guidelines

1. Background to intimate and personal care for the person
    *   Who leads and coordinates intimate and personal care for that person.
    *   The role of the manager and key-worker.
    *   Where more detailed information or accounts on intimate and personal care needs are held.

2. Outline of intimate and personal care task needed
    *   The actual tasks the person needs help with.
    *   Information on when and where help is usually required.
    *   Guidance on how each task is best completed.

3. Care responsibilities
    *   Who is best placed to conduct each task and why.
    *   Who else is best placed to provide assistance.
    *   What should happen in the absence of key staff.

4. Guidance on the care interaction
    *   How to communicate most effectively with the person.
    *   Responding to the person's preferences and choices.
    *   Advice on how to make the interaction enjoyable and positive.

What might statements in individual care guidelines look like? The following provides an example.

Spare pads, pants and communication book are in Claire's shoulder bag. One member of staff to assist. Claire will walk only if holding onto someone's hand or with her walking frame, plus a little assistance and reassurance. She will need assistance in adjusting clothing and in sitting on the toilet. Tuck the toilet paper out of sight as Claire will often pull as much as possible onto the floor. Leave her for about ten minutes, checking discreetly from time to time. When she is ready she will take a proffered hand and stand up. If she is not ready she will refuse to take it. Then assist her to dress and walk. Female staff should remind each other that Claire is on the toilet and to record in her daily communication book for her mother, whether or not she has had a bowel movement. Toilet times: 9.30, 11.45 (unless she prefers to go straight to the dining room), 1.45 and 3.45.

Currently we are trying to find out whether or not she wipes her bottom and whether we need to wipe her bottom for her. We are also trying to find out more about the significance of the different timings and why the careful monitoring of her bowel movements is necessary. Is it for her health or her mother?

NOTE

1   Protection of Vulnerable Adults Scheme, which 'acts as a workforce ban on those professionals who have harmed vulnerable adults in their care. It will add an extra layer of protection to…stop known abusers from entering the care workforce' (Department of Health 2004).

REFERENCES

Ahmad, W. and Atkin, K. (1996) *Race and Community Care*. Buckingham: Open University Press.

Alaszewski, A., Harrison, L. and Manthorpe, J. (eds) (1998) *Risk, Health and Welfare: Policies, Strategies and Practice*. Buckingham: Open University Press.

Alaszewski, H., Parker, A. and Alaszewski, A. (1999) *Empowerment and Protection: The Development of Policies and Practices in Risk Assessment and Risk Management in Services for People with Learning Disabilities*. London: Mental Health Foundation.

Alaszewski, A., Alaszewski, H., Ayer, S. and Manthorpe, J. (2000) *Managing Risk in Community Care: Nursing, Risk and Decision-making*. London: Bailliere Tindall.

Bergh, P., Hoekman, J. and Ploeg, D. (1997) 'Case file research: nature and gravity of sexual abuse and the work method of an advisory team.' *NAPSAC Bulletin No. 18*, January. Nottingham: University of Nottingham.

Brown, H. and Cambridge, P. (1997) 'Policies and their contribution to coherent decisionmaking.' In P. Cambridge and H. Brown (eds) *HIV and Learning Disability*. Kidderminster: British Institute of Learning Disabilities.

Brown, H. and Stein, J. (1998) 'Implementing adult protection policies in Kent and East Sussex.' *Journal of Social Policy 27*, 3, 371–396.

Brown, H., Stein, J. and Turk, V. (1995) 'The sexual abuse of adults with learning disabilities: report of a second two year incidence survey.' *Mental Handicap Research 8*, 1, 1–22.

Buchanan, A. and Wilkins, R. (1991) 'Sexual abuse by the mentally handicapped: difficulties in establishing prevalence.' *Psychiatric Bulletin 15*, 601–605.

Buckinghamshire County Council (1998) *Independent Longcare Inquiry*. Buckingham: Buckinghamshire County Council.

Cambridge, P. (1999a) 'The first hit: a case study of the physical abuse of people with learning disabilities and challenging behaviours in a residential service.' *Disability and Society 14*, 3, 285–308.

Cambridge, P. (1999b) 'Building care management competence in services for people with learning disabilities.' *British Journal of Social Work 29*, 393–415.

Cambridge, P. (2002)'Taking the risk: assessing and managing risk.' In S. Carnaby (ed.) *Learning Disability Today.* Brighton: Pavilion.

Cambridge, P. and Carnaby, S. (2000a) *Making it Personal: Providing Intimate and Personal Care for People with Learning Disabilities.* Brighton: Pavilion.

Cambridge, P. and Carnaby, S. (2000b) 'A personal touch: managing the risks of abuse during intimate and personal care for people with learning disabilities.' *Journal of Adult Protection 2*, 4, 4–16.

Cambridge, P., Carnaby, S. and McCarthy, M. (2003) 'Responding to masturbation in supporting sexuality and challenging behaviour in services for people with learning disabilities.' *Journal of Learning Disabilities 7*, 3, 251–266.

Cambridge, P. and McCarthy, M. (1997) 'Developing and implementing sexuality policy for a learning disability provider service.' *Health and Social Care in the Community 5*, 4, 227–236.

Cambridge, P. and McCarthy, M. (2001) 'User focus groups and best value in services for people with learning disabilities.' *Health and Social Care in the Community 9*, 6, 476–489.

Cambridge, P. and Parkes, T. (2004) 'Good enough decision-making? Improving decision-making in adult protection.' *Social Work Education 23*, 6, 711–729.

Carnaby, S. and Cambridge, P. (2002) 'Getting personal: an exploratory study of intimate and personal care provision for people with profound and multiple learning disabilities.' *Journal of Intellectual Disability Research 46*, 2, 120–132.

Department of Health (2000) *No Secrets: Guidance on Developing and Implementing Multi-Agency Policies and Procedures to Protect Vulnerable Adults from Abuse.* London: The Stationery Office.

Department of Health (2001) *Valuing People: A New Strategy for Learning Disability for the 21st Century.* London: Department of Health.

Department of Health (2004) *Protection of Vulnerable Adults (POVA) Scheme in England and Wales for Care Homes and Domiciliary Care Agencies: A Practicala Guide.* London: Departmt of Health.

Dunne, T. and Power, A. (1990) 'Sexual abuse and mental handicap: Preliminary findings of a community based study.' *Mental Handicap Research 3*, 111–125.

Emerson, E. and Hatton, C. (1999) 'Future trends in the ethnic composition of British society among British citizens with learning disabilities.' *Tizard Learning Disability Review 4*, 4, 28–32.

Hannah, C. (1994) 'The context of culture in systemic therapy: an application of CMM.' *Human Systems: The Journal of Systemic Consultation and Management 5*, 69–81.

Hard, S. and Plumb, W. (1987) *Sexual Abuse of Persons with Developmental Disabilities: A Case Study.* Unpublished manuscript.

Harris, J. (2002) 'From good intentions to improved practice – developing effective policies.' In D. Allen (ed.) *Ethical Approaches to Physical Interventions.* Kidderminster: British Institute of Learning Disabilities.

Kent Social Services Department (2000) *Multi-agency Adult Protection Policy/Protocols/Procedures for Kent and Medway.* Maidstone: Kent County Council Social Services Directorate.

Lee-Treweek, G. (1994) 'Bedroom abuse: the hidden work in a nursing home.' *Generations Review 4*, 1, 2–4.

Macintyre, D. (1999) *Macintyre Undercover,* BBC1, 16 November.

McCarthy, M. and Thompson, D. (1996) 'Sexual abuse by design: an examination of the issues in learning disability services.' *Disability and Society 11*, 2, 205–217.

Murphy, G. (2003) 'Capacity to consent to sexual relationships in adults with learning disabilities.' *Journal of Family Planning and Reproductive Health Care 29*, 3, 148–149.

Murphy, G. and O'Callaghan, A. (2004) 'Capacity to consent to sexual relationships among people with intellectual disabilities.' *Psychological Medicine 34*, 1347–1357.

Newland, J. (1999) 'Assessing cultural identity in people with learning disabilities.' *Tizard Learning Disability Review 4*, 4, 20–24.

Nind, M. and Hewett, D. (1994) *Access to Communication: Developing the Basics of Communication with People with Severe Learning Disabilities through Intensive Interaction.* London: David Fulton.

Skellington, R. (1992) *Race in Britain Today.* London: Sage.

Sobsey, D. and Varnhagen, C. (1989) 'Sexual abuse and exploitation of people with disabilities: towards prevention and treatment.' In M. Wapo and L. Gougen (eds) *Special Education Across Canada.* Vancouver: Centre for Human Development and Research.

Turk, V. and Brown, H. (1993) 'The sexual abuse of adults with learning disabilities: results of a two year incidence survey.' *Mental Handicap Research 6*, 3, 193–216.

Wheeler, P. (2004) 'Sex, the person with a learning disability and the changing legal framework.' *Learning Disability Practice 7*, 3, 32–38.

Part 2

Developing Best Practice in Intimate and Personal Care with People with Learning Disabilities

CHAPTER 7

Multi-Disciplinary Working and Care Coordination

Paul Cambridge and Steven Carnaby

INTRODUCTION

The primary function of the care management process has been identified as matching resources to needs (Challis and Davies 1986). Ovretveit (1993) has similarly identified the purpose of care management and multi-disciplinary teams as matching the person's needs with available skills and resources.

Staff teams supporting people with learning disabilities who need help with intimate and personal care are, however, very unlikely to be multi-disciplinary in character, although those managing the services providing care may have nursing or social work backgrounds. Consequently, most frontline staff delivering intimate and personal care to people with learning disabilities are very unlikely to have a discipline or wider organisational rationales to draw on. They may have received some induction training and be completing a national vocational qualification in social care, but this will not address the theoretical aspects of their work. Staff will probably get some advice or guidance on how to do specific care tasks such as helping Mandy to dress or helping John to bathe, but are very unlikely to get any theoretical background or explanation as to why things are done in a certain way. Home carers are even more unlikely to have received help or guidance on how to effectively deliver intimate and personal care and will be doing this in ways they have found work for them, generally outside any understanding of the potentials or disadvantages of their approach or alternative approaches. Staff teams in residential or day services or family carers providing intimate and personal care will consequently be unlikely to possess the wide range of skills, experience and training characteristics of multi-disciplinary teams.

This is not to devalue their contribution nor to say that their skills and working experience may not be considerable, but to recognise that this is developed from a different perspective. Frontline staff and carers therefore sometimes find themselves in situations where they will be expected to take responsibility for supporting and implementing the work and recommendations of specialists as well as their line managers or supervisors. These people may be social workers, communication therapists, community learning disability nurses, challenging needs workers, clinical psychologists and so on, but they have one thing in common, in that they generally provide support from peripatetic teams that operate in a locality, such as an area or division in a social services department of a county council or across a London borough. As such they are generally not part of the services or staff team actually supporting people with learning disabilities on a daily basis and providing intimate and personal care. This often raises problems, such as split line management or professional accountability, and may lead to fractures in working relationships if case coordination and responsibilities are not transparent.

The role of multi-disciplinary workers and teams and of care managers is potentially very important for supporting people with complex support needs, including those who need help with intimate and personal care. However, not every service or service user will have ready access to multi-disciplinary resources or a care manager. This chapter explores some of the theoretical and practice issues that can emerge in the multi-disciplinary context.

THE POTENTIALS AND LIMITS OF MULTI-DISCIPLINARY WORKING

The rationale for multi-disciplinary working is strong. Multi-disciplinary working in social care is seen as a route for developing integrated support for service users and staff across agencies, professional perspectives and disciplines. It is seen as the main device for promoting the integration of the health and social care aspects of service provision for people with learning disabilities, but also as a way of preventing the loss or dilution of particular disciplines or specialisms. In learning disability, it can also help to promote wider social policy initiatives such as partnership working and has been an important part of developing joint working at the practice level between health and social services.

Currently, joint learning disability teams are working alongside learning disability partnership boards (Department of Health 2001), in much the same way as multi-disciplinary and community learning disability teams have worked to support the development of community care itself. Whatever their formal titles, such teams generally include a range of 'disciplines' or professional and specialist interests or skills. These invariably include clinical psychology, social work, community nursing, occupational therapy, speech and language therapy and psychiatry. Community multi-disciplinary teams have been defined as:

> a small group of people, usually from different professions and agencies, who relate to each other to contribute to the common goal of meeting the health and social needs of one client or those of a client population in the community. (Ovretveit 1993, p.55)

The function of such teams tends to reflect their genesis, and is both part of promoting inter-agency working and ensuring that a range of integrated provisions and supports are provided for people with learning disabilities living in a range of community-based services or informal family care. Indeed, a function of most teams is also to ensure equity in support across formal and informal care settings. However, by their very existence such teams can sometimes provide stark inequities between local areas, depending on their coverage and the access or eligibility criteria to referral or service receipt.

How such teams operate and their remit also needs to be considered in the context of other functional responsibilities in social care for people with learning disabilities. These include care management and specialist support for people with challenging behaviours. In both cases, separate care management or challenging needs teams may operate, creating the potential for functional and operational ambiguities to develop with multi-disciplinary teams. In some cases care management responsibilities can be met through specialist or generic care management teams and in others by integrating care management with the work of multi-disciplinary teams. In some cases challenging needs teams operate separately from multi-disciplinary teams and in others specialists in challenging needs workers are members of multi-disciplinary teams.

There appears to be a seemingly endless series of options and permutations for multi-disciplinary working, which makes it difficult to recommend ways staff and families supporting people with learning disabilities can access multi-disciplinary skills. In some cases, it may be a responsibility of the service manager or the care manager, whose job it is to coordinate such inputs from different agencies outside their availability on a formal 'team'. Reflecting on such complexity and variability, it may sometimes be difficult to appreciate how intimate and personal care fits into such a diverse organisational and operational context. At its simplest, however, it is evident that all professional disciplines have a potential role to play and these are now briefly explored.

The clinical psychologist

A clinical psychologist and/or challenging needs nurse might become involved with an individual in cases where challenging behaviour presents during intimate or personal care interactions. Due to the intimate nature of the activity in question, their work is likely to be indirect, relying on information for assessment from the staff or family members involved in providing direct support. After information has been collected as part of this assessment, the function that behaviour serves for the individual would be established as far as possible. Advice in the form of proactive and reactive strategies would then be offered.

Speech and language therapist

Speech and language therapists and their assistants focus on the communication partnerships that operate between the individual and those providing support. In the context of intimate and personal care, the therapist might be looking at ways in which the supporters might be able to develop a person's expressive communication and identify their choices and preferences. There is likely to be an emphasis on enabling the individual to exert as much control over the process as possible and influence the pace and approach that is adopted. Specific approaches might include the use of Makaton and on-body signing, use of picture and visual timetables, objects of reference and attention to the ways in which stimuli in the environment affect the individual's receptive communication. Speech and language therapists are also often experts in dysphagia, offering assessment and advice around issues of eating, drinking and swallowing.

Community learning disability nurse

The community nurse is able to respond to health issues noticed or raised during intimate and personal care, as well as giving specific advice around issues such as sexual health screening (e.g. mammograms, smear tests and prostate assessment). Community nurses might also accompany individuals to primary care appointments (e.g. GP clinics) or act as a liaison when people with learning disabilities require specialist mainstream health care support (e.g. kidney dialysis, input from a diabetic nurse or a GUM [Genito-Urinary Medicine] clinic).

The care manager

Care management is likely to be more distant from the intimate care arena, but would be responsible for undertaking needs assessments and identifying who is able to ensure that intimate and personal care is consistently provided across residential and day support services or between family and respite care. Care managers would, for example, coordinate decision-making concerning the funding implications of any intimate and personal care support that is needed or provided.

ORGANISATIONAL CONTEXT

The fragmented history of health and social services working together suggests fundamental difficulties for multi-disciplinary teamworking. In the 1970s joint finance and joint planning had disincentives for longer-term collaboration or was focused on particular groups or projects rather than being strategically driven (Knapp *et al.* 1992; Webb and Wistow 1985; Wistow and Hardy 1986). The main difficulties that emerged were the lack of co-terminosity between health and local authorities, with different systems of accountability, organisational cultures and professional orientations. Although respective roles and responsibilities were clarified in the 1990 community care reforms (Department of Health 1989), with the emergence of a social services lead for planning, purchasing and coordinating community care, and later reforms in the NHS, various permissive approaches to exploring joint commissioning emerged reflecting a lack of central direction (Cambridge 1999a; Department of Health 1995; Poxton 1994; Waddington 1995).

The development of primary care trusts (PCTs) led to wider variation in responsibilities between health and social care for people with learning disabilities. *Partnership in Action* (Department of Health 1998) offered new ways in which health and social services could work towards achieving mutual goals and more integrated services through pooled budgets, agreed lead or integrated provisions and the development of partnership boards for the main adult client groups between social services and primary care trusts. Single management and joint teams have certainly aided joint-working although implementation has been patchy. Particular issue base initiatives such as *No Secrets* (Department of Health 2000), have also encouraged the development of multi-agency perspectives and practices, although they are unable to prescribe the ways practitioners and managers from agencies work together on the ground. *Valuing People* (Department of Health 2001) finally signalled the importance of partnership working through learning disability partnership boards and related mechanisms such as joint investment plans in services for people with learning disabilities, setting a baseline for new joint teams and more integrated multi-disciplinary working and care management practice.

However, we need to remember that partnership working is a relatively new concept in social care, so we are still learning how to develop partnership approaches at team, service planning and commissioning levels. Integrated approaches in health and social care sit between organisational domains (Huxham and Vangen 2000), which is where partnership working provides potential solutions. However, single management and budgetary devices seem essential, as recommended for learning disability as long ago as 1986 by the Audit Commission (Audit Commission 1986), although it has to be remembered that learning disability partnership boards do not enjoy executive powers.

As with multi-disciplinary working they depend on the participation and involvement of different stakeholders and more importantly their cooperation and do not necessarily have authority over those working in services. Partnerships need organisational form (Meads and Ashcroft 2000) and as with teamworking, require negotiation and the selection of appropriate partners or members. The effective features of partnership working, amongst others, include trust, collaboration, clarity in objectives, accountability, performance review and probity (Audit Commission 2002; Frye and Webb 2002).

LESSONS FOR MULTI-DISCIPLINARY WORKING

Multi-disciplinary working at the team and practice levels has tended to mirror developments in joint and inter-agency working and indeed partnership working, although it has often been more difficult for organisational and cultural reasons to develop integrated working at the macro-organisational level. Consequently, multi-disciplinary teams have often been at the sharp end of inter-agency working and health and social care partnerships. More recently, partnership working through Learning Disability Partnership Boards (Department of Health 2001) has meant greater integration of learning disability services at all levels across health and social care, including joint teams.

The rationale for multi-disciplinary working whether at management or practice levels is that having a number of different disciplines in health and social care working together should result in a more integrated approach to supporting the needs of people with learning disabilities living in community settings or community-based services. Traditionally, such services and supports have been isolated from professionals. Families supporting their relatives with learning disabilities or provider services with managers and often largely inexperienced and unqualified support workers have found it difficult to access specialist professional support and advice, unless things go seriously wrong. Fire-fighting has tended to come before preventive work and regular support. Having a peripatetic team means that in theory services can be delivered in non-institutional ways to people according to individual needs and support situations. Different professionals can provide advice or direct support such as therapy or develop individual interventions within the context of a broad multi-disciplinary perspective.

The 'scarcity' of multi-disciplinary support, such as psychology and communication therapy, can mean not everyone who needs such help receives it and that the support received may vary widely in coverage or intensity as well as territorially in relation to the operation of multi-disciplinary teams or local authority/PCT areas. However, the rationale behind multi-disciplinary working is that the person's needs are more likely to be recognised and responded to in a balanced and holistic way. Some teams such as community support teams also work with families and staff in developing plans and support as well as with service users. Care managers should also work across a range of interests in services, from those who plan and commission services, specialists and professionals in health and social services, to informal carers and service users themselves.

Community multi-disciplinary teams and care management teams are not without their own management and operational challenges. The mere fact of having different disciplines on a team brings its own tensions and conflicts. For example, decision-making and accountability can sometimes be difficult, with role ambiguity and role conflict identified risks of teamworking (Ovretveit 1993). Much will hinge on team management skills and on actual team composition (Onyett 1992; Ovretveit 1993) as well as on the value and function of teams themselves. Care management teams can be very differently organised for example, with generic disability or specialist teams (Cambridge 1999b; Cambridge et al. 2005). It is important therefore that those working on multi-disciplinary teams and staff working with them in supporting people with complex needs acknowledge that the inter-professional system is complex and that a number of obstacles are likely to exist to effective inter-professional working (Braye and Preston-Shoot 1995).

At least two key questions for the relationship between multi-disciplinary working and intimate and personal care are evident. First, how can practitioners working with a large number of clients, maybe up to one hundred for care managers and potentially every person with a learning disability in a local area for a multi-disciplinary team, be expected to help with making sure good intimate and personal care is in place for the people with whom they have working contact? Second, how can they help develop staff and family carer competence in providing intimate and personal care to people with learning disabilities? Answers will vary according to the nature of multi-disciplinary working, the composition of teams and the specialist skills and experiences represented and the level and nature of contact with individuals and their carers.

THE NATURE OF MULTI-DISCIPLINARY WORKING

Multi-disciplinary assessment provides information about an individual's situation and context from a range of professional perspectives. These perspectives can be seen as both separate (in that each forms a 'strand' of the assessment according to a particular set of theoretical models and principles) and linked, because each professional concerned is working towards the same goal or goals. The people involved in conducting a multi-disciplinary assessment will vary according to:

- the service setting
- the nature of the service user's needs
- the issue of interest
- local issues relating to service design and availability of resources.

Whitehouse (1951, cited in Orelove and Sobsey 1996) suggests:

> We must understand that there are no discrete categories of scientific endeavours. Professions are only cross-sections of the overall continuum of human thought. Fundamentally no treatment is medical, social, psychological or vocational – all treatment is total. Yet members of each profession within the narrowness of their own training and experience will attempt to treat the whole person. Obviously, no one profession can do this adequately under present conditions.

Assessment models

Orelove and Sobsey (1996) suggest that the demands presented by complex support needs and environments require a re-evaluation of the appropriateness of more 'traditional' approaches taken by multi-disciplinary teams. They set out the characteristics of the more familiar multi-disciplinary approach along with two alternative models – inter-disciplinary and trans-disciplinary working:

Multi-disciplinary working

Organisation
Professionals work with the person individually, with little consideration of overlap between disciplines. This model was designed to meet the needs of patients within medical settings who had problems in one domain.
Disadvantages

- Assessment process: as team members work in isolation, there is more risk of generating information that does not meet the individual's needs. There is risk of inaccurate and inconsistent recommendations.

- Planning: implementation of the plans can be difficult, as there are so many generated, many of which may contain conflicting ideas. Team members may also end their responsibilities at the stage of making recommendations, leaving implementation to frontline support staff.

Inter-disciplinary working

Organisation
Team members work within a structure that encourages communication and sharing of information between them. Key decisions are made by group

consensus but assessment and implementation remain tied to each discipline. Therefore, planning is more collaborative than the multi-disciplinary model but implementation remains isolated.

Disadvantages

- Group decision-making: this tends to happen in theory only, rather than in practice.

- Still a 'discipline-referenced' model: decisions about planning, assessment, intervention and evaluation and team interactions are still driven by the orientations of each discipline. This can also lead to competitiveness between disciplines.

- Role of therapists: both models are at risk of using therapists as 'hands-on' specialists rather than acting as consultants to support staff. This implies a 'pull-out' model, where the service user leaves the service setting to receive 'therapy'. This in turn can lead to inappropriate interventions, as assessments are not conducted in 'natural' settings.

Trans-disciplinary working

The trans-disciplinary approach is characterised by sharing or transferring of information and skills across traditional disciplinary boundaries. It differs from the other two models in that one team member acts as primary facilitator of services and other team members act as consultants.

Characteristics of the trans-disciplinary model

- Indirect therapy approach (e.g. monitoring; consultation).

- Role release (sharing and exchange of certain roles and responsibilities across team members).

Applications of the trans-disciplinary model

- Assessment (e.g. initial assessment in a community learning disability team).

- Goal setting.

The main features of each of the three models are described in more depth in Table 7.1.

THE INTEGRATING ROLE OF CARE MANAGEMENT

Care management is about linking services across agencies and performing core tasks such as individual service planning (Cambridge 1999b; Challis and Davies 1986), so it is both a process and a function. Care management processes

Table 7.1 Analysis of teamworking: A comparison of three team models (Orelove and Sobsey 1996)

	Multi-disciplinary	Inter-disciplinary	Trans-disciplinary
Assessment	Separate assessments by team members	Separate assessments by team members	Team members and family conduct a comprehensive developmental assessment together
Parent participation	Parents meet with individual team members	Parents meet with team or team representative	Parents are full, active and participating members of the team
Service plan development	Team members develop separate plans for their discipline	Team members share their separate plans with one another	Team members and the parents develop a service plan based on family priorities, needs and resources
Service plan responsibility	Team members are responsible for implementing their section of the plan	Team members are responsible for sharing information with one another as well as for implementing their section of the plan	Team members are responsible and accountable for how the primary service provider implements the plan
Service plan implementation	Team members implement the part of the service plan related to their discipline	Team members implement their section of the plan and incorporate other sections where possible	A primary service provider is assigned to implement the plan with the family
Line of communication	Informal lines	Periodic case-specific team meetings	Regular team meeting where continuous transfer of information, knowledge and skills are shared among team members
Guiding philosophy	Team members recognise the importance of contributions from other disciplines	Team members are willing and able to develop, share and be responsible for providing services that are a part of the total service plan	Team members make a commitment to teach, learn and work together across discipline boundaries to implement a unified service plan
Staff development	Independent and within their discipline	Independent within as well as outside of their discipline	An integral component of team meetings for learning across disciplines and team building

and functions can be part of the work of multi-disciplinary teams. Care managers often have a variety of professional backgrounds and their task is to assess needs and coordinate a package of individually tailored services. People with profound and multiple learning disabilities relying on others for intimate and personal care clearly should be a high priority when it comes to care management coordination. However, in many cases practice is different from theory and falls short of expectations. Care managers can be under major pressure and may have to target carefully and prioritise resources and their time. Widely varying care management arrangements also exist within and between social services authorities (Cambridge 1999b), leading to inequities and differences in practice.

Person centred planning (Department of Health 2001) and other micro-organisational devices such as direct payments and individual service planning are relevant to care management coordination. It will be essential that intimate and personal care needs are assessed and included in micro-planning and micro-budgeting arrangements, with due regard to the expressed wishes of the person or their advocate or representative. Someone such as a care manager or service manager, or for people receiving direct payments, the broker of the independent living organisation helping to coordinate the resources, will need to work across these various arrangements to ensure the best outcomes for intimate and personal care – namely that it is of the best quality and that the risks of abuse or neglect are minimised.

Although case coordination is a task of care managers and, at the service level, key-workers and service managers, not everyone receiving intimate and personal care will have a care manager. Person centred planning is a potentially helpful mechanism, but still not everyone will have a person-centred plan and where they do exist, there is a risk that they will become organisationally-led and largely paper exercises (Mansell and Beadle-Brown 2004) at the expense of the individual. Evidence also suggests they perform best when operating within wider person-centred perspectives such as organisations or teams (Sanderson 2002). Whatever arrangements apply to individual cases, it will be important for someone to take responsibility for coordinating the micro-organisation of intimate and personal care for each individual. In many cases, there will be sensible reasons why this should not be the person providing intimate and personal care, as there could be conflicts of interest with caring or organisational responsibilities. These might be in terms of management of professional accountability or adult protection in relation to the risk of neglect, physical, sexual or financial abuse, depending on the wider roles and responsibilities of carers. This is not the same as saying that the main carer or carers should not be consulted and fully involved however.

Care managers also hold responsibility for community care needs assessment and review, making their role potentially critical for case coordination, particularly considering the other forms and models of assessment outlined above. When working with people with profound and multiple learning disabilities, intimate and personal care needs will invariably form an important part of care management.

Care managers may also need to be professional advocates for people with learning disabilities and complex needs, as such individuals are generally excluded from making many decisions of their own and establishing wider relationships outside services. Care management is particularly important for people receiving intimate and personal care because it is likely that more than one agency is funding care and that a number of support services, staff and different professionals are involved in providing care. Care managers may themselves come from a variety of professional backgrounds including nursing and social work. Intimate and personal care requires good planning, coordination and delivery if people are to receive consistent and continuous support of a high standard across different services, such as residential, day support and respite care. Regular review is also required if intimate care is to respond to the changing needs of service users or the changing demands on staff groups, individual support workers or carers. Care managers are also consequently well placed to monitor service quality and appropriateness.

CONCLUDING OBSERVATIONS AND EXAMPLES

In conclusion, we examine how responsibilities for case coordination may be articulated within a multi-disciplinary working context and a macro-organisational environment in which partnership approaches to service planning and development operate. A number of examples illustrate how different professionals and staff can become involved in helping to plan intimate and personal care.

Example A

A relatively able person with a learning disability who is able to articulate his or her care needs and express preferences but who needs help with intimate and personal care because of a physical disability. It may be that the key-worker or care manager simply needs to ensure that a person-centred plan is in place as part of, or separate from, the care management process and that the person has had an opportunity to voice their preferences for intimate and personal care. This might also be addressed in the individual service plan, which sometimes operates alongside the person-centred plan. The key-worker or care manager may need to check that the person is given the necessary choices in the first place and that the required support to meet the expressed or identified needs is provided. Thus the key-worker or care manager can act as a sort of professional advocate. In this case it might be better for the care manager to lead this as there may well be conflicts of interest as the key-worker is likely to be part of the service responsible for providing intimate and personal care to the person.

Example B

A person with a learning disability receiving a direct payment with the help of an independent living organisation and who is living with a family member. Some physical care is provided by the family carer but also by others such as a community nurse and also carers paid for via the direct payment. Here the task will be for the care manager or person centred planning facilitator to ensure that intimate and personal care is addressed through the person-centred plan and that those providing intimate and personal care are doing it not only in ways that the person wants and when they want it, but that this is consistent between the different people providing different or identical intimate and personal care tasks.

Some level of information exchange and review will also need to be conducted, ideally managed by the person themselves, on experiences and lessons to do with intimate and personal care needs and how these are met. The family member will not be best placed to lead on these things, as again there are likely to be potential conflicts of interest. Also, the risk of abuse is highest when a number of different people provide intimate and personal care and we are also only just beginning to recognise the high risk of abuse from carers of those receiving direct payments (Williams 2005). At least this approach will help provide some level of scrutiny by linking between the different professionals and carers involved and give the person safe opportunities to disclose abuse.

Example C

A person with profound and multiple learning disabilities who has no expressive or receptive communication and is totally dependent on others. The service manager and psychologist from a local community team will need to work together to ensure that a group of people who know the person and their needs and preferences well, are able to meet together to discuss, formulate and plan the person's intimate and personal care and then oversee the coordination of provision (Cambridge and Carnaby 2000). Such working groups can help protect the person from neglect by providing a level of scrutiny and quality control, helping ensure that appropriate intimate and personal care is provided in effective ways that respect the person and maximise the quality of the care interaction as well as attending to the person's basic physical care needs.

Example D

A person with severely challenging behaviour who reacts violently during intimate care and who attempts to smear faeces. Here a worker from a challenging needs team will need to work with the service manager and staff team to help develop a plan of intervention to deal with challenging behaviour that has been increasing in intensity and duration. The objective will be to reduce the frequency and severity of the challenging behaviour to enable the intimate care interaction to be a positive experience for the person and the carer or member of staff providing the intimate and personal care. To achieve this the function of the challenging behaviour will need to be identified – how, when and why the behaviour happens and what the behaviour is achieving for the person will need to be better understood. Only when this is understood will it be possible to design intimate and personal care provision in an effective way, possibly alongside other interventions with the purpose of addressing the function of the challenging behaviour. It may be that the challenging behaviour simply presents during intimate care as this is the only time the person has an opportunity to interact or communicate intensively with staff.

Example E

A communication therapist will work intensively with someone receiving intimate and personal care by developing an individualised vocabulary using non-traditional forms of communication, mainly symbols but also some signs. For the first time the person will be able to use expressive communication to ask for things and let their preferences for how different intimate care tasks are provided, and by whom, be known. The communication therapist will also need to work with other staff helping them develop their expressive and receptive communication skills using the person's individualised vocabulary. A focus will be provided on those tasks relevant to intimate and personal care for those undertaking this, but on choices and decision-making more widely for other staff on the team, providing a broader foundation for empowering the user and for feeding into choices in intimate and personal care.

Example F

A man with severe learning disabilities and autistic spectrum disorder has deteriorating health due to renal failure. A steering group to support his health care is set up comprising his mother, his day centre worker, local learning disability team members (clinical psychologist, community nurse and care manager), and the renal nurse from the specialist unit at the local hospital. The group develops protocols and risk assessments around dialysis, including desensitisation to the catheter, familiarisation with the ward and strategies for addressing behavioural issues arising from spending long periods in one place.

REFERENCES

Audit Commission (1986) *Making a Reality of Community Care.* London: Audit Commission, HMSO.

Audit Commission (2002) *Developing Productive Partnerships.* London, Audit Commission.

Braye, S. and Preston-Shoot, M. (1995) *Empowering Practice in Social Care.* Buckingham: Open University Press.

Cambridge, P. (1999a) 'More than just a quick fix? The potential of joint commissioning in services for people with learning disabilities.' *Research, Policy and Planning 17,* 2, 12–22.

Cambridge, P. (1999b) 'Building care management competence in services for people with learning disabilities.' *British Journal of Social Work 29,* 393–415.

Cambridge, P. and Carnaby, S. (2000) *Making it Personal: Providing Intimate and Personal Care for People with Learning Disabilities.* Brighton: Pavilion.

Cambridge, P., Carpenter, J., Forrester-Jones, R., Tate, A., Knapp, M., Beecham, J. and Hallam, A. (2005) 'The state of care management in learning disability and mental health services twelve years into community care.' *British Journal of Social Work 35,* 7, 1039–1162.

Carnaby, S. and Cambridge, P. (2002) 'Getting personal: an exploratory study of intimate and personal care provision for people with profound and multiple learning disabilities.' *Journal of Intellectual Disability Research 46,* 2,120–132.

Challis, D. and Davies, B. (1986) *Case Management in Community Care.* Aldershot: Gower.

Department of Health (1989) *Caring for People: Community Care in the Next Decade and Beyond.* London: HMSO.

Department of Health (1995) *Practical Guidance on Joint Commissioning for Project Leaders.* London: HMSO.

Department of Health (1998) *Partnership in Action.* London: HMSO.

Department of Health (2000) *No Secrets: Guidance on Developing and Implementing Multi-agency Policies and Procedures to Protect Vulnerable Adults from Abuse.* London: HMSO.

Department of Health (2001) *Valuing People: A New Strategy for Learning Disability for the 21st Century.* London: Department of Health.

Frye, M. and Webb, A. (2002) *Effective Partnership Working.* London: HM Treasury.

Huxham, C. and Vangen, S. (2000) 'Leadership in the shaping and implementation of collaboration agendas: how things happen in a (not quite) joined up world.' *Academy of Management Journal 43,* 6, 1159–1175.

Knapp, M., Cambridge, P., Thomason, C., Beecham, J., Allen, C. and Darton, R. (1992) *Care in the Community: Challenge and Demonstration.* Aldershot: Gower.

Mansell, J. and Beadle-Brown, J. (2004) 'Person-centred planning or person-centred action? Policy and practice in intellectual disability services.' *Journal of Applied Research in Intellectual Disabilities 17,* 1–19.

Meads, G. and Ashcroft, J. (2000) *Relationships in the NHS.* London: RSM Press.

Onyett, S. (1992) *Case Management in Mental Health.* London: Chapman & Hall.

Orelove, F.P. and Sobsey, D. (eds) (1996). *Educating Children with Multiple Disabilities: A Transdisciplinary Approach*. Third Edition. Baltimore: Paul H. Brookes.

Ovretveit, J. (1993) *Co-ordinating Community Care*. Buckingham: Open University Press.

Poxton, R. (1994) *Joint Commissioning: The Story So Far*. London: King's Fund.

Sanderson, H. (2002) 'A plan is not enough: exploring the development of person-centred teams.' In S. Holburn and P. Vietze (eds) *Person-Centred Planning: Research, Practice and Future Directions*. London: Brookes.

Waddington, P. (1995) 'Joint commissioning of services for people with learning disabilities; review of the principles and practice.' *British Journal of Learning Disabilities* 23, 1, 2–10.

Webb, A. and Wistow, G. (1985) 'Social services.' In S. Ransom, G. Jones and K. Walsh (eds) *Between Centre and Locality*. London: Allen and Unwin.

Williams, B. (2005) 'The abuse of direct payments.' *Journal of Adult Protection* 7, 3, 38–39.

Wistow, G. and Hardy, B. (1986) 'Transferring care: can financial incentives work?' In A. Harrison and J. Gretton (eds) *Health Care UK 1986*. London: Policy Journals.

CHAPTER 8

Adults with Mild Learning Disabilities – Promoting Independence

Neil James and Paul Wheeler

INTRODUCTION

Whilst in the past the provision of care to service users may have been the main role of those working with adults with a mild learning disability, this should no longer be the case. Rather, the role of people working with such adults as outlined, not only in the most recent key policy documents (Department of Health 2001; National Assembly for Wales 2001; Scottish Executive 2000) but also those dating back over three decades (e.g. Department of Health and Social Services and the Welsh Office 1971) is to support individuals to live more independently, exercise more control over their daily lives and be a part of their local community. Another key aim of services is to improve the quality of life of those who use the services.

This chapter outlines some of the reasons why it is important for people with a learning disability to participate actively in ordinary activities as independently as possible. It then provides the reader with an overview of the key principles of the philosophy and social policy driving service change along with some practical examples of how such aims might be realised. A number of learning theories are then briefly described in order to demonstrate that individuals learn in a variety of ways. Knowledge of such theories is necessary in order to ensure that individuals are supported in their learning using the method(s) most effective for them. The chapter then outlines other issues that warrant consideration when planning teaching strategies. Techniques for teaching new skills such as 'shaping' and 'chaining' are outlined and the reader is provided with activities aimed at helping them to develop a teaching programme in Appendices 4 and 5 at the end of the book.

WHY PROMOTE PARTICIPATION AND INDEPENDENCE?

Although policy documents, training manuals, service managers and others may promote such things as inclusion, independence and choice, the reasons for this are not often stated. This section of the chapter outlines some of the reasons for such policies in order that the reader may understand the relevance of encouraging greater participation and independence in those using their services.

One reason for promoting participation and independence is that participating in daily activities and developing one's independence is considered a normal part of adult life. In the past, people with a learning disability have frequently been viewed as eternal or perpetual children who need to have things done *to* or *for* them. This is not the case, for although people with learning disabilities may not achieve some of the milestones that signify the transition from childhood to adulthood, such as learning to drive, there is no reason why they should not achieve many others, including developing relationships and participating in work or leisure activities, if they are provided with appropriate support.

A second reason for promoting participation in activity and developing independence is that participation in activity is considered to be important both to one's physical and mental health. For example, there is evidence that non- or under-employment may result in ill health, despair, chronic lethargy and other symptoms similar to the loss of a friend or relation (Archer and Rhodes 1987). Reactions to being non-employed depend on various things, including the extent of social networks a person has; the way a person interprets their non-employment; the ability a person has to control their environment; and the opportunities a person has to use their skills to make social contacts, achieve external goals, accumulate money, acquire personal security and maintain a valued status. Given that people with a learning disability often have low self-esteem, have limited social networks, and may lack communication and other skills required in order to attain things mentioned here, it is likely that non-employment may have a more adverse effect on people with learning disabilities than people who have such skills. In order for people with learning disabilities to become accepted members of a community, they need to participate within, or contribute to, that community. Although one way of achieving this is through paid employment, this option may not be available to many people with a learning disability. It is important, therefore, that people with learning disabilities are offered the opportunity to participate in meaningful activities and relationships. Being offered broad experiences and the opportunity to learn skills, which can then be carried out more independently, thereby affording individuals greater choice and control over their lives, may enable them to achieve greater inclusion in society (Mansell and Beadle-Brown *et al.* 2004).

The final reason to be considered here is that participation and independence are important factors in the development of the 'self' or the individual's 'self-concept'. 'Self-concept', or the attitude an individual holds towards him or herself is generally regarded as being comprised of three aspects: 'self-image', 'self-esteem' and 'ideal self'. It is also seen as being open to influence by such things as the reaction others display towards us, the social roles we have and, our comparing ourselves to others (Gross 1996).

The first component of self-concept, 'self-image', is concerned with the way in which we think of and see ourselves. One way of finding out about a person's self-image is to ask them, 'Who are you?' When asked 'Who are you?', people often give answers relating to their social role, their personality traits and physical characteristics (Gross 1996). It is often the social role of the person that is given immediate consideration by others as to the value they and other members of society accord that individual. If an individual does not appear to have a recognised social role, does not participate in valued activities or does not demonstrate their independence it is likely that they will be viewed less positively by society than those who do. Physical characteristics are also likely to be given early consideration by others as they are readily observed. Whilst a person may not be able to change some of their physical features, a person who is dressed appropriate to their age and the situation, and is clean and groomed is more likely to be accepted by others than a person who presents as dirty, unkempt and inappropriately dressed. Physical characteristics can thus increase or decrease the likelihood of inclusion and the development of relationships.

Although in the past some people have suggested that people with a learning disability do not experience such concepts as self-esteem, research suggests that people with a learning disability are aware of their self-concept. For example, Jahoda and Markova's (2004) small-scale phenomenological study not only demonstrated that individuals with a learning disability were aware of the stigma associated with learning disability, but also that they sought to reject prejudice displayed towards them or sought to distance themselves from stigmatising services and other individuals with a learning disability. A larger-scale study of 101 children undertaken by Kelly and Norwich (2004) in the south-west of England found that over 90 per cent of their sample of pupils were aware of their learning disabilities. Although 23 per cent of the pupils expressed the view that they were 'not bothered about' having a learning disability, 44 per cent expressed negative feelings, saying such things as they felt 'hurt', 'sad', or 'lonely' because of their learning disability.

It is evident from such studies, that people with a learning disability are aware of their learning disability and the stigma attached to it. If they are not provided with the opportunity to participate in valued activities and become more independent, it is likely that their self-concept will diminish even more.

Being able to attend to your own intimate and personal care is thus an important aspect in the development of a positive self-concept.

PROMOTING INDEPENDENCE THROUGH SERVICE CHANGE

Although learning disability is a lifelong impairment, people can still learn and develop skills that enhance their autonomy. This is especially important to remember when considering the continued endeavour of philosophies and social policies in aiming to develop socially valued roles for people with a learning disability. Over the last 30 or more years services for people with learning disabilities have been directed by philosophies and social policy that aim to improve the quality of life for this group of people. Social policy is set out by the serving government as a result of needs expressed by members of society. Social policy seeks to address a range of issues that have consequences, not only for a particular population within society, but also for service providers and agencies (Evans *et al.* 1992). Such policies allocate a set of values, aimed at altering the lives of those concerned, via a process of decisions and actions that need to be carried forward (Ham 1999; Hill 1993).

Between 1913 and 1959, legislative definitions have included terms such as 'defective', 'idiots', 'imbeciles', and 'subnormality'. The Mental Health Act of 1959 superseded all previous legislation for the treatment of people with a learning disability and it also removed the damaging and restrictive 'moral defective' category. It introduced the term 'mental disorder' and established new provisions in relation to the care and treatment of people with learning disabilities. In particular it placed an emphasis on community care. Despite the 1959 Act, some ten years later in 1969, reports emerged like the *Report of the Committee of Enquiry into Ely Hospital* (DHSS 1969). These reports highlighted the poor standard of care in learning disability hospitals across the country and can be seen to have instigated the government's white paper *Better Services for the Mentally Handicapped* (Department of Health and Social Services and the Welsh Office 1971). This promoted the development of normalisation principles for people with learning disabilities by emphasising community living and involvement.

The concept of normalisation upon which social role valorisation is based dates back to over 40 years ago and is based on the work of Bank-Mikklesen (1959), which was further developed by Bengt Nirje in 1969 and Wolf Wolfensberger in 1970. Nirje (1980) defines normalisation as 'making available to all mentally retarded people patterns of life and conditions of everyday living which are as close as possible to the regular circumstances of life of society' (p.33). Wolfensberger in 1983 proposed that normalisation be renamed 'social role valorisation' because this phrase would not only incorporate 'the most explicit and highest goal of normalisation' but would also entail 'the creation, support, and defence of valued social roles for people who are at risk of devaluation'. Normalisation is concerned with allowing people to develop to their fullest potential and to extend, as far as possible, the person's competence in dealing with matters of everyday living. In trying to achieve this it requires that people with learning disabilities are offered individualised care and opportunities of experience, thereby resulting in increased decision-making and learning opportunities.

The principles of normalisation and social role valorisation have guided subsequent social policies aimed at optimising independence and the maintenance of community care for people with learning disabilities. Such policies include the Jay Committee Report (DHSS 1979), the *Welsh Office: All Wales Strategy for the Development of Services for Mentally Handicapped People* (Welsh Office 1983), The Cumberlege Report (DHSS 1986) and the Griffiths Report, *Community Care: An Agenda for Action* (HMSO 1988). These all described aims such as optimising independence, empowerment, choice and a consumer-led service. In the mid-1980s, O'Brien's Five Service Accomplishments provided standards against which services may be assessed in terms of the principles of normalisation. The accomplishments by which services are judged are 'dignity and respect'; 'community presence'; 'community participation'; 'choice'; and 'competence'.

These reports and policies were subsequently followed by the white paper, *Caring for People: Community Care in the Next Decade and Beyond* (Department of Health 1989) and the NHS and Community Care Act (1990), which continued with the objectives of promoting independence, creating opportunities and providing care packages that made community care more flexible (Gladden 1997). More recent policy documents, including *Valuing People* (Department of Health, 2001), *Fulfilling the Promises* (National Assembly for Wales 2001) and *Same As You* (Scottish Executive 2000), continue to promote the integration of people with learning disabilities into the wider community and their access to recreational and occupational activities.

Living valued lives, undertaking activities that other people have the opportunity to do, promoting the view that people with learning disabilities should live, work, shop, and spend their leisure time in the same places as the majority population brings into the fore the issues of empowerment and advocacy. If the quality of life of a person with a mild learning disability is to be enhanced then they themselves must be empowered to challenge service provision and be vociferous in seeking changes that promote their independence. Parrish and Birchenall (1997) predict that by endeavouring to empower people with a learning disability self-advocacy may be achievable. It may be pertinent to initially have an independent advocate for the person as they are less likely to experience conflicting demands on their loyalties and through such a service the person can be taught and supported to develop their self-advocacy skills.

The process of empowering and promoting independence for any person with a learning disability can be greatly enhanced by the use of such planning tools as a 'quality of life framework' and 'person centred planning'. Using a quality of life framework such as that described by Northway and Jenkins (2003) provides a process of assessment; identification of areas for intervention; setting of goals and strategies; and finally, evaluation in a person-centred format via the eight core dimensional model developed by Schalock (1996). Person centred planning (PCP) can be undertaken with the aid of a variety of different tools that include 'Essential Lifestyle Planning', 'PATH' (Planning Alternative Tomorrows with Hope) and 'Personal Futures Planning'. PCP will be addressed in greater depth later in Chapter 13 of this book. However, it is important to highlight that in promoting independence the PCP process supports the individual to direct their own lives and develop relationships within their community with the ultimate goal of increasing independence (Sanderson 2003). When devising intervention plans for teaching skills then the philosophies of person centred planning and quality of life should be at the forefront of the planning process.

LEARNING THEORIES

As part of the PCP process and the subsequent development of any teaching programme that seeks to enhance and develop skills and promote personal control it must be recognised that everyone is different and that each individual may have their own particular learning style. There are a number of theories concerning the way that people learn and it is worth considering these now, albeit briefly, in order to support the identification of the most fitting way to support someone's learning.

A much used and well-known learning theory within learning disability services is that of behaviourism. In behaviourism the teaching of new skills uses methods such as learning by association and reinforcement of behaviour that result in the learning being automatic (Quinn 1995). Within this type of learning it is believed that the success or reward that a person gains from a particular behaviour is likely to result in it being repeated. Behaviourism focuses on what is observable and measurable and overlooks internal processes such as thought and feelings that may influence the way a person responds to their environment (Good and Brophy 1990). In contrast to behaviourism, humanistic theory attempts to understand the learner as a human being who has thoughts, feelings and experiences that explain their behaviour. It is argued that these inner processes lead to personal growth and individual fulfilment (McKenna 1995; Quinn 1995). Social cognitive theory suggests that the learning of new behaviours results from an individual observing relationships and the behaviours of other people and their environment and modelling their behaviours on these (Dembo 1994; Smith 1999).

Learning by understanding and putting meaning to what is experienced is the basis of experiential learning and Kolb (1984) suggests that this process involves four stages that are sequential. The first stage is that of the experience itself, followed by personal reflection on this experience leading to action which becomes another experience on which reflection will occur (Atherton 2003; Kelly 1997). The timescale over which this process occurs can vary in time length from a very short period to months (Atherton 2003).

In constructivist theories of learning the person constructs their responses and behaviours to situations based on the knowledge and meaning that they have gained from previous events along with their understanding of the world (Mergel 1998).

When planning teaching, in addition to considering learning theories it is necessary to be aware of conditions that will affect the way a person learns. These include motivation, attitude, enthusiasm, determination and interest in learning the skill that you are trying to teach.

PLANNING TEACHING

The initial stages of planning a teaching strategy must involve the person themselves in order for them to be contributors to the planning process. It is important that the person is given the opportunity to understand what, why and how they are going to be supported to develop the identified skill. Part of this process involves asking 'What is the skill that needs to be taught?' Within this question one must recognise the value and relevance of the skill and for whom the skill is more important (i.e. the service or the person). It may be necessary to distinguish between what skills are essential and what skills are desired. The skill that is then identified should be one that is within the scope of the person's ability. A question that could be asked at this stage would be, 'Will the new skill produce lasting changes and benefits to the person's lifestyle?'

The starting point of the overall skill teaching strategy should be the undertaking of an assessment to ascertain the person's current skill level. It is essential to identify whether the person needs to be taught a skill from the very beginning or whether there exists the foundation of a skill that may be built upon. If the skill identified is not one the person will be able to achieve totally then one should consider teaching them to develop functionally equivalent behaviour to the target behaviour. Planning should also take into account the level of difficulty of a task when prioritising interventions so that easier skills are taught first. Doing so should enable the person to build upon their successes, maintain motivation and build self-esteem. Assessors must be clear on what the skill encapsulates in order to identify the need for intervention. An example of this may be preparing a sandwich: the person may get the bread, butter and jam but be unable to use a knife to spread or cut the sandwich. Providing reinforcement for the first parts of this activity that they are already able to carry out will maintain their consistency and teaching programmes can be developed covering using a knife to first spread the butter, then the jam, cut the sandwich, put the sandwich onto a plate and then put the ingredients away in their appropriate place.

Providing achievable goals, whether long or short term, will help maintain the focus of teaching an individual and provides a target to be worked towards. However, it is important that when setting goals they are objective, observable, realistic and achievable within a time schedule that maintains motivation (Zarkowska and Clements 1994). Breaking the overall task down into smaller steps and focusing on one step at a time can be used to identify short-term goals, while the long-term goal could be the overall task that it is hoped the person is able to achieve (Zarkowska and Clements 1994). In the example of the sandwich-making discussed earlier, the short-term goals could include: using the knife to spread the butter, while the long-term goal would be the completion of the whole process.

A variety of techniques may be utilised to help with teaching the new skill, including 'shaping', 'forward' and 'backward chaining', 'partial participation', 'precision teaching' and 'incidental teaching' (Gates, Gear and Wray 2000; Yule and Carr 1987; Zarkowska and Clements 1994). Using reinforcers to support teaching can help to maintain and strengthen the occurrence of the behaviour in the future (Yule and Carr 1987). Reinforcers (things that when presented after the behaviour occurs result in a future increase of that behaviour) can be varied in form and include verbal praise, favoured activities, attention, material reinforcers such as tangible items and tokens that are exchanged at a later time for a material or activity reinforcer. The choice of reinforcement used will depend on the person and this must be discussed with them in order to establish which would be of greatest value to them. When using reinforcement it is important to maintain consistency, be aware that overuse of a reinforcer may reduce its effectiveness and the need to plan for its fading out. It is important that agreement is attained as to when is the most appropriate time to provide reinforcement during the development of a skill.

Using a task analysis helps to break down a skill into sequential (step by step parts) and also provides a structure on which objective measurement of skill acquisition can be undertaken to monitor progress. For example, the activity of making a sandwich as previously considered may involve not only the sandwich preparation but also hand washing prior to undertaking the activity and cleaning up after completion of task. An example of a task analysis for this activity is included in Appendix 4 at the end of the book.

Case study: John

John is a 26-year-old man with a mild learning disability. He has recently visited the dentist and has been advised to clean his teeth twice a day in order to prevent future decaying problems and the need for fillings. As John has stated that he cleans his teeth regularly everyday staff have offered to undertake an assessment of his oral hygiene to see whether he needs support to develop the skill further.

Activity

Devise a task analysis of teeth cleaning that can be used for the assessment process and then adapt it so it can be used as a teaching programme. Once you have completed this please refer to Appendix 5 at the end of this book as a guide to what it might look like.

When considering how to effectively support the development of a skill it may be that part-task chaining may be appropriate. This involves the teaching of one task at a time until the person has mastered it and then moving onto the next task (Zarkowska and Clements 1994). When using this teaching approach the skill can be developed by either forward or backward chaining. With forward chaining the skill is taught from the beginning (i.e. the first task on the task analysis) whereas in backward chaining the skill is taught by starting at the last task. Zarkowska and Clements (1994) tell us that by using backward chaining, success is gained every time because the last stage of the task is always completed by the person. If necessary a task may be broken down into very small detailed written steps that may be more time-consuming. This is referred to as 'precision teaching' and the teaching of this task would be scheduled with written prompts that aim to ensure success.

What appears to be a less informal teaching style is that of 'incidental teaching'. Here, the person themselves is more in control of the learning as they themself initiate the event. The 'teacher' follows the lead of the person, offering prompts and reinforcements whether or not the task or skill is achieved successfully. An example of an incidental teaching event may be that of the person asking to go to the shops, whereby the skills of getting their shoes and coat followed by putting them on can be taught. Another example may be that the person enjoys going swimming, incidental teaching may occur around them drying and changing after having been for a swim.

There may be parts of a skill that a person finds difficult or does not wish to undertake. If this is the case, the use of 'shaping' can help them to complete the task. In shaping you reinforce the behaviour or action that is closest to the desired objective and once this response is established you reinforce the next behaviour or action that is closest to the desired objective (Tsoi and Yule 1987; Zarkowska and Clements 1994). It may also be the case that a person will initially require prompting to help them complete a task. Prompting can take many different forms including verbal instruction, practical demonstration, the use of visual cues and gentle physical guidance. The level of prompting required and the types of prompts utilised will depend on the needs of the person. However it should be remembered that if too much prompting is given the person may become reliant on prompting and not develop the skill independently. Conversely, if too little or inappropriate prompting is given, the individual may not achieve the task and may be left with a deficit in skill acquisition and/or feelings of failure (Zarkowska and Clements 1994).

When identifying the skill to be taught it is important to recognise how achievable a skill is for the individual and whether they are going to be able to undertake it independently. If the person is unable to undertake the skill independently this should not preclude them from participating in the skill to an extent to which they are able. As discussed earlier in this chapter the use of short- and long-term goals must be realistic and in line with the needs and consideration of the abilities of the person. The person may be able to complete some tasks, partially complete others and may not be able to undertake others at all. Building on those that they can undertake either totally or partially should be the focus for attention and development.

CONCLUSION

Teaching of self-care skills is an important part of promoting independence. Not only is it recommended by policy but it is also important in raising an individual's self-concept and thus improving their mental and physical health and quality of life. As has been illustrated within this chapter, those who provide support and opportunities for people with learning disabilities must be able to work creatively and positively when helping an individual develop their self-help skills. Although an outline of learning theories and teaching interventions have been provided, such interventions should not be attempted without input from multi-disciplinary teams including the individual services user, clinical psychologists, family and other carers.

REFERENCES

Archer, J. and Rhodes, V. (1987) 'Bereavement and reactions to job loss: a comparative review.' *British Journal of Social Psychology 26*, 3, 211–224.

Atherton, J.S. (2003) *Learning and Teaching: Learning from Experience.* www.learningandteaching.info/learning/experience.htm (accessed 23 March 2005).

Bank-Mikklesen, N. (1959) Cited by Swann, C. (1997) 'Development of Services' In B. Gates (ed.) (1997) *Learning Disabilities.* Edinburgh: Churchill Livingstone.

Dembo, M.H. (1994) *Applying Educational Psychology* (Fifth Edition). White Plains, NY: Longman Publishing Group.

Department of Health and Social Services (1969) *Ely Report. Report of the Committee of Enquiry into Allegations of Ill Treatment of Patients and Other Irregularities at the Ely Hospital, Cardiff.* Cmnd 3975. London: HMSO.

Department of Health and Social Services and the Welsh Office (1971) *Better Services for the Mentally Handicapped.* Cmnd 4683. London: HMSO.

Department of Health and Social Services (1979) *Report of Enquiry into Mental Handicap Nursing (Jay Report).* London: HMSO.

Department of Health and Social Services (1986) *Neighbourhood Nursing: A Focus for Care (Cumberledge Report).* London: HMSO.

Department of Health (1989) *Caring for People: Community Care in the Next Decade and Beyond.* Cmnd 849. London: HMSO.

Department of Health (2001) *Valuing People: A New Strategy for Learning Disability for the 21st Century.* London: HMSO.

Evans, G., Todd, S., Beyer, S., Felce, D., and Perry, J. (1992) *A Four-Year Longitudinal Study of the Impact of the All Wales Strategy on the Lives of People with Learning Difficulties.* Cardiff: Mental Handicap in Wales Applied Research Unit.

Gates, B., Gear, J. and Wray, J. (eds) (2000) *Behavioural Distress – Concepts and Strategies.* London: Bailliere Tindall.

Gladden, R. (1997) 'Legislation and social policy over the past 100 years.' In B.Gates (ed.) *Learning Disabilities* (Third Edition). Edinburgh: Churchill Livingstone.

Good, T.L. and Brophy, J.E. (1990) *Educational Psychology: A Realistic Approach.* (Fourth Edition). White Plains, NY: Longman.

Gross, R. (1996) *Psychology: The Science of Mind and Behaviour.* London: Hodder and Stoughton.

Ham, C. (1999) *Health Policy in Britain* (Fourth Edition). London: Macmillan Press Ltd.

Her Majesty's Stationary Office (1988) Griffiths, Sir R. *Community Care: Agenda for Action.* London: HMSO.

Hill, M. (1993) *Understanding Social Policy* (Fourth Edition). Oxford: Blackwell Publishers.

Jahoda, A. and I. Markova (2004) 'Coping with social stigma: people with intellectual disabilities moving from institutions and family home.' *Journal of Intellectual Disability Research 48*, 8, 719–729.

Kelly, C. (1997) 'David Kolb, the theory of experiential learning and ESL.' *The Internet TESL Journal 3*, 9. http://iteslj.org/Articles/Kelly-Experiential (accessed 3 March 2005).

Kelly, N. and Norwich, B. (2004) 'Pupils' perceptions of self and of labels: moderate learning difficulties in mainstream and special schools.' *British Journal of Educational Psychology 74*, 411–435.

Kolb, D.A. (1984) *Experiential Learning: Experience as the Source of Learning and Development.* New Jersey: Prentice-Hall.

Mansell, J. and Beadle-Brown, J. *et al.* (2004) *Person-Centred Active Support.* Brighton: Pavilion Publishing.

McKenna, G. (1995) 'Learning theories made easy: humanism.' *Nursing Standard 9*, 31, 29–31.

Mergel, B. (1998) 'Instructional design and learning theory.' www.usask.ca/education/coursework/802papers/mergel/brenda.htm (accessed 14 March 2005).

National Assembly for Wales (2001) *Fulfilling the Promises: Proposals for a Framework for Services for People with Learning Disabilities.* Cardiff: Learning Disability Advisory Group, National Assembly for Wales.

Nirje, B. (1980) 'The normalisation principle.' In R.J. Flynn and K.E. Nitsch (eds) *Normalisation, Social Integration and Community Services.*' Baltimore: University Park Press.

Northway, R. and Jenkins, R. (2003) 'Quality of life as a concept for developing learning disability nursing practice?' *Journal of Clinical Nursing 12*, 1, 57–66.

Parrish, A. and Birchenall, P. (1997) 'Learning disability nursing and primary health-care.' *British Journal of Nursing 6*, 2, 92–98.

Quinn, F.M. (1995) *The Principles and Practice of Nurse Education.* London: Chapman & Hall.

Sanderson, H. (2003) 'Person centred planning.' In B. Gates (ed.) *Learning Disabilities – Toward Inclusion.* Edinburgh: Churchill Livingstone, pp.369–389.

Schalock, R.L. (1996) 'Reconsidering the conceptualisation and measurement of quality of life.' In R.L. Schalock (ed.) *Quality of Life: Vol. 1. Conceptualization and Measurement.* Washington DC: American Association on Mental Retardation, pp.123–139.

Scottish Executive (2000) *The Same As You? A Review of Services for People with Learning Disabilities.* Edinburgh: Scottish Executive.

Smith, M.K. (1999) 'Learning theory', *The Encyclopaedia of Informal Education.* www.infed.org/biblio/b-learn.htm (accessed 14 March 2005).

Tsoi, M. and W. Yule (1987) 'Building up new behaviours: shaping, prompting and fading.' In W. Yule, and J. Carr (eds) *Behaviour Modification: For People with Mental Handicaps.* London: Chapman & Hall.

Welsh Office (1983) *All Wales strategy for the development of services for mentally handicapped people.* Cardiff: Welsh Office.

Wolfensberger, W. (1983) 'Social role valorisation: a proposed new term for the principal of normalisation.' *Mental Retardation 21*, 234–239.

Yule, W. and Carr, J. (eds) (1987) *Behaviour Modification for People with Mental Handicaps.* London: Chapman & Hall.

Zarkowska, E. and Clements, J. (1994) *Problem Behaviour and People with Severe Learning Disabilities.* Cheltenham: Stanley Thornes (Publishers) Ltd.

FURTHER READING/RESOURCES

Book

Brown, H. and Smith, H. (eds) (1992) *Normalisation – A Reader for the Nineties*. Kent: Tavistock/Routledge.

Website

www.learningandteaching.info/learning (information on learning theories).

CHAPTER 9

Adults with Profound and Multiple Learning Disabilities – Supporting Planned Dependence

Steven Carnaby

INTRODUCTION

> I want to know, as far as possible, how [people with profound disabilities] perceive their world – how it feels to them. Within the parameters of where they feel safe, how can we enlarge and enrich their experience? How can we increase their confidence and help them to 'feel good' about themselves and others? (Caldwell with Stevens 1998, p.4)

People with profound and multiple learning disabilities (PMLD) form a small but significant section of the wider population of people with learning disabilities. It is increasingly recognised that people with PMLD need specific types of support that are likely to differ in nature and intensity from that needed by individuals with moderate or mild learning disabilities (PMLD Network 2001). Indeed, in order to plan and provide support, there needs to be honest recognition of the true extent of an individual's disabilities and how their functioning is affected in order to identify effectively how that individual enjoys spending time and what they need from others in order to live life with as much autonomy as possible.

The vast majority of people with PMLD need significant support if not total assistance with many aspects of intimate and personal care, and are therefore most vulnerable to poor practice, abuse and inappropriate approaches. This chapter will look at specific issues relating to the lives of people with PMLD and assess ways in which these issues influence both how they themselves experience the world, and how supporters of people with PMLD are likely to perceive them. This will lead to specific discussion of the approach to intimate and personal care, with suggestions for best practice.

WHO ARE WE TALKING ABOUT?

Various labels and terms have been used for the needs of people requiring significant levels of support in most areas of their lives, including:

- severe disabilities

- profound disabilities

- profound and multiple disabilities

- high support needs

- complex needs

- complex and multiple disabilities.

All of the above terms may be useful, but the language used must be agreed and used consistently within an organisation or service to avoid confusion. Being consistent with language also helps to ensure that the extent of an individual's disability is acknowledged and respected. While labels of any kind have the potential to stigmatise, sensitive use of clear terminology maps out what people need and indicates the types of support that are likely to be required. Unclear and inconsistent use of labelling can put people at risk of receiving inadequately planned support. This can compromise the individual's quality of life, and in some cases could lead to poor physical and/or psychological health (Carnaby 2002).

The *Diagnostic and Statistical Manual of Mental Disorders* Fourth Edition (*DSM-IV*: published by the American Psychiatric Association (1994)) states that 'the group with profound mental retardation [sic] constitutes approximately 1%–2% of people with mental retardation', but practice prevalence is difficult to establish as figures vary with the type of definitions adopted. The definitions of profound intellectual disability most often cited include having an IQ of below 20 (World Health Organization 1992 in Lacey and Ouvray 1998), below 20–25 (*DSM-IV*), or functioning with an IQ estimated to be five standard deviations from the norm (Hogg and Sebba 1987). All of these references to IQ are notional, as clinicians conducting assessment of cognitive ability would find it a significant challenge to achieve accurate and reliable results in this range of functioning. While using IQ scores is problematic and arguably inappropriate, its use in this notional way can be helpful in appreciating the ways in which levels of understanding may differ between people with profound disabilities and those with severe disabilities, as well as from those with mild learning disabilities.

Other literature takes a more functional approach to describing PMLD. For example, Jean Ware (1996) suggests that people with a profound learning disability have a 'degree of learning difficulty so severe that they are functioning at a developmental level of two years or less (in practice well under a year)'. The World Health Organization (1992, in Lacey and Ouvray 1998) suggests that people with PMLD are 'severely limited in their ability to understand or comply with requests or instructions. Most such individuals are immobile or severely restricted in mobility, incontinent, and capable at most of only the rudimentary forms of non-verbal communication.' Finally, people with PMLD can be described or defined in terms of their support needs. Such definitions include the following:

- Being a member of 'High Dependency Group IV' – the criteria for which includes multiple physical disabilities, double incontinence and severe epilepsy (National Development Team, cited in Lacey and Ouvray 1998).

- Requiring constant help and supervision and having little or no ability to meet personal care needs (WHO 1992, cited in Lacey and Ouvray 1998).

- Requiring a highly structured environment with constant aid and supervision and an individualised relationship with a caregiver in order to attain optimal development (American Psychiatric Association 1994).

Profound learning disabilities and multiple impairment can often be traced to extensive damage that results from what are often identifiable neurological conditions (American Psychiatric Association 1994). Individuals may experience any one or more severe physical disability, severe visual impairment, severe hearing impairment, epilepsy and other complex health conditions for which medication is usually required, for example, chronic pulmonary disease (Hogg 1992). There may also be impairments in the ability to detect touch, pressure, temperature and pain (Oberlander, O'Donnell and Montgomery 1999). The significant brain damage leading to profound cognitive impairment increases the likelihood of the individual experiencing additional disabilities (Foundation for People with Learning Disabilities 2001).

In turn, their communication skills are also likely to be at an early developmental level, involving signals such as reflex responses, actions, sounds and facial expressions (Porter et al. 2001). People with profound learning disabilities are reported to have lower receptive communication skills than individuals with severe learning disabilities (Cascella 2004).

SUPPORT NEEDS

Jean Ware (1996) takes a functional perspective to defining PMLD, referring to people as functioning at two years or less. This is a highly useful and practical approach, as it enables us to think clearly about how people with PMLD experience the world, how they are likely to manage information that they receive from others and importantly, what they need in order to feel safe, in control and able to influence their environment.

Providing effective support for people with PMLD requires a collaborative approach that is developmentally appropriate for the individual concerned (see Lacey and Ouvray 1998; Sobsey and Wolf-Schein 1996). Some find this approach difficult, as they feel that it compromises the individual's dignity and right to be respected as an adult. However, the increasing evidence base, emerging to support the use of developmental approaches (e.g. Bradley 1998; Bradshaw 2001; Dick and Purvis 2005; Goldbart 1994; Nind and Hewett 1994), suggests that acknowledging an individual's level of functioning is essential if we are to support their development, enhance their engagement and encourage them to form meaningful relationships with other people. If handled sensitively, it can be argued that adopting a developmental approach is the clearest way of showing respect for an individual.

Assessment

Identifying good support stems from thorough, detailed assessment, and some key principles are highlighted below:

Principles of the assessment process

- Spend time with the person in a range of different settings (e.g. at home and at the day centre). Watch how s/he responds to different people and different situations.

- Try to establish how the person shows like or dislike.

- Support and participate in the completion of standardised assessment tools used by professionals from the local community team. These tools are used to assess areas such as the individual's communication skills, their vision and hearing or their level of social functioning. Many of these require information from informants other than the service user – give careful thought to who the most appropriate informants might be.

- Consult with the individual's GP or the local community learning disability nurse and ask for a health assessment to be completed (e.g. the 'OK Health Check').

- Spend time getting to know the individual's family and/or significant others. Respect for the individual's personal history is a key element of good practice.
- Observe the individual's personal relationships, and the extent to which they seem meaningful to him or her.

(Carnaby 2002)

The assessment process is likely to show that people with PMLD need particular supports that are carefully individualised to meet their needs. Involving people with PMLD in personally relevant activities of daily living may range from assisting the individual to gain complete independence with the provision of equipment and/or training, or it may enable control of an aspect of the activity. The principle here is to give the person as much control as possible over their personal activities, while also establishing the importance that they place on those specific activities to ensure motivation to participate (Miller 1998).

SENSORY NEEDS

Given that the vast majority of people with PMLD will experience both limited communication skills *and* impairments in vision and hearing, considerations of sensory needs are essential. The role of sensory function cannot be over-estimated in that information required through the senses is the basis for learning about and acquiring a conceptual understanding of the physical world (Warren 1994).

Seven major types of sensory input have been identified – visual, tactile, vestibular, proprioceptive, auditory, olfactory and gustatory (Rosen 1997). A distinction can also be made between *external* input received from the environment (e.g. light) and *internal* sensory information from within the body system (e.g. proprioceptive information about the body's position in space) (Brown, McLinden and Porter 1998). Attention needs to be paid to the extent of sensory impairment, how this affects the nature and quality of information the individual receives about their surroundings – and most importantly, how this information will affect feelings of security and safety.

Where sensory impairment has been identified, interventions can assist with maximising the amount and quality of information available to the person. For example, much has been learned about how to create visual distinction and clarity by using colour contrast, borders and edging, by thinking about lighting positioning, troublesome reflection and glare (Best 1992). Less consideration has been paid to creating acoustically meaningful surroundings (e.g. thinking about how an individual with sensory loss makes sense of chatter, chair legs scraping on the floor and other incidental sound sources) (Rikhye, Gotheif and Appell 1989).

Other key issues that are often neglected include managing situations where individuals with sensory loss are sharing the environment with people who do not have those impairments. Some adaptations are likely to be of benefit to all. Equally, the use of touch can act as interpretation and reassurance in a world that is experienced as overwhelming and chaotic (Brown *et al.* 1998). Specialists (e.g. optometrists and audiologists) can be approached to contribute to a collaborative and multi-disciplinary approach.

Monitoring responses in the five categories of awareness, attending, localising, recognising and understanding is recommended when assessing vision (Aitken and Buultjens 1992) but can also underpin assessment of functioning in other sensory modalities (Brown *et al.* 1998). Crucially, it is suggested that sensory reinforcement can be used to enhance awareness and support the individual in developing a sense of self – particularly those with visual impairment and/or hearing loss (Bunning 1997).

Eating and drinking

Eating and drinking is a key area of daily living that can present people with PMLD with a range of complex problems. Specific difficulties include primitive reflexes (such as bite or gag reflex), tongue thrust, swallowing difficulties, affected facial muscles, poor lip/tongue control, excessive drooling, sensory impairment, reinforced and learnt behaviours and roles, communication difficulties and limited physical abilities. Recognised techniques are available for practitioners to help address these issues (Miller 1998). In addition, a thorough assessment from an occupational therapist is likely to lead to recommendations regarding the use of appropriate equipment. A person-led approach intent on involving the individual by considering motivation, communication and other aspects of their perspective and experience is essential (e.g. McCurtin 1997).

Provision of physical care and support

The physical care of people with PMLD can be seen as either very simple or very complex – supporting basic life needs can be done with little intervention, but enabling a more fulfilled and meaningful life can be a more complicated challenge (Goldsmith and Goldsmith 1998). Practitioners usually understand the implications of limited movement for the body, and a wide range of assessment tools has been developed for this purpose (Poutney, Mulcahy and Green 1990). A common theme is apparent in many of the approaches based on physiotherapeutic principles, namely that quality in the performance of movement is an important aim, with more 'normal' movement and posture being the eventual goal. This 'functional' approach sets short-term goals as part of an ongoing programme (Partridge 1996). While there may be benefits observed in the young child (e.g. with cerebral palsy) the effective parts of treatment long term are likely to be those that become part of the individual's daily life (Scrutton 1984).

The carer's or parent's role in the individual's physical management is clearly crucial and the dependency of the individual with PMLD can lead to a sense of needing to protect against 'outside' intervention. Great sensitivity is needed to enable a collaborative relationship between carers and services to gradually evolve (Hornby 1994).

As with anybody, proper rest and quality sleep are essential to good health, but there might be specific barriers preventing this for people with PMLD, such as having difficulty in changing position (Goldsmith and Goldsmith 1998). Polysomnographic evidence suggests increased obstructive apnoea (where breathing is interrupted), as well as epileptiform discharges in the sleep of people with severe cerebral palsy (Kotagel, Gibbons and Stith 1994). Circadian rhythms may be disturbed, so the usual pattern of waking during the day and sleeping at night does not occur (Okawa, Takahashi and Sasaki 1986). Here behavioural interventions have been unsuccessful, although there is some evidence that prescribing melatonin can be beneficial (Jan, Espezel and Appleton 1994). Considering postural support can also ameliorate the situation (Turrill 1992). The importance of positioning at night is recognised by therapists, as more damage is likely to be caused by uncontrolled lying than uncontrolled sitting (Pope 1997).

INTIMATE AND PERSONAL CARE AND PEOPLE WITH PROFOUND AND MULTIPLE LEARNING DISABILITIES

The breadth and complexity of likely issues relating to the daily lives of people with PMLD require a sophisticated level of response, if needs are to be met in an individualised, appropriate fashion. The provision of intimate and personal care is a particular activity where thorough assessment of sensory impairment, physical disability, communication skills, health issues and self-awareness all need to be coordinated to inform the approach that is to be adopted. A useful starting point when attempting to create an individualised approach to intimate and care support may be the sharing of perspectives. This may be done through person centred planning (see Cambridge and Carnaby 2005), the main process through which the individual's perspective is placed at the centre of assessment, planning and intervention. However, when working with people with PMLD, there is higher potential for the individual's voice to be at best distal and at worst totally absent from the decision-making process. Transparent and long-term collaborative working within, across and outside agencies is needed if a holistic perspective of the individual's perspective is to be established.

Underpinning values

Many policies regarding the delivery of intimate and personal care refer to 'dignity' and 'respect' with little discussion of what these terms may mean in practice. For people with PMLD these terms will also have individual meaning, but there are core principles that might help us think about our approach.

People with PMLD have usually required significant or total assistance with their intimate and personal care needs from birth and have therefore been socialised into a sense of self that accepts intimate touch from others (sometimes strangers), perhaps in ways over which they have no influence or control. Providers of intimate care need to acknowledge this phenomenon and incorporate practices that place current practice into the individual's personal and historical context. Who has supported the individual in the past? Has the person been subjected to abusive support (which can range from rough handling to sexual assault)? Working in a dignified and respectful way is therefore working in the context of the individual's experience and adapting our practice accordingly. The intention behind the way that we touch others should always be discussed and documented where possible to avoid misinterpretation and encourage the use of appropriate and positive interpersonal boundaries.

We also need to offer support that aims to enhance autonomy and involvement in the process. This might manifest itself in very practical ways, for example:

- using objects of reference (a pad/a bottle of wash cream) to inform the individual that we are going to change their continence pad

- placing a small amount of wash cream on the person's hand, then on their hip before finally using it on their genitals as a way of priming them for the task to be completed

- where appropriate, playing the individual's favourite music in the bathroom during intimate care activities

- recognising that for many people with PMLD and significant physical disabilities and limited communication skills, controlling their food intake is a primary medium through which they can control their environment: give people time to eat, make it as enjoyable and relaxed as possible and resist the temptation to 'fit it in' between other activities

- supporting people with eating at their pace, giving them time to smell, taste and where appropriate touch the food they are being offered

- where pureeing food is required, ensuring that each element of the meal is pureed separately to maximise the flavour and experience of the food.

Throughout the use of these strategies, the individual's developmental level of functioning, communication skills, sensory and physical disabilities and particular psychological idiosyncrasies need to be carefully borne in mind. Intimate and personal care is an activity in and of itself with a wide range of benefits aside from the actual physical health and hygiene outcome, and should not be rushed in order for the individual to return to the previous activity. It is an ideal opportunity for building relationships, teaching self-awareness and developing communication skills.

The levels of increasing involvement can also be measured on an individual basis. McInnes and Treffrey (1982) identified an eight-stage sequence through which they believe people who have multiple impairments progress when introduced to a new activity:

Resistance

Using the example of interactive hand massage, the person may pull their hands away.

Tolerance

If the activity is continued sensitively – so as not to distress the person unduly – s/he may begin to tolerate it.

Cooperates passively

Using hand massage as the example, the person would begin to tolerate touch for longer periods of time.

Enjoys

With increased passive cooperation (e.g. allowing their hand to be turned over during massage), signs of enjoyment might be observed.

Responds cooperatively

The person begins to be more actively involved, e.g. turning their hand over themselves.

Leads

Using the hand massage example, begins to offer their hands to be massaged.

Imitates

Might make stroking movements themselves, or try to massage another person's hands.

Initiates

May finally reach the stage that they want the activity to begin (e.g. looking at the bottle of massage lotion, or communicating this in some other way).

This is a valuable framework for helping an individual's support network develop a consistent approach that has the development of autonomy at its centre.

SUGGESTIONS FOR BEST PRACTICE

The following list of principles incorporates those suggested by Bradley and Ouvray (1999):

1. Good relationships are fundamental in working with people with PMLD. It is important to build an atmosphere of acceptance, trust and respect, which will nurture interaction and communication.

2. Respond promptly when you notice that someone is trying to communicate. Look for the subtle actions or sounds that a person with PMLD makes and think about what they might mean.

3. People with PMLD will only communicate when they have a reason, and if they are given the opportunity to do so. Encourage them to express themselves by whatever means they can.

4. Some people with PMLD have had long experience of their signals being unrecognised or ignored, with the result that they have given up trying. It is important to encourage them to try again, so that they can learn to express their needs, interests and feelings.

5. Make sure that service users are in a situation that allows them to communicate easily – in a good position, near to people they like to be with and in interesting surroundings.

6. Think carefully when you interpret people's attempts to communicate, and check in whatever way you can that this really is what they mean.

7. Some people with PMLD may not have experienced satisfactory early relationships, and may need a lot of help in developing meaningful relationships.

8. Try to make your relationship with the people you work with more equal. Find out all you can about each person as an individual, rather than concentrating exclusively on their learning and care needs.

9. Make sure you acknowledge the sexuality and sexual needs of every person with PMLD. Consider what s/he may need to know in relation to his or her own sexuality, and ways of giving this information. Talk to colleagues about the needs of service users, and how to provide appropriate support for each person's individual needs.

10. Devise detailed individualised care plans derived from discussion taking place as part of the individual's person-centred plan. Review and evaluate regularly to maintain consistency and efficacy.

11. Make sure that strategies for support are created from a multi-disciplinary perspective as far as possible, in order to acknowledge the complexities associated with the person's lifestyle.

12. Working closely with colleagues from speech and language therapy to develop ways of understanding how the individual could be supported to further influence *how* and *when* things are done to them.

13. Remember that people with PMLD are people first and should be respected as such. Avoid:

    • calling out across a crowded room that 'It's time to change your pad'; instead, approach them discreetly and use the individual's preferred method of communication to inform them what is happening

    • emerging from a bathroom wearing apron and gloves so that everyone knows what has been happening

    • talking about an individual's bowel movement or personal habits in an inappropriate forum (e.g. on the bus or in the canteen).

14. Throughout an intimate or personal care activity, inform people about what is being done to and with them using a form of communication they can understand and with which they are familiar (e.g. objects of reference or on-body signing).

15. Use reflective practice to limit the risk of depersonalising practice, particularly when supporting individuals who need others to speak on their behalf.

REFERENCES

Aitken, S. and Buultjens, M. (1992) *Vision for Doing: Assessing Functional Vision of Learners who are Multiply Disabled.* Edinburgh: Moray House Publications.

American Psychiatric Association (1994) *Diagnostic and Statistical Manual of Mental Disorders (DSM-IV)* Fourth Edition. American Psychiatric Association.

Best, A. (1992) *Teaching Children with Visual Impairments*. Milton Keynes: Open University Press.

Bradley, H. (1998) 'Assessing and developing successful communication.' In P. Lacey and C. Ouvray (eds) *People with Profound and Multiple Learning Disabilities: A Collaborative Approach to Meeting Complex Needs*. London: David Fulton.

Bradley, A. and Ouvray, C. (1999) *Better Choices – Fuller Lives: Working with People with Profound Learning Disability and Complex Support Needs, Unit 1 – Services, Staff and Service Users*. Kidderminster: BILD Publications.

Bradshaw, J., (2001) 'Communication partnerships with people with profound and multiple learning disabilities.' *Tizard Learning Disability Review 6*, 2, 6–15.

Brown, N., McLinden, M. and Porter, J. (1998) 'Sensory needs.' In P. Lacey and C. Ouvray (eds) *People with Profound and Multiple Learning Disabilities: A Collaborative Approach to Meeting Complex Needs*. London: David Fulton.

Bunning, K. (1997) 'The role of sensory reinforcement in developing interactions.' In M. Fawcus (ed.) *Children with Learning Difficulties: A Collaborative Approach to their Education and Management*. London: Whurr.

Caldwell, P. with Stevens, P. (1998) *Person to Person: Establishing Contact and Communication with People with Profound Disabilities*. Brighton: Pavilion Publishing.

Cambridge, P. and Carnaby, S. (eds) *Person Centred Planning and Care Management with People with Learning Disabilities*. London: Jessica Kingsley Publishers.

Carnaby, S. (2002) 'Being who you are.' In S. Carnaby (ed.) *Learning Disability Today*. Brighton: Pavilion Publishing.

Cascella, P. (2004) 'Receptive communication abilities among adults with significant intellectual disability.' *Journal of Intellectual and Developmental Disability 29*, 1, 70–78.

Dick, D. and Purvis, K. (2005) 'Total communication, person centred planning and person centred services.' In P. Cambridge and S. Carnaby (eds) *Person Centred Planning and Care Management with People with Learning Disabilities*. London: Jessica Kingsley Publishers.

Foundation for People with Learning Disabilities (2001) *Learning Disabilities: The Fundamental Facts*. London: Foundation for People with Learning Disabilities.

Goldbart, J. (1994) 'Pre-intentional communication: opening the communication curriculum to students with profound and multiple learning difficulties.' In J. Ware (ed.) *Educating Children with Profound and Multiple Learning Difficulties*. London: David Fulton.

Goldsmith, J. and Goldsmith, L. (1998) 'Physical management.' In P. Lacey and C. Ouvray (eds) *People with Profound and Multiple Learning Disabilities: A Collaborative Approach to Meeting Complex Needs*. London: David Fulton Publishers.

Hogg, J. (1992) 'The administration of psychotropic and anticonvulsant drugs to children with profound intellectual disability and multiple impairments.' *Journal of Intellectual Disability Research 36*, 473–488.

Hogg, J. and Sebba, J. (1987) *Profound Retardation and Multiple Impairment: Development and Learning*. Rockville, MD: Aspen Publishers.

Hornby, G. (1994) *Counselling in Child Disability: Skills for Working with Parents*. London: Chapman & Hall.

Jan, J.E., Espezel, H. and Appleton, R.E. (1994) 'The treatment of sleep disorders with melatonin.' *Developmental Medicine and Child Neurology 36*, 97–107.

Kotagel, S., Gibbons, V.P. and Stith, J.A. (1994) 'Sleep abnormalities in patients with severe cerebral palsy.' *Developmental Medicine and Child Neurology 36*, 304–311.

Lacey, P. and Ouvray, C. (eds) (1998) *People with Profound and Multiple Learning Disabilities: A Collaborative Approach to Meeting Complex Needs.* London: David Fulton.

McCurtin, A. (1997) *The Manual of Paediatric Feeding Practice.* Bicester: Winslow Press.

McInnes, J. and Treffrey, J. (1982) *Deaf-blind Children: A Developmental Guide.* Milton Keynes: Open University Press.

Miller, J. (1998) 'Personal needs and independence.' In P. Lacey and C. Ouvray (eds) *People with Profound and Multiple Learning Disabilities: A Collaborative Approach to Meeting Complex Needs.* London: David Fulton.

Nind, M. and Hewett, D. (1994) *Access to Communication: Developing the Basics of Communication in People with Severe Learning Difficulties through Intensive Interaction.* London: David Fulton.

Oberlander, T.F., O'Donnell, M.E. and Montgomery, C.J. (1999) 'Pain in children with significant neurological impairment.' *Journal of Developmental and Behavioural Paediatrics 20,* 235–243.

Okawa, M., Takahashi, K. and Sasaki, H. (1986) 'Disturbance in circadian rhythms in severely brain damaged patients correlated with CT findings.' *Journal of Neurology 233,* 274–282.

Partridge, C.J. (1996) 'Physiotherapy approaches to the treatment of neurological conditions – an historical perspective.' In S. Edwards *Neurological Physiotherapy: A Problem Solving Approach.* Edinburgh: Churchill Livingstone.

PMLD Network (2001) *Valuing People with PMLD.* London: Mencap.

Pope, P. (1997) 'Management of the physical condition in people with chronic and severe neurological disabilities living in the community.' *Physiotherapy, March, 83,* 3.

Porter, J., Ouvray, C., Morgan, M. and Downs, C. (2001) 'Interpreting the communication of people with profound and multiple learning difficulties.' *British Journal of Learning Disabilities 29,* 1, 12–16.

Poutney, T.E., Mulcahy, C. and Green, E. (1990) 'Early development of postural control.' *Physiotherapy 76,* 12, 799–802.

Rikhye, C., Gothelf, C. and Appell, M. (1989) 'A classroom environmental checklist for students with dual sensory impairments.' *Teaching Exceptional Children 22,* 1, 44–46.

Rosen, S. (1997) 'Kinesiology and sensorimotor function.' In B. Blasch, W. Wiener and R. Welsh (eds) *Foundations of Orientation and Mobility.* New York: American Foundation for the Blind.

Scrutton, D. (1984) *Management of the Motor Disorders of Children with Cerebral Palsy.* London: Spastics International Medical Publishers.

Sobsey, D. and Wolf-Schein, E. (1991) 'Sensory impairments.' In F. Orelove and D. Sobsey *Educating Children with Multiple Disabilities: A Transdisciplinary Approach.* Baltimore: Paul H. Brookes.

Turrill, S. (1992) 'Supported positioning in intensive care.' *Paediatric Nursing, May,* 24–27.

Ware, J. (1996) *Creating Responsive Environments for People with Profound Learning and Multiple Disabilities.* London: David Fulton.

Warren, D. (1994) *Blindness and Children: An Individual Differences Approach.* Cambridge: Cambridge University Press.

World Health Organization (1992) *The ICD-10 Classification of Mental and Behavioural Disorders.* Geneva: WHO.

CHAPTER 10

Children and Young People with Learning Disabilities: Developing Good Practice in Intimate and Personal Care Provision

Steven Carnaby and Angela Mallett

INTRODUCTION

As with intimate and personal care more widely, discourse relating specifically to services for children with learning and/or physical disabilities has been very limited. A developmental factor is operating here, in that intimate care for very young children and infants *with and without* disabilities is clearly commonplace. It is understood and expected that they have high levels of dependency in terms of continence and personal hygiene, and need a significant level of support, teaching and modelling in order to acquire increasing levels of independence. The support of adults with continence and other intimate aspects of daily life is likely to be considered by society as non-standard (e.g. usually associated with dependence, illness or incapacity). A key issue here is the role of normalisation in Britain and the ways in which it influences both our thinking about how to support children and young people and our gradually shifting attitudes about the nature of supporting individuals with intimate care as they develop from small children to become young adults.

This chapter explores some of the particular issues relating to the direct support of intimate and personal care for children and young people with learning disabilities, drawing from three main sources – small-scale research, feedback from staff training workshops and our own personal experiences of providing intimate and personal care for children. As well as the wider social and political context, we consider issues relating to best practice and emphasise the role of communication between all involved parties as a way of ensuring safe, appropriate and effective support.

THE WIDER CONTEXT

Considerations of the provision of intimate and personal care for children with learning disabilities brings with it an additional bundle of issues, including the adjustments required as children make the transition into adult services and, of particular policy and practice importance, considerations of child protection. Such factors make it critically important that we get right:

1. the planning and delivery of intimate and personal care for children with learning and/or physical disabilities

2. the support and guidance staff need to provide high-quality intimate and personal care

3. the facilitation of positive interactions between staff, children and their parents and carers (e.g. Griffiths 1994).

These three areas can be combined to create a framework for best practice. First, as in many aspects of health and social care, careful assessment and planning helps ensure that the child receives support of a high quality. This means the development of thorough assessment tools that ask the appropriate questions about what the child needs in terms of support, how she or he can influence the delivery of intimate care and how the care itself can be monitored and evaluated (Orelove and Sobsey 1996).

Second, staff providing intimate and personal care need training, support and guidance in order to keep themselves and the children they support as safe as possible by minimising risks that occur in relating to the absence of clear interpersonal boundaries, inconsistent practice and inadequate attention to physical health and hygiene issues. In turn, the recent policy and practice focus on child protection (e.g. Department of Health 2004) is likely to magnify concerns about safety in children's services, with implications for managing defensive practice and the perceived risks of physical and sexual abuse. It could be consequently argued that such pressures constrain practice in intimate and personal care by encouraging closed and minimal interactions between staff and service users.

Third, ways in which services attempt to understand and communicate with the families of children and young people with learning disabilities around the practice of intimate care is a key element of any good practice framework. The biological need for direct support with intimate and personal care inherent in all young children is likely to make the specific needs of young children with learning disabilities relatively invisible until they reach the age where children without disabilities begin to develop skills in continence and self-care more generally. Failure to reach these milestones, or reaching them in part at a later stage than the majority of children, may for some parents and carers be the first concrete signal that their child in not developing in standard ways.

The emotional impact of such a realisation is likely to be hard to bear, and as the child grows older, may be an area of life that remains difficult and emotionally complex for the family. It is essential therefore that services (e.g. schools and respite provision) are able to acknowledge the significance of intimate care to the child's family. Not only is it an area of life that may serve as a regular reminder of the child's disability, but it is also an area of life more often associated with risks of abuse and poor practice in general. The facilitation of positive interaction with children during intimate care is more likely to result when paid carers have made concerted efforts to work in partnership with parents and carers to develop child-centred practice. The nature of this facilitating can range from simple regular telephone contact to more direct involvement where parents and carers 'model' the ways in which tasks need to be carried out, or become involved in staff training. The ways in which facilitation occurs needs ongoing review and evaluation. This can ensure both that parents and carers feel heard and that staff are encouraging a two-way dialogue that continues to develop the approach taken to the child's support.

THE NATURE OF THE CHALLENGE

Most commonly, children with learning disabilities will receive intimate and personal care in three main settings outside of the family home: school (specialised education or mainstream), respite or short breaks and residential provision. Many of the issues relating to the delivery of intimate care are common to all three settings, but specific issues or dilemmas can also arise.

Issues relating to children attending special or mainstream schools

While it might be assumed that staff working in special schools would be familiar with the intimate and personal care needs of pupils, it cannot be assumed that all staff would be comfortable (or necessarily competent) in carrying out this support. There may well be cultures of demarcation, where intimate and personal support is viewed as the domain of teaching assistants rather than more qualified staff, such hierarchy perhaps being symptomatic of the devalued status ascribed to intimate care in wider society.

The range of tasks is likely to be wide. Some students might need simple prompting at regular points throughout the day, while other pupils will need to use changing benches, hoists and two staff to support them. Many children with learning disabilities need supervision at mealtimes, while some need total assistance. An increasing number of children and young people use PEG (percutaneous endoscopic gastrostomy) feeding, or need oxygen or other complex health interventions to sustain life. Teaching and support staff are therefore required to manage what might be seen as competing demands (i.e. the educational curriculum and intimate and personal care), and such juggling may present particular difficulties and challenges. One solution would be to combine these two agendas rather than attempting to view them separately, looking at how the provision of high-quality, child-centred care can provide a fertile arena for developing a wide range of skills as recommended by the curriculum – for example, the development of self-esteem, communication and an understanding of how the body works (see Marvin 1998 for useful discussion on the curriculum and children with complex needs).

The increase in supporting children with learning disabilities to attend mainstream school – in some cases this can be on a very part-time basis – can also lead to a number of specific challenges. Some studies suggest that children with learning disabilities in mainstream schools have lower social status than their non-disabled peers, and are at risk of suffering psychologically as a consequence (Nabuzoka 2000). Requiring substantial support with personal care might exacerbate this situation. The hierarchy referred to previously in terms of special schools also has the potential to operate in this context, as care assistants may be employed specifically to support children with intimate care needs. The fact that the child requires support to leave the classroom and his or her peers on a regular basis in order to attend to something that those peers can do independently and during lunch and other planned breaks in the day also has the potential to stigmatise the young person with disabilities.

Issues relating to children using respite services

The use of respite or short breaks can be a valuable resource for the child with learning disabilities as well as the family or carer, in many cases giving everybody space and time for themselves away from intense family dynamics. Here issues for staff are likely to relate to consistency as it relates to the regularity of respite stays. Where respite is used regularly there are more opportunities for developing routines and familiarity in such areas as the ways in which personal care tasks are carried out and at what time. More irregular visits might lead to more attention being paid to developing confidence in everybody.

As with parents of adults with learning disabilities, parents and carers of children and young people may be reticent about leaving them in the care of others, even where time is spent offering reassurance and visits are built up gradually. Trust is more likely to be developed when effort is put into building open and transparent communication around the child's needs, giving the parent or carer opportunities for sharing their concerns and anxieties as well as providing key information about the nature of support required. Here staff are likely to suggest that the parent or carer physically demonstrate to them what is needed as well as it being written in a care plan. This serves a number of functions. As well being a concrete demonstration of what is needed, the child is being given a message that the carer or parent is happy with the staff to be providing intimate support, thus facilitating positive interaction between staff and the child. Equally, the parent or carer is more likely to feel valued and listened to, as their ideas and approach are leading the work of staff.

Issues relating to children living in residential care

Many issues relating to children using respite care are likely to apply to those living in residential care, but an obvious difference is the permanence of a staff role and its significance as *locus parentis*. Children and young people are supported by paid carers rather than significant others, and from an early age they are subject to close physical scrutiny from people outside their immediate family. The necessary boundaries that need to be placed between the child and his or her carers have the potential to impact upon self-esteem and sense of self for a number of reasons. Staff turnover can lead to inconsistency of support as well as fragmented or fragile attachments with adults, while the intimacy shared between parent and child takes on a different hue when acted out and witnessed in a formal care environment.

The developmental issue raised earlier has particular significance in the formal care environment. At which stage does a female member of staff adapt her physical contact with the boys she works with? How do male members of staff manage the issues that emerge when the very tactile girl they have known since she was three years old still demands hugs and holding hands aged 15 years? As children with learning disabilities grow up, their role in society changes and so the messages they receive from formal carers needs to change accordingly.

Risks of abuse

As with provision for adults with learning disabilities, children and young people with learning disabilities are at risk of abuse as a result of their need for intimate and personal support. This abuse can be physical, sexual, psychological or in the form of neglect. The Department of Health (2004) suggests: 'Disabled children are more likely to experience abuse than non-disabled children. Children living away from home are particularly vulnerable'. The Department of Health National Service Framework for Children (2004, 6.2) provides advice on the nature of safeguarding protocols to minimise the risks of abuse, all of which are highly relevant to the provision of intimate and personal care:

- Consulting with disabled children, and organisations advocating on their behalf, about how best to safeguard them.

- The development of emergency placement services for disabled children who are moved from abusive situations.

- The systematic collection and analysis of data on disabled children subject to child protection processes.

- Safeguarding guidance and procedures for professional staff working with disabled children.

- Training for all staff to enable them to respond appropriately to signs and symptoms of abuse or neglect in disabled children.

- Guidance on contributing to assessment, planning and intervention and child protection conferences and reviews.

- Disability equality training for managers and staff involved in safeguarding children work.

- Regular reviews and updating of all policies and procedures relating to disabled children.

FACING THE CHALLENGE: DEVELOPING STAFF TRAINING

In recognition of the paucity of guidance and resources for supporting good practice in intimate and personal care for children and young people, a two-day training programme was developed and rolled out across one local authority in the East Midlands. This authority had requested support after reflecting on the current approach to intimate and personal care in its statutory children's services, this agenda arising after service development personnel had become familiar with issues emerging in services for adults with learning disabilities elsewhere.

The training programme was developed in consultation with the local authority and was facilitated by teachers from a local special school and an independent consultant. The benefit of involving local teaching staff in the delivery of the workshops was that where necessary and appropriate, individual children common to all settings could be discussed in relation to particular issues that were being raised, and action planning could be established to prevent any benefits of such networking being lost.

As with previous work carried out with services supporting adults with learning disabilities (e.g. Carnaby 2000), the main emphasis in providing training and practice development opportunities for those working with children and young people was the creation of a space for open dialogue. This is required to allow concerns to be shared, assumptions safely and appropriately challenged and suggestions for good practice recorded in order to inform the drafting of more detailed child-centred care plans. This discursive approach was combined with psycho-educational elements and briefings on local policy and national guidance as an attempt at integrating policy, practice and personal perspective.

The training workshops aimed to achieve the following:

- Identify key tasks in the area of intimate and personal care.
- Place intimate and personal care within the context of the child's life and support structures.
- Enable the design of individualised approaches to meeting needs.
- Consider the importance of collaborative working.
- Establish principles of good practice.

Prior to the training in each case, participants were asked to complete a questionnaire (see Appendix 2), which had been adapted from research carried out with staff working with adults with learning disabilities (see Chapter 2). This aimed to establish attitudes and perspectives among group members and was used to prime the workshop facilitators to focus on key issues where necessary. The programme of the workshop ran as follows:

Introductions and ground rules

This was an essential part of the workshop, as it created a safe space for dialogue and addressed issues such as confidentiality and appropriate sharing of information. Incorporated into this first section was a 'name game' where participants were asked to share something about their own name with the wider group. This exercise was used to illustrate the observation that if we are uncomfortable talking about our own name, we are very likely to find it almost impossible to talk about sensitive and taboo topics such as intimate care and children.

Understanding the source of knowledge and information

Participants were asked to consider how people gain their understanding of three important areas of life that are related to intimate and personal care – sex and sexuality, the use of touch and the nature of relationships with others. Observations were made that we gain our knowledge in these areas from a variety of sources including the media (i.e. from television, film, the news, magazines and books), our friends and family, personal experience and from formal education.

When asked to think about children and young people with learning disabilities, it was suggested that their knowledge may come from some or all of these sources but in many cases, the information acquired may be incomplete, distorted or inconsistent because of the cognitive limitations involved. In addition, children with learning disabilities might get a skewed picture of issues relating to intimacy through abusive relationships or because their bodies are more likely to be open to public scrutiny from an early age as a result of their intimate care needs.

Legislative and knowledge frameworks

Participants were asked to consider their own understanding of the legal context along with their own knowledge about sex and sexual behaviour in order to explore their confidence in modelling appropriate boundaries and behaviour with the young people they support. This was conducted through the use of multiple choice questionnaires. Issues focused on here included the age of consent, the physiological signs of sexual arousal and the position surrounding relationships between paid staff and people with learning disabilities as enshrined in law. The legal context around intimate care appeared to be the subject evoking most anxiety amongst workshop participants, and was without fail the one area that people asked to be covered during the opening discussion.

Use of case studies

These aimed to address a wide variety of complex issues relating to intimate and personal care, and encouraged participants to discuss the importance of consistent practice that is carefully recorded and monitored. Examples are shown on pp.151–2.

The case studies enabled open discussion about personal values as well as the acknowledgement of the wider context of people's lives and how these experiences can impact upon the practice and experience of intimate and personal care. This part of the workshop appeared to be particularly useful for developing consistency between staff members.

Feedback from pre-workshop questionnaire

This brief presentation provided participants with an overview of what they as a group appeared to be feeling about intimate and personal care, and a number of themes emerged:

Issues for service users

Participants were aware that there was an interface between the provision of intimate care and the emerging sexuality of their service users. The practice of continuing intimate and physical support for the young child as s/he develops into adolescence was thought to influence the individual's emerging sense of self, affecting the ability to physically separate self from others. Similarly,

Case study: Mark

Mark is ten years old and appears to have an aspect of autism. He presents as more able in the SLD school than his peers, and there is a question as to whether he should have a diagnosis of Asperger's Syndrome.

Mark can be challenging at home, sometimes hitting his mother and tipping over furniture. For the last year he has received respite care. Mark's father left the parental home when Mark was four years old.

Mark is sometimes incontinent of urine and faeces during the day. Mark's mother ensures he wears a pad during the day to avoid 'accidents', and he always wears a pad at night.

During the last few respite breaks, some of the staff team have noticed that by introducing a clear routine to Mark, he is able to go without his pad during the night. Mark's mother feels that she will not be able to continue this strategy at home.

- What are the issues for Mark?
- What are the issues for Mark's mother?
- What are the issues for the staff team?
- How can all of those involved in Mark's care work more effectively?

the regular need for intimate support was seen as resulting in more limited opportunities for the development of dignity, privacy and accompanying self-esteem. Staff struggled with the challenge of shifting their approach to the individual as s/he developed from childhood into adolescence.

A practical example of this was related by a group of female staff who were refusing to support a boy of 15 since he had started to become regularly sexually aroused during intimate care. They admitted to feelings of embarrassment and shame, as they had known him since he was five years old – but no longer felt able to support him. Further discussion explored the need to consider the boy's experience and understanding of what was going on, but also to recognise their own feelings of loss for the child who was now clearly becoming a man.

Issues for parents/families

Participants spoke about conversations with parents and families concerning the feelings of guilt at not 'coping' and needing others to provide intimate care

Case study: Paul

Paul is 13 years old and has profound and multiple learning disabilities. He has limited vision and hearing and uses a moulded wheelchair.

Paul attends a special school, and much of his care needs are met by his doting grandmother, who appears to have a lot of influence over Paul's mother.

Paul has been using respite care for the last eight months, but Paul's grandmother has become increasingly critical of the care provided, feeling that Paul's family should meet his needs.

Soon after Paul started using respite care services, his family noticed that he had begun to masturbate at home, which they report had not happened before. Paul's grandmother stated at a recent meeting that she no longer wants him to use respite care, implying that staff must have shown him how to masturbate while he was staying with them.

- What are the issues for Paul?

- What are the issues for his mother and grandmother?

- What are the issues for the local authority?

- What are the issues for the staff team in the respite service?

for their own child. Further, there were examples where family members had expressed concerns that the staff would not 'do it right' – or might abuse the child in some way.

A common theme in all of the workshops was where to locate the expertise around good practice in supporting a particular child with intimate and personal care. Staff themselves may view the parent or carer as the 'expert' in supporting the child, sometimes leading to pressure being placed on the parent. The converse may be the case, where parents and carers assume that staff have the expertise and leave the development of good practice to them. There may also be situations where staff see themselves as 'experts' and contradict the advice and/or wishes of the family.

Discussion led to a consensus that all three of these positions can have clear disadvantages and that an arguably more appropriate approach is to focus on collaboration within a 'best interests' mode. Here, information, skills and knowledge are shared between interested and involved parties to enable the construction of a consistent agreed approach that is supported by all.

Issues for staff

Inter-agency collaboration was a main theme when considering issues for staff, namely the development of open dialogue between the school, the respite service and the residential establishment where this applied. Sensitive collaboration between school, family (or residential services) and respite services was felt to be important around the following:

- Boundary setting (i.e. what happens, who does it, how is it done, at what time and in what location).

- Child protection issues (e.g. keeping body charts to monitor any changes in physical appearance).

- 'Managing' transition from childhood into adolescence – adapting procedures to maximise autonomy or at least maximise the extent to which the young person can influence the way that any particular procedure is conducted.

As with the one administered to staff working with adults, the pre-workshop questionnaire for staff working with children and young people asked participants to rate their attitudes towards particular intimate and personal care tasks on a scale of 1 to 5, where 1 signified the lowest level of discomfort. The slight addition was that the questionnaire made a differentiation between younger children under ten years and older children/young people aged ten to eighteen years. This aimed to explore the hypothesis that people might feel more comfortable in supporting younger children – perhaps because such support is more 'socially acceptable'.

A sample summary from some of these data is shown in Table 10.1. It suggests that participants were most uncomfortable about carrying out associated tasks such as laundry and clearing up body fluids, and were on average more uncomfortable generally when carrying out more invasive intimate tasks (average rating = 2.9) compared with less invasive tasks (average rating = 2.4). There was a slight indication that they were more uncomfortable supporting older children with more intimate tasks (average rating = 3.2) compared with younger children (average rating = 2.6).

CONCLUDING SUGGESTIONS FOR BEST PRACTICE

This chapter has explored a hitherto neglected area of practice, namely the support of intimate and personal care for children and young people with learning disabilities, and raised a number of issues relating to the development of good practice. While it is clearly inappropriate to establish any specific gold standards around particular tasks, it might be helpful for services to ensure that

Table 10.1 Average ratings made by staff working with children and young people with learning disabilities about their relative discomfort in carrying out intimate and personal care tasks

	Average ratings		
	<10-year-olds	10–19-year-olds	Both groups
Intimate care tasks			
Dressing/undressing underwear	2.1	2.7	2.4
Using toilet	2.1	2.6	2.4
Changing continence pads (faeces)	2.9	3.3	3.1
Changing continence pads (urine)	3.0	3.3	3.2
Bath/shower	2.4	2.8	2.6
Washing intimate parts of body	2.9	3.2	3.1
Menstrual care	2.7	3.3	3.0
Enemas	3.0	4.0	3.5
Intimate care domain (all tasks)	2.6	3.2	2.9
Personal care tasks			
Skin care	2.6	2.2	2.4
Eating	2.1	2.1	2.1
Haircare	2.4	2.2	2.3
Brushing teeth	3.0	2.6	2.8
Dressing/undressing outer clothes	2.5	2.4	2.5
Washing non-intimate parts of body	2.7	2.4	2.5
Prompting to use toilet	2.2	2.3	2.3
Personal care domain (all tasks)	2.5	2.3	2.4
Associated tasks			
Soiled laundry	3.1	3.0	3.1
Vomit	3.4	3.6	3.5
Faeces	3.3	3.6	3.5
Urine	3.3	3.5	3.4
Blood	3.4	3.8	3.6
Associated tasks domain (all tasks)	3.3	3.5	3.4

Rating: 1 = most satisfaction or least discomfort and 5 = least satisfaction or most discomfort their staff are supported to work consistently in ways underpinned with certain key principles. A suggested list for these principles might include:

- open discussion of the need for intimate care support in job descriptions and interviews

- specific team-based training that looks at personal values, social context and boundary setting issues

- the development of collaborative practice across agencies and in partnership with children and their families

- close working with clinical staff (e.g. speech and language therapists or clinical psychologists) where necessary to develop specific strategies for addressing issues as they arise, particularly important for young people with autism, profound and multiple disabilities and other complex needs

- the provision of regular time for staff reflection on their practice

- development of detailed care plans that are written jointly with the young person wherever possible and involving their family where appropriate

- maintenance of effective coordination by a named individual to ensure that effective and consistent care is provided across settings

- a lifespan approach to intimate care that recognises a young person's changing needs, acknowledges the importance of responsive support and also works at addressing behavioural and other difficulties as early as possible to prevent them becoming entrenched as the individual ages.

REFERENCES

Carnaby, S. (2000) 'Workshop presentation: individual planning in intimate and personal care for people with intellectual disabilities.' 'Making it Personal' National Conference, ORT House, London. 13 June.

Department of Health (2004) National Service Framework for Children, Young People and Maternity Services: Disabled Children and Young People and Those with Complex Health Needs. London: HMSO.

Griffiths, M. (1994) Transition to Adulthood: The Role of Education for Young People with Severe Learning Difficulties. London: David Fulton.

Marvin, C. (1998) 'Teaching and learning for children with profound and multiple learning difficulties.' In P. Lacey and C. Ouvray (eds) People with Profound and Multiple Learning Disabilities: A Collaborative Approach to Meeting Complex Needs. London: David Fulton.

Nabuzoka, D. (2000) Children with Learning Disabilities: Social Functioning and Adjustment. Leicester: British Psychological Society

Orelove, F.P. and Sobsey, D. (1996) *Educating Children with Multiple Disabilities: A Transdisciplinary Approach.* Baltimore: Paul H. Brookes.

FURTHER READING/RESOURCES

Books

The Shepherd School, Nottingham has been a key player in the new edition of *Living Your Life,* published by Brook in November 2003. This is a comprehensive curriculum of SRE designed for those working with young people and adults with learning difficulties. Supported by the Teenage Pregnancy Unit, this resource has been well received. Future publications from the school include *Bodyworks,* aimed at those pupils with profound and multiple learning difficulties, and a new pack on citizenship. For further details on these, please contact Angela Mallett at Shepherd School or Sarah Bustard at sarah.bustard@nottinghamcity-pct.nhs.uk.

Other resources recommended by the school:

British Institute of Learning Disabilities (BILD), Campaign House, Green Street, Kidderminster, Worcestershire DY10 1JL Tel: 01562 723010; email: enquiries@bild.org.uk. See BILD Good Health Series (1998): *Exercise; Breathe Easy; Eating and Drinking; Alcohol and Smoking; Looking After Your Teeth; Seeing and Hearing; Sex; If You are Ill; Using Medicine Safely; Coping with Stress.*

Craft, A. and Stewart, D. (1996) *What About Us?* Sheffield: Home and School Council.

Learning Development Aids, Duke Street, Wisbech, Cambridgeshire PE13 2AE publish the following: *Living Your Life; Chance to Choose; Picture Yourself;* pictures to support *Living Your Life* and *Chance to Choose; The Protection Pack,* by the Shepherd School.

Massey, D. (ed.) (1995) *Sex Education Resource Book.* London: fpa.

Schwier, K. and Hingsburger, D. (2000) *Your Sons and Daughters with Intellectual Disabilities.* London: Jessica Kingsley Publishers.

Scull, L. and Kerr-Edwards, L. (1999) *Talking Together – A Resource for Parents.* London: fpa.

Stewart, D. and Ray, C. (2001) *Ensuring Entitlement: Sex and Relationships Education for Disabled Children.* London: Sex Education Forum.

Wetton, N. and Williams, T. (2000) *Health for Life – Ages 4–7.* Cheltenham: Nelson Thornes Ltd.

CHAPTER 11

Providing Care for Older People with Learning Disabilities

Eleni Hatzidimitriadou and Alisoun Milne

OVERVIEW

Changes in lifestyle, improvements in care and better access to medical treatment have resulted in increased longevity among people with learning disabilities. Despite wider recognition of this 'new' older population by policy-makers and service providers, the needs arising from the cumulative challenges of ageing with a learning disability have yet to be fully understood and addressed. In this chapter, the authors explore the care implications of growing older with a learning disability, offer an overview of the main age-related needs and discuss the service context of their care. They also highlight the needs of family carers. The key challenges facing service provision are also explored and a number of recommendations made, focusing particularly on the development of effective and safe intimate and personal care.

INTRODUCTION

Old age has only recently been conceptualised as a distinctive life stage for people with learning disabilities. Enhanced longevity is a consequence of changes in lifestyle, improvements in care and better access to medical treatment (Herr and Weber 1999; Tinker 1997; Victor 1997). For the learning disabled population as a whole, life expectancy has increased from 20 years in 1930 to 70–74 years in 1990 (Foundation for People with Learning Disabilities 2002). The greatest increase has been among people with mild learning and physical disabilities – mainly women (McDonald 2002). Life expectancy of people with Down's Syndrome has increased spectacularly with over 40 per cent now surviving to the age of 60 years (Holland 2000). In addition to higher numbers, older people with learning disabilities are also more visible as they live in community settings instead of being 'hidden' in institutions or within family homes (Walker and Walker 1998).

Despite this emerging 'new' population, limited attention has been paid to reviewing or meeting their needs; the majority focus of work in the learning disability field has been on childhood and early adulthood (Hatzidimitriadou and Milne 2005; Hogg and Lambe 1998; Robertson, Moss and Turner 1996). In this chapter, we present an overview of existing evidence about the needs of older[1] people with learning disabilities and their family carers, and discuss the service context of their care. We also highlight key issues for addressing the intimate and personal care needs of this group and make a number of recommendations for future service developments.

HEALTH, AGEING AND LEARNING DISABILITY

Although there is no definitive age at which 'later life' begins in learning disabled populations, 50 years is generally accepted as the threshold. That age-related problems impact at an earlier age than for the general population is more widely recognised (Jenkins, Brooksbank and Miller 1994; McDonald 2002). Differential morbidity – the tendency for people with more severe levels of disability to experience age-related ill health at an earlier age than their more able counterparts – produces a particular demographic pattern (Foundation for People with Learning Disabilities 2002). The population of older people with learning disabilities tends to be relatively able with good health and functional skills (Cooper 1997a; Hogg et al. 2001; Moss, Lambe and Hogg 1998).

The most common physical health problems are arthritis, rheumatic illnesses, cardiac and pulmonary conditions. These difficulties usually lead to loss of mobility and sight and hearing may also decline (McDonald 2002). The impact of such age-related health symptoms tends to be greater for this group as there are limited opportunities to maintain fitness and prevent deterioration (Bland et al. 2003). Yet general practitioners do not routinely monitor the age-related health status of people with learning disabilities; it is unclear whether this is due to a lack of interest or knowledge (Grant 2001). Evenhuis et al. (2000) suggest a number of service-related barriers to accessing health care; these include minimal training of staff in assessment, diagnosis and treatment; lack of consent procedures; and limited time for informant-based medical history-taking or capacity for accommodating behavioural challenges. Mental health issues have particularly attracted the attention of researchers. Evidence can be located around two areas: functional mental illness and dementia.

Functional mental illness

Similar to the general older population, there is a prevalence rate of 20 per cent for major psychiatric disorders in learning-disabled people aged 65 years and over (Day and Jancar 1994). The majority of reported cases are diagnosed with depression or anxiety; in particular, people experience reactive depression due to age-related physical illness, or bereavement related to loss of their carer (Cooper 1999). Behavioural problems also account for a third to a half of cases with psychiatric disorders (Davidson et al. 1999). At all ages, people with learning disabilities are at enhanced risk of developing psychosis and autism (Cooper 1999; Driessen et al. 1997; Gustafsson 1997; Moss et al. 1998).

Despite the relatively high prevalence of mental ill health in this population, few people are referred to psychiatric services for help (Cooper 1999; Moss et al. 1998). Identification of mental health problems in people with learning disabilities can be complex: lack of cooperation and communication problems make assessment and diagnosis difficult, while co-morbidity issues further complicate the picture (Bouras 1999; Holland 2000; Janicki and Dalton 1999). As a result, high levels of unmet psychiatric needs exist and ensuring access to, and support from, mental health services remains an ongoing challenge.

Dementia

Dementia is the global impairment of higher mental functioning including the loss of memory, problem-solving ability, the use of learned skills, social skills and emotional control (Alzheimer's Society 2003). It is progressive and usually irreversible. Longevity is the key risk factor for Alzheimer's disease, the most common form of dementia in the general as well as learning disabled populations (Dalton and Janicki 1999). Prevalence is the same as (Janicki and Dalton 2000), or higher than (Cooper 1999) that of the general population; it increases with age from 6 per cent in the 40–64 years cohort to 70 per cent in the 85–94 years age group (Holland 2001). People with Down's Syndrome are evidenced as particularly at risk of developing dementia: of those aged 50–59 over a quarter is affected whilst for those aged 60–69 over a half have dementia (Hutchinson 1999; Turk, Dodd and Christmas 2001).

Dementia-related symptoms such as impairment of daily activities, abnormal emotional and social behaviours, aggressive behaviour, eating and sleep disturbances, are likely to be similarly severe in people with learning disabilities as in the age-matched general population. Symptoms tend to manifest themselves in those areas of function that are already impaired. Depression is also common, a co-morbidity often overlooked (Cooper 1997b; Janicki and Dalton 1999). US work suggests that early assessment and appropriate interventions can alleviate symptoms and help with care planning (Janicki et al. 1995; Wilkinson and Janicki 2002).

PROFILE AND NEEDS OF OLDER PEOPLE WITH LEARNING DISABILITIES

- Improvements in care and treatment have resulted in many more people with learning disabilities reaching old age.

- The greatest increase has been amongst people with mild learning and physical disabilities – mainly women.

- Older people with learning disabilities tend to be relatively able with good health and functional skills.

- Common age-related physical illnesses for this population are arthritis and rheumatic illnesses, cardiac and pulmonary conditions.

- Key age-related mental health problems are depression, anxiety and dementia.

- Dementia is at least as prevalent amongst older people with learning disabilities as the general age-matched population; it is more prevalent in people with Down's Syndrome. Prevalence increases with age.

- There are a number of disability and service-related barriers to accessing health care; primary care does not routinely monitor the health status of people with learning disabilities as they age.

- Few older people with learning disabilities are referred to psychiatric services for help; however, evidence indicates that early assessment and support from professionals can alleviate symptoms.

FAMILY CARERS

It is estimated that a third of adults with learning disabilities live with a family carer aged 70 or over; the vast majority of them are parents, while the remainder are grandparents or siblings (Department of Health 2001a; Foundation for People with Learning Disabilities 2003; Magrill 2005; Ward 1998). These carers tend to have limited social networks as a consequence of relatives and friends dying or moving away to 'retire'; many are also widowed (Bigby 1997). Due to providing intensive care over many years they are at significant risk of becoming physically and/or mentally ill; familiar aspects of caring can become difficult (Foundation for People with Learning Disabilities 2002; Milne *et al.* 2001). For some older carers the caring relationship may be partially 'reversed', with the cared for person taking on domestic tasks such as cleaning or cooking that used to be done by the carer (Hatzidimitriadou and Forrester-Jones 2002; Magrill *et al.* 1997).

The ageing profile of the learning disabled population often results in the loss of their primary carer during their middle or later years. As many will not have spouses or children, they are not only bereft of a familiar lifestyle, and often their lifelong home, but also their primary source of emotional support and care (Foundation for People with Learning Disabilities 2002; Magrill 2005). The consequences are immense. It is often at this 'crisis point' that formal services become involved, with residential care often being the only option for people with complex or challenging needs (Herr and Weber 1999; Robertson *et al.* 1996). It is to service provision that we now turn.

CARE PROVISION FOR OLDER PEOPLE WITH LEARNING DISABILITIES AND THEIR CARERS

Policy context

Over the last few years there have been major learning disability policy reviews by governments in England, Wales and Scotland (Foundation for People with Learning Disabilities 2002). The white paper *Valuing People* (Department of Health 2001b) is a key strategy document, which provides a new vision for learning disability services based on the principles of rights, independence, choice and inclusion. The importance of person centred planning for older people with learning disabilities is specifically highlighted; learning disability partnership boards (LDPBs) are tasked with planning and commissioning services for this population, including long-term care (Foundation for People with Learning Disabilities 2003; Towell 2002).

Valuing People also draws attention to the need to support older family carers (Department of Health 1999, 2001b). The Older Family Carers Initiative (OFCI) – launched by the Foundation for People with Learning Disabilities in 2002 – aimed to support LDPBs identify and meet the needs of older family carers (Magrill 2005). It offers a number of examples of good practice.

Summary of policy context

- The white paper *Valuing People* highlights a need for agencies to develop services for older people with learning disabilities and their carers.

- The importance of person centred planning is specifically highlighted.

- Learning disability partnership boards are tasked with planning and commissioning services for users and carers.

- The 'new vision' for learning disability services extends across the life span incorporating the principles of rights, independence, choice and inclusion.

- The Foundation for People with Learning Disabilities, Older Family Carers Initiative offers a number of examples of good practice with carers.

THE IDEOLOGICAL CONTEXT OF SERVICE PROVISION

In addition to the role played by policy, a number of ideological influences are also significant in underpinning service development for the population under review. Space only permits a brief review of two key issues: social construction of ageing and social integration.

The social construction of ageing

The 'social construction of ageing' refers to the relationship between attitudes to old age, our conceptualisation of ageing and the care and treatment of older people. Ageism is a particularly powerful influence on attitudes, treatment and services for older people. It is defined by Hughes (1995, pp.42–43) as:

> a matrix of beliefs and attitudes which legitimises the use of age as a means of identifying a particular social group which portrays the members of that group in negative, stereotypical terms and which consequently generates and reinforces a fear of the ageing process and a denigration of older people.

The consequences of ageism are observable everywhere – in the social and economic policies that discriminate against older people, in the attitudes and values of people generally and the ways these shape the treatment and behaviour towards older people in both personal and professional encounters. The ways in which old age, and attitudes to it, interact with other aspects of social identity such as race, gender, sexuality and disability has also been noted. It has been suggested that older people with learning disabilities are doubly disadvantaged by the combined effects of ageism and discrimination related to learning disability (Walker and Walker 1996, 1998). This 'double jeopardy' has the effect of lowering expectations and legitimising the provision of inadequate services.

There is evidence that ageism and the social construction of ageing underpin both the development of services for older people and the delivery of care (Hughes 1995). Many services are imbued with a dependency culture, which characterises old age as associated with inevitable decline in functioning, passivity and withdrawal from 'life' (Biggs 1993). This limited perspective is echoed in work with older people, which is routinely regarded as requiring lower levels of skill, knowledge and qualification than work with other user groups. For example, the needs of older people, as constructed by social services, emphasise the 'routine' nature of the work, and the delivery of short-term instrumental, standardised packages of care. This practice is then perpetuated by the habitual allocation of older service users to unqualified or assistant staff. These trends combine to form a reinforcing cycle of disadvantage; the low status attached to older users reinforcing the low status attached to unqualified staff. This issue is linked to the devalued status of intimate and personal care, an issue that is explored later in this chapter.

Social integration

Walker and Walker (1998) extend this argument into the service delivery arena, critiquing the ideological shift experienced by people with learning disabilities once they become 'older' service users. They note that: 'as soon as a person is transferred from one service provider category to another, merely as a result of chronological ageing, the orientation of services shifts from supporting independence to reproducing dependence' (p.127). The ageist assumptions and dependency culture that underpin services for older people results in older people with learning disabilities facing more restrictive and segregated lives than was the case when they were in receipt of services for younger adults (McDonald 2002; Thompson 2002).

Whether normalisation – the key principle underpinning the majority of services for people with learning disabilities – continues to be as relevant, or appropriate, for services for older people is, however, debatable (Walker and Walker 1996). Walker and Walker (1998) propose a model of 'social integration', an adaptation of the 'supportive environment model' outlined by Zarb and Oliver (1993). This provides a basis for extending the principles of integration whilst accommodating the need for support arising from age-related ill health. The key components of this model – proactivity; creative provision; services that anticipate crises and reflect user need; user-led services; and an emphasis on user rights and entitlements – would ensure improved service quality, the maintenance of independence and the provision of support in a community-based setting.

Space does not permit discussion of the relevance of recent developments in dementia care but evidence suggests that a shift away from a biomedical model towards a social and interpersonal model enhances quality of life and reduces challenging behaviours amongst people with dementia (Kitwood and Bredin 1992). There may be lessons to be learned from innovative services in this field particularly, long-term care (Wilkinson et al. 2004).

SUMMARY OF THE IDEOLOGICAL CONTEXT OF SERVICE PROVISION

- Ageism is a powerful influence on our attitudes towards, and treatment of, older people.

- Older people with learning disabilities are disadvantaged by the combined effects of ageism and discrimination related to disability.

- Work with older people is regarded as requiring lower levels of skill and interventions tend to be 'standardised'.

- The ageist assumptions and dependency culture that underpin services for older people results in older people with learning disabilities facing restrictive and segregated lives.

- Whilst normalisation continues to be relevant a model of 'social integration' may be more appropriate; this provides a basis for extending the principles of integration while accommodating the need for support arising from age-related ill health.

- Recent developments in dementia care may also be relevant, particularly innovations in long-term care.

SERVICES FOR OLDER PEOPLE WITH LEARNING DISABILITIES

As might be expected, there is limited consensus about whether services for older people with learning disabilities should be integrated with generic older people's services or whether specialist services need to be developed. What is clear, however, is that at present, when people with learning disabilities reach 'old age' they are expected to 'leave' specialist learning disability services and make use of services for older people. As noted above, these tend to be of lower quality and are often imbued with a dependency culture; few have specialist expertise in learning disability (McDonald 2002; Thompson and Wright 2001).

The present picture of service provision for this population is mixed. In her study of service provision for this user group, Fitzgerald (1998b) found considerable geographical variation and widespread confusion about which agencies are responsible for providing services. Common problems include lack of investment in services; low expectations of users; limited commitment to maintaining user independence; very low levels of consultation with users; and few opportunities for users to develop social networks (Fitzgerald 1998a, 1998b; Learning Disability Task Force 2004). A 2004 report by the Learning Disability Task Force confirms that these shortcomings of service provision are still evident despite the significant changes in policy-making (2004).

Severe criticisms about the lack of, and low quality of, services for older people with learning disabilities have also been made by professionals working in the learning disability sector (Aspray et al. 1999; Duff, Hoghton and Scheepers 2000; Hassiotis, Barron and O'Hara 2000). Specific concerns focus on limited access to psychiatric and general health care services, lack of access to recreational or leisure activities, and staff's limited awareness of age-related physical and mental health difficulties (Bailey and Cooper 1997). In a study that examined disparities in service provision between different groups of people with learning disabilities living in the community, two-thirds of those working with people over 50 thought that the general level of service for this user group was 'poor' or 'very poor' and included the almost 'routine' practice of placing people with learning disabilities aged 50 and over in residential care (Walker and Walker 1998). A specific deficit relates to care for older people with learning disabilities who develop dementia. Evidence suggests many providers have no guidance for managing dementia-related needs or accessing dementia expertise (Wilkinson and Janicki 2002).

Choice and control by service users

Of core relevance to any discussion about service development are issues of choice and control. Despite the priority accorded the enablement of younger people with learning disabilities to exercise control over their lives, this emphasis is largely absent in work with older people (Fitzgerald 1998a; Grant 1997).

A study by Stalker and colleagues found wide variations in the opportunities available for older users to express their views and be involved in care or treatment decisions (Stalker, Duckett and Downs 1999). While a limited degree of choice over everyday matters is common, for example, what to eat at meal times, involvement in more significant choices is often restricted, partial or contested. Specifically, there is limited or no choice about accommodation, day activities or types of support. The study concludes that there are a number of barriers and facilitators to user involvement in decision-making. Barriers include negative staff attitudes; carers' views being regarded as more important than those of the service user; and lack of time. The factors that facilitate choice are knowledge of the service users' tastes and needs; time to explore ways of communicating; accessible information; and acknowledgement that the vast majority of people – however old or frail – can express their preferences given appropriate support and encouragement. Evidence from the US reveals that older people with learning disabilities who have verbal skills do display insights into age-related changes in their personal and social lives and can be engaged in discussions about the nature of services they want to meet their needs (Ansello and Coogle 2000). As noted above, lessons about effective engagement can also be learned from the field of dementia care. For example, the development of person-centred care has led to a much greater level of involvement of people with dementia in care and treatment decisions (Cheston and Bender 1999; Marshall 1996).

Failure to recognise the heterogeneity of the learning disabled population is a central barrier to creative service development. This tendency results in the whole user group receiving an unnecessarily restrictive level of care and standard packages of support – the 'one size fits all' philosophy. There is also an accompanying tendency to minimise the significance of losses such as mobility or incontinence, and to underestimate the impact of 'needing help' with activities of daily living (Wilkinson *et al.* 2004). As noted earlier, packages for older people tend to be routine and practical in nature; whilst many contain elements of personal and intimate care this issue is rarely addressed, or even acknowledged, in any meaningful way. The older person with a learning disability is more likely to need help with activities of daily living and personal care as a consequence of suffering from a range of age-related illnesses. S/he is also more likely to be admitted to a care home. Issues relating to personal and intimate care are thus of core relevance to service provision for this group and are the focus of the next section.

SUMMARY OF SERVICES FOR OLDER PEOPLE WITH LEARNING DISABILITIES

- There is limited consensus about whether services for older people with learning disabilities should be integrated with older people's services or whether specialist services are needed.

- When people with learning disabilities reach 'old age' they are expected to access older people's services, which tend to be of lower quality and are often imbued with a dependency culture; few have expertise in learning disability.

- Service provision is fragmented and piecemeal and it is not clear which agencies are responsible for service development.

- Professionals working in the learning disability sector have been very critical of the low quality of services for older people with learning disabilities.

- There is very limited opportunity for older users to express their views and be involved in care and treatment decisions.

- Barriers to user involvement include negative staff attitude, the dominance of carers' views, lack of time and the 'one size fits all' approach.

- Factors that facilitate choice are knowledge of the service users' wishes, time to explore ways of communicating and full assessment of changing needs.

- Person-centred care has improved the engagement of people with dementia care and may be applicable to older people with learning disabilities.

- As this group is more likely to need help with activities of daily living and personal care as a consequence of suffering from a range of age-related illnesses, personal and intimate care is of core relevance to service provision.

INTIMATE AND PERSONAL CARE

A key component of high quality care for the group under review is the provision of effective and appropriate intimate and personal care. Personal care is a contentious and contested arena; it lies on the fault line between the medical and social care spheres and is delivered by a range of workers with widely differing status, roles, pay and employers (Twigg 2000). It is also the focus of much debate concerning the long-term care of older people – including those with learning disabilities – as it constitutes a significant and costly proportion of the overall cost of care.

Despite its centrality to the care of adults with dependency needs, good practice in intimate and personal care has received little attention by service planners or care providers. Twigg (2002) offers two reasons for this negligence: the non-bodily nature of social work, which traditionally focuses on psychosocial aspects of care, and societal taboos concerning the body and its management. Body care is widely regarded as a 'private matter' that should be dealt with alone or in the company of intimates. Furthermore, as noted earlier, personal care tasks are devalued by health and social care agencies and are delivered by low status frontline staff whose needs for support and training go largely unrecognised (Twigg 2000, 2002). In part, this is explained by the gendered nature of informal care. There is a widespread belief that as women ordinarily provide unpaid care to their children and dependent relatives it is not only unproblematic as a task but also unworthy of financial recompense when delivered in the formal sector.

However, there is significant evidence that failing to address this issue increases the risk of staff engaging in inconsistent and institutionalised practices and exposes people with learning disabilities – especially those with complex age-related needs – to potential abuse (Cambridge and Carnaby 2000b; Garner and Evans 2000). This risk is magnified by the 'private' and 'closed' nature of the majority of long-term care settings (Garner and Evans 2000) and is compounded by the multiple vulnerabilities experienced by older people with learning disabilities. These include: high levels of dependency; the likely prevalence of dementia; severely impaired communication; the fact that most older users have few relatives; and very limited service options. Reliance on care staff for survival is a particularly notable dimension of risk. The double jeopardy status discussed earlier may also increase vulnerability to abuse or neglect.

SUMMARY OF INTIMATE AND PERSONAL CARE

- A key component of high quality care for older people with learning disabilities is the provision of effective and appropriate intimate and personal care.

- Personal care is a contentious and contested arena and is the focus of much debate concerning long-term care.

- Despite its centrality to the care process, good practice in intimate and personal care has received little attention by service planners or providers.

- However, failure to address the issue increases the risk of staff engaging in inconsistent and institutionalised practices and may expose older people with learning disabilities to potential abuse.

- This risk is magnified by the 'private' and 'closed' nature of long-term care settings.

- It is also compounded by the multiple vulnerabilities experienced by older people with learning disabilities. These include significant dependency, dementia and impaired communication, physical frailty, few relatives, limited care options, and reliance on service providers.

RECOMMENDATIONS

Recommendations are located around the following themes: planning and service development; assessment of need; family carers; and intimate and personal care.

Planning and service development

Strategic service planning lies at the heart of high quality service development (Hogg 2000). Guidance accompanying *Valuing People* suggests that the most effective model for developing services for older people with a learning disability is for strategic planning on a local or regional basis to ensure partnership between learning disability trusts, older people's services and social services (Department of Health 2004a). Housing departments also have a role in providing housing with care for people who are relatively able bodied. Barriers between agencies and a weak culture of collaboration undermine joint working in many areas (Department of Health 2004b).

Learning disability partnership boards need to take account of the growing number of older people in the learning disabled population in their area. This requires acknowledgement of the fact that 'old age' begins earlier and that ageing is associated with a number of physical and mental health risks. Taking account of those users who are upcoming elderly is also important, particularly when they are living with an older family carer. A particular group that requires attention is people with Down's Syndrome; many will need services that can accommodate the challenges arising from Alzheimer's disease. Recent evidence identifies relatively few local authorities as having fully developed plans for meeting the needs of the population under review: this suggests that the *Valuing People* guidance is timely and urgently needed (Towell 2002).

Whilst it is difficult to stipulate the range and types of services needed, it is clear that *both* residential and community-based services are required. The local service context will be important in influencing decisions about where to develop new services or adapt existing ones. Whilst there is mixed evidence about whether services for this user group are best located within older people's services or learning disability services, some needs can only be met in specialist care settings, for example, older people with complex needs and challenging behaviour. The development of appropriate psychiatric services, including early detection of, and appropriate care for, dementia in older people with learning disabilities is a particular requirement, especially in people with Down's Syndrome.

Assessment of need

The *Valuing People* guidance proposes that a specific person-centred plan should be in place for every service user with a learning disability when they reach 50. This may need to be done earlier if the user already has a number of age-related needs or has Down's Syndrome (Department of Health 2004a). There is an accompanying need for primary care to assess proactively the health care needs of the population under review. Improved monitoring has the potential to identify health problems at an early stage and offer preventive treatment and advice (Hogg 2000). The advantage of general practitioners conducting the assessment is that they are very likely to be familiar with the service user and their carer, have knowledge of their health history, and awareness of their care needs These assessments should dovetail with the person centred planning process as well as with any specialist assessments.

Assessment of mental health needs is a specialist priority. Jenkins *et al.* (1994) suggest that all people with a learning disability aged 50 and over receive a regular psychiatric assessment to prevent the onset of functional mental problems; ensure early treatment for depression and anxiety; and minimise the effects of long-standing psychiatric disorders. Early detection of dementia is also important (Janicki and Dalton 1999). Whilst there is some way to go in terms of developing appropriate assessment tools, Janicki and Dalton propose that initial evaluations are done for all people with Down's Syndrome from the age of 40 years and for all other people with learning disabilities from the age of 50 years. These need to be done by psychiatric services as they are often complex and require specialist skill.

Family carers

There is a pressing need to plan care and support systems with both carers and cared for well before the curtailment of care, or death of the primary carer. A number of the 'Growing Older with Learning Disabilities' (GOLD) projects and the 'Older Family Carers Initiative' (OFCI) identified positive ways to help family carers plan for the future care of their relative (Foundation for People with Learning Disabilities 2002, 2003; Magrill 2005). Of particular note is recognising that what many older carers want is to continue caring for as long as possible; and the services that most help carers are respite care, support in an emergency, support groups and access to information. Further, the majority of older carers are prepared to engage in future planning for their relative, if the issue is dealt with sensitively and carefully by a known and trusted worker.

Intimate and personal care

Providing quality intimate and personal care to older service users with a learning disability is a complex challenge, which, to date, has received very limited attention. Research evidence suggests that minimal guidance is offered to care workers (Carnaby and Cambridge 2002). Where policies do exist, they tend to be very general, taking little account of differences between user groups, age, life stages, gender issues, or cultural or dependency needs. Carnaby and Cambridge (2002) recommend the development of both specific policy guidance and staff training and have developed a training 'resource pack' upon which service providers and workers can draw with the aim of developing 'best practice' (Cambridge and Carnaby 2000a). The pack contains sections on supporting older people with learning disabilities, incorporating a number of the issues that have been reviewed here such as taking account of declining physical and mental health and supporting users and family carers to continue living a full and independent life.

The little work that has been done in this area indicates that delivering appropriate intimate and personal care requires detailed understanding of an individual's needs and wishes, for example, preference for a particular soap (Cambridge and Carnaby 2000b; Carnaby and Cambridge 2002; Dodd, Turk and Christmas 2002). Knowledge of this nature depends to a large extent on effective communication between the care worker and user and familiarity with the user's views and character traits (Carnaby and Cambridge 2002). We have noted that the health needs of many service users with learning disabilities change and multiply when they become old. Staff who do not have a pre-existing or well-established link with the service user are likely to find it much more difficult to offer sensitive and individualised care. Trust and effective communication are key elements of good practice in this intimate arena and are particularly significant for service users who develop dementia. That residential care workers are unlikely to know a user before admission and that staff turnover is very high in both community and residential settings undermines the acquisition of personal knowledge, the development of intimacy and continuity of care.

Recent policy emphasis on raising the standards of service provision and staff may offer an opportunity to enhance practice. The National Minimum Standards for Care Homes for Older People state that 'arrangements for health and personal care must ensure that the service user's privacy and dignity are respected at all times' (Department of Health 2002 'Privacy and Dignity', Standard 10.1). Training initiatives such as the Learning Disability Awards Framework (LDAF), introduced by the Department of Health, also address issues relating to personal care and unlike care standards guidance, locate it within a 'good practice' framework. These awards emphasise the role of underpinning principles in enhancing all care practice: user empowerment, collaborative communication between staff and service users and the development of an inclusive model of care. They also confirm the importance of quality of life principles such as choice, rights and self-actualisation in training staff to work effectively (Alcoe, Carnaby and Duerdoth 2002).

User involvement and empowerment are significant dimensions of quality care. Much like their minimal involvement in care and treatment decisions, older people with learning disabilities are very unlikely to be involved in service development. Whilst in part this reflects communication difficulties, it is also a consequence of their disempowered and dependent status (Ansello and Coogle 2000). While there is some expectation that their views will be taken account of in the person centred planning process, issues of body care are often neglected. Frontline staff should be actively encouraged to facilitate users to voice their preferences in personal care matters and independent advocates should be used in situations where the user's capacity is compromised. Flexible methods of working and allocating sufficient time to personal care tasks are essential pre-requisites for the delivery of a service, which promotes user dignity, individuality and independence (Fitzgerald 1998a, 1998b).

There is considerable scope for developing collaborative, individualised and flexible approaches to personal care, drawing on experience from other fields and other countries. Work in the dementia field has already been noted, as has work from the USA specifically focusing on the needs of older people with learning disabilities. There is additional scope to take account of work with younger adults with learning disabilities, complex needs and challenging behaviour (Carnaby and Cambridge 2002).

A significant training agenda exists for health and social care staff – and agencies – if quality personal care is to be assured for the population under review. At the very least generic care staff require training about the needs of people with learning disabilities and staff working in services for the learning disabled need training about the ageing process and age-related ill health. In addition to a focus on personal and intimate care the training agenda needs to incorporate work on communication, managing loss and bereavement, and supporting users with complex and cumulative needs As agencies are dealing with an increasing number of people in this group, more staff will need training in the recognition, assessment and management of dementia, including intimate and personal care (Wilkinson and Janicki 2002).

Summary of intimate and personal care recommendations

- Personal care needs to change and multiply as the service user ages; dementia poses a particular challenge to the delivery of user-led care.

- Intimate and personal care needs should be reviewed as a part of the PCP process, taking full account of the views of the user.

- The delivery of effective care depends on detailed knowledge of the service user's wishes and preferences, effective communication, familiarity and trust.

- Responsibility for taking this forward rests with policy-makers, agencies providing care and those charged with implementing national care standards and training.

- Staff training for intimate and personal care issues should be based on quality of life principles including empowerment, choice, rights and self-actualisation.

- Staff should be encouraged to work flexibly and collaboratively with users in defining the parameters of intimate and personal care.

- Much can be learned from the dementia care field and from work with younger adults with learning disabilities with complex needs.

- Generic care staff require training about the needs of people with learning disabilities and staff working in services for the learning disabled need training about age-related ill health, including dementia.

CONCLUSION

While there is some recognition of the growing number of people with learning disabilities surviving into old age, little account is taken of the implications of this demographic trend for the development of appropriate care (Hatzidimitriadou and Milne 2005). The multiple and often complex nature of the physical and mental health needs of this population is a significant challenge for services. That they experience the double jeopardy of being old *and* learning disabled and are rarely coherently provided for by agencies compounds their disadvantage. The review of evidence offered in this chapter suggests that the provision of quality care requires a multi-agency proactive approach, which involves both strategic *and* individualised planning with service users and their carers before 'old age' is reached. The provision of intimate and personal care is identified as pivotal to the delivery of effective support. While training can go part way to addressing the current skill deficit, the twin agendas of resourcing services appropriately and developing models of care that can accommodate the voices and choices of older users, are equally important dimensions of developing safe, effective and individualised intimate and personal care for one of the most vulnerable groups in UK society.

NOTE

1   Controversially, in the learning disabilities field there is no consistent definition of 'old' and evidence is not gathered around similar age cohorts or in a similar method by various groups or agencies; therefore, we are obliged to accept the definitions employed by researchers and summarise evidence taking account of definitional and geographical variation.

REFERENCES

Alcoe, J., Carnaby, S., and Duerdoth, N. (2002) 'Training for competence: the new certificates in working with people who have learning disabilities.' *Tizard Learning Disability Review 7*, 2, 3–7.

Alzheimer's Society (2003) *Information Sheet – What is Dementia?* www.alzheimers.org.uk/Facts_about_dementia/PDF/400_WhatIsDementia.pdf (accessed 17 June 2005).

Ansello, E., and Coogle, C. (2000) 'Activating consumers and families.' In M. Janicki and E. Ansello (eds) *Community Supports for Aging Adults with Lifelong Disabilities.* Baltimore: Paul H. Brookes Publishing, pp. 137–152.

Aspray, T.J., Francis, R.M., Tyrer, S.P. and Quilliam, S.J. (1999) 'Patients with learning disability in the community.' *British Medical Journal 318*, 7182, 476–477.

Bailey, N.M. and Cooper, S.-A. (1997) 'The current provision of specialist health services to people with learning disabilities in England and Wales.' *Journal of Intellectual Disability Research 41*,1, 52–59.

Bigby, C. (1997) 'When parents relinquish care: informal support networks of older people with intellectual disability.' *Journal of Applied Research in Intellectual Disabilities 10*, 4, 333–344.

Biggs, S. (1993) *Understanding Ageing: Images, Attitudes and Professional Practice.* Buckingham: Open University Press.

Bland, R., Hutchinson, N., Oakes, P. and Yates, C. (2003) 'Double jeopardy? Needs and services for older people who have learning disabilities.' *Journal of Learning Disabilities 7*, 4, 323–344.

Bouras, N. (1999) 'Editorial – mental health and learning disabilities: planning and service developments.' *Tizard Learning Disability Review 4*, 2, 4–16.

Cambridge, P. and Carnaby, S. (2000a) *Making it Personal: Providing Intimate and Personal Care for People with Intellectual Disabilities.* Brighton: Pavilion Publishing.

Cambridge, P. and Carnaby, S. (2000b) 'A personal touch: managing the risks of abuse during intimate and personal care.' *Journal of Adult Protection 2*, 4, 4–16.

Carnaby, S. and Cambridge, P. (2002) 'Getting personal: an exploratory study of intimate and personal care provision for people with profound and multiple intellectual disabilities.' *Journal of Intellectual Disability Research 46*, 2, 120–132.

Cheston, R. and Bender, M. (1999) *Understanding Dementia: The Man with the Worried Eyes.* London: Jessica Kingsley Publishers.

Cooper, S.A. (1997a) 'Deficient health and social services for elderly people with learning disabilities.' *Journal of Intellectual Disability Research 41*, 331–338.

Cooper, S.A. (1997b) 'A population-based health survey of maladaptive behaviours associated with dementia in elderly people with learning disabilities.' *Journal of Intellectual Disability Research 41*, 6, 481–487.

Cooper, S.A. (1999) 'Psychiatric disorders in elderly people with developmental disabilities.' In N. Bouras (ed.) *Psychiatric and Behavioural Disorders in Developmental Disabilities and Mental Retardation.* Cambridge: Cambridge University Press, pp.212–225.

Dalton, A. J., and Janicki, M. (1999) Aging and Dementia. In M. Janicki and A. Dalton (eds) *Dementia, Aging and Intellectual Disabilities: A Handbook*, pp.5–31. Philadelphia: Brunner/Mazel.

Davidson, P.W., Houser, K.D., Cain, N.N., Sloane-Reeves, J., Quijano, L., Matons, L., Giesow, V. and Ladrigan, P.M. (1999) 'Characteristics of older adults with intellectual disabilities referred for crisis intervention.' *Journal of Intellectual Disability Research 43*, 1, 38–46.

Day, K. and Jancar, J. (1994) 'Mental and physical health and ageing in mental handicap: a review.' *Journal of Intellectual Disability Research 38*, 241–256.

Department of Health (1999) *Caring about Carers: A National Strategy for Carers.* London: Department of Health.

Department of Health (2001a) *Carers and Disabled Children Act – Carers and People with Parental Responsibility for Disabled Children: Policy Guidance.* London: Department of Health.

Department of Health (2001b) *Valuing People: A New Strategy for Learning Disability for the 21st Century* (No. Cm5086). London: The Stationery Office.

Department of Health (2002) *Care Homes for Older People: National Minimum Standards.* London: The Stationery Office.

Department of Health (2004a) *New Provision for Older People with Learning Disabilities.* London: Department of Health.

Department of Health (2004b) *Valuing People: Moving Forward Together – The Government's Annual Report on Learning Disability.* London: The Stationery Office.

Dodd, K., Turk, V. and Christmas, M. (2002) *Down's Syndrome and Dementia: Resource Pack for Carers and Staff.* Kidderminster: BILD Publications.

Driessen, G., DuMoulin, M., Haveman, M.J., and van Os, J. (1997) 'Persons with intellectual disability receiving psychiatric treatment.' *Journal of Intellectual Disability Research 41*, 512–518.

Duff, M., Hoghton, M. and Scheepers, M. (2000) 'More training is needed in health care of people with learning disabilities.' *British Medical Journal 321*, 7257, 385.

Evenhuis, H.M., Henderson, C., Beange, H., Lennox, N. and Chicoine, B. (2000) *Healthy Ageing – Adults with Intellectual Disabilities: Physical Health Issues.* Geneva: World Health Organization.

Fitzgerald, J. (1998a) 'It's never too late: empowerment for older people with learning difficulties.' In L. Ward (ed.) *Innovations in Advocacy and Empowerment*, pp.151–159. Chorley: Lisieux Hall Publications.

Fitzgerald, J. (1998b) *Time for Freedom? Services for Older People with Learning Difficulties.* London: Values into Action and Centre for Policy on Ageing.

Foundation for People with Learning Disabilities (2002) *Today and Tomorrow: The Report of the Growing Older with Learning Disabilities Programme.* London: The Mental Health Foundation.

Foundation for People with Learning Disabilities (2003) *Planning for Tomorrow: Report on the Findings of a Survey of Learning Disability Partnership Boards about Meeting the Needs of Older Family Carers.* London: The Mental Health Foundation.

Garner, J. and Evans, S. (2000) *Institutional Abuse of Older Adults* (No. CR84). London: Royal College of Psychiatrists.

Grant, G. (1997) 'Consulting to involve or consulting to empower?' In P. Ramcharan, G. Roberts, G. Grant and J. Borland (eds) *Empowerment in Everyday Life: Learning Disability.* London: Jessica Kingsley Publishers.

Grant, G. (2001) 'Older people with learning disabilities: health, community inclusion and family caregiving.' In M. Nolan, S. Davies and G. Grant (eds) *Working with Older People and Their Families: Key Issues in Policy and Practice.* Buckingham: Open University Press.

Gustafsson, C. (1997) 'The prevalence of people with intellectual disability admitted to general hospital psychiatric units: level of handicap, psychiatric diagnoses and care utilization.' *Journal of Intellectual Disability Research 41*, 6, 519–526.

Hassiotis, A., Barron, P. and O'Hara, J. (2000) 'Mental health services for people with learning disabilities.' *British Medical Journal 321*, 7257, 583–584.

Hatzidimitriadou, E. and Forrester-Jones, R. (2002) *The Needs of Older People with Learning Disabilities and Mental Health Difficulties in the Medway Area.* Canterbury: Tizard Centre, University of Kent.

Hatzidimitriadou, E. and Milne, A. (2005) 'Planning ahead: meeting the needs of older people with intellectual disabilities in the United Kingdom.' *Dementia: The International Journal of Social Research and Practice 4*, 3, 341–359.

Herr, S.S. and Weber, G. (1999) 'Aging and developmental disabilities: concepts and global perspectives.' In S.S. Herr and G. Webber (eds) *Aging, Rights, and Quality of Life: Prospects for Older People with Developmental Disabilities.* Baltimore: Paul H. Brookes Publishing Co., pp.1–18.

Hogg, J. (2000) *Improving Essential Health Care for People with Learning Disabilities: Strategies for Success.* Dundee: University of Dundee.

Hogg, J. and Lambe, L. (1998) 'Older people with learning disabilities: a review of the literature on residential services and family caregiving.' Dundee: White Top Research Unit, University of Dundee.

Hogg, J., Lucchino, R., Wang, K. and Janicki, M. (2001) 'Healthy ageing – adults with intellectual disabilities: ageing and social policy.' *Journal of Applied Research in Intellectual Disabilities 14*, 3, 229–255.

Holland, T. (2000) 'Ageing and learning disability.' *British Journal of Psychiatry 176*, 26-31.

Holland, T. (2001) *Ageing and its consequences for people with Down's syndrome.* www.intellectualdisability.info/lifestages/ds_ageing.htm (accessed 24 August, 2004)

Hughes, B. (1995) *Older People and Community Care: Critical Theory and Practice.* Buckingham: Open University Press.

Hutchinson, N.J. (1999) 'Association of Down's syndrome and Alzheimer's disease: review of the literature.' *Journal of Learning Disabilities for Nursing, Health and Social Care 3*, 4, 194–203.

Janicki, M. and Dalton, A.J. (1999) 'Dementia in developmental disabilities.' In N. Bouras (ed.) *Psychiatric and Behavioural Disorders in Developmental Disabilities and Mental Retardation.* Cambridge: Cambridge University Press, pp.121–153.

Janicki, M. and Dalton, A.J. (2000) 'Prevalence of dementia and impact on intellectual disability services.' *Mental Retardation 38*, 276–288.

Janicki, M., Heller, T., Seltzer, G. and Hogg, J. (1995) *Practice Guidelines for the Clinical Assessment and Care Management of Alzheimer and Other Dementias among Adults with Mental Retardation.* Washington: American Association on Mental Retardation.

Jenkins, R., Brooksbank, D. and Miller, E. (1994) 'Ageing in learning difficulties: The development of health care outcome indicators.' *Journal of Intellectual Disability Research 38*, 2, 257–264.

Kitwood, T. and Bredin, K. (1992) *Person to Person: A Guide to the Care of Those with Failing Mental Powers.* Loughton: Gale Centre Publications.

Learning Disability Task Force (2004) *Rights, Independence, Choice and Inclusion.* London: Learning Disability Task Force.

Magrill, D. (2005) *Supporting Older Families: Making a Real Difference.* London: Mental Health Foundation.

Magrill, D., Dagnan, D. and Fitzgerald, J. (1997) *Crisis Approaching – Sharing Caring Project.* Sheffield: Sheffield Mencap.

Marshall, M. (1996) *I Can't Place this Place at All: Working with People with Dementia and their Carers.* Birmingham: Venture.

McDonald, A. (2002) '"Not as young as we used to be": Supporting Older People with Learning Disabilities.' In S. Carnaby (ed.) *Learning Disability Today,* pp.225–235. Brighton: Pavilion.

Milne, A., Hatzidimitriadou, E., Chryssanthopoulou, C., and Owen, T. (2001) *Caring in Later Life: Reviewing the Role of Older Carers.* London: Help the Aged.

Moss, S., Lambe, L. and Hogg, J. (1998) *Ageing Matters: Pathways for Older People with a Learning Disability – Manager's Reader.* Kidderminster: BILD.

Robertson, J., Moss, S. and Turner, S. (1996) 'Policy, services and staff training for older people with intellectual disability in the UK.' *Journal of Applied Research in Intellectual Disabilities 9*, 2, 91–100.

Stalker, K., Duckett, P. and Downs, M. (1999) *Going with the Flow: Choice, Dementia and People with Learning Difficulties.* Brighton: Pavilion.

Thompson, D. (2002) 'Editorial – Growing older with learning disabilities.' *Journal of Learning Disabilities 6*, 2, 115–122.

Thompson, D. and Wright, S. (2001) *Misplaced and Forgotten? People with learning Disabilities in Residential Services for Older People.* London: The Mental Health Foundation.

Tinker, A. (1997) *Older People in Modern Society* (Fourth Edition). London: Longman.

Towell, D. (2002) *Partnership Boards and User Engagement: What do you Think of the Show So Far?* (No. Topic Paper 9). London: Institute for Applied Health and Social Policy, King's College.

Turk, V., Dodd, K. and Christmas, M. (2001) *Down's Syndrome and Dementia: Briefing for Commissioners.* London: The Mental Health Foundation.

Twigg, J. (2000) 'The medical–social boundary and the location of personal care.' In A.M. Warnes, L. Warren and M. Nolan (eds) *Care Services in Later Life: Transformations and Critiques.* London: Jessica Kingsley Publishers, pp.119–134.

Twigg, J. (2002) 'The body in social policy: mapping a territory.' *Journal of Social Policy 31,* 3, 421–439.

Victor, C.R. (1997) *Community Care and Older People.* Cheltenham: Stanley Thomas.

Walker, A. and Walker, C. (1996) 'Older people with learning disabilities leaving institutional care: a case of double jeopardy?' *Ageing and Society 16,* 125–150.

Walker, A. and Walker, C. (1998) 'Normalisation and 'normal' ageing: the social construction of dependency among older people with learning difficulties.' *Disability & Society 13,* 1, 125–142.

Ward, C. (1998) *Preparing for a Positive Future: Meeting the Age-related Needs of Older People with Learning Disabilities.* Chesterfield: ARC.

Wilkinson, H. and Janicki, M. (2002) 'The Edinburgh Principles.' *Journal of Intellectual Disability Research 46,* 3, 279–284.

Wilkinson, H., Kerr, D., Cunningham, C. and Rae, C. (2004) *Home for Good? Preparing to Support People with a Learning Disability in a Residential Setting when they develop Dementia.* London: Joseph Rowntree Foundation.

Zarb, G. and Oliver, M. (1993) *Ageing with a Disability.* London: University of Greenwich.

CHAPTER 12

Developing Best Practice in Intimate and Personal Care for People with Learning Disabilities

Steven Carnaby and Paul Cambridge

> Encounters, whether fleeting or longer term or intense, can bring to them an intention to co-ordinate with the other person or to ignore them – to treat them in effect as a cipher rather than as a whole human being. To co-ordinate successfully requires absolutely a commitment to recognise, respect and seek to understand the other's position but, equally, a commitment to respect and seek to understand one's own position. (Brechin 2000, p.160)

Brechin's observation about the nature of human interaction in many ways encapsulates the spirit of this book. Recognising and respecting the position of another person while equally striving to understand our own is particularly important when a power imbalance exists between us and other individuals or where the purpose of the interaction predicates an inherent potential for inequality (Brechin 2000). Supporting people with learning disabilities with intimate and personal care meets both criteria. There will invariably be an imbalance in power based on intellectual disability. This will be heightened by the nature of the dependency relationship existing between the two people, as well as the general construction of dependency in services for people with learning disabilities. The latter is part of systemic factors such as the total dependency of many people receiving intimate and personal care on others for literally sustaining their lives and physical being, lack of advocacy for people with profound and multiple learning disabilities and so on. The former is part of a myriad of contextual factors such as a limited capacity to communicate effectively on the part of both parties, the conduct of intimate and personal care in private spaces, and so on.

A key message from contributors in this volume is that working sensitively and appropriately with people when providing intimate and personal care (in Brechin's words, 'to co-ordinate successfully') requires a level of reflection, planning, discussion and collaboration generally not permitted in services for people with learning disabilities where resource pressures and lack of social spaces and opportunities for exchange tend to exclude such micro-level case coordination. It also necessitates that those providing direct support are enabled to acknowledge their own attitudes, feelings and reactions to the work. These themselves may sometimes stem from difficult experiences associated with sexuality of personal identities, often the result of exclusion or oppression on the basis of gender, race, sexuality or age. Such forces are present in all our lives and can become acutely critical in our work supporting people with learning disabilities in intimate and personal care. Only through establishing and evaluating these complex processes can we begin to develop confidence in constructing best practice and in so doing develop competence in providing intimate and personal care in person-centred ways.

In this concluding discussion we review the main themes emerging from our contributors. This provides not only a summary of learning points from the book but in drawing them together, we also aim to provide a framework for developing high quality intimate and personal care. These themes are discussed below as they relate to service users, direct support staff and wider organisation and support systems.

THE EXPERIENCE OF RECEIVING INTIMATE AND PERSONAL CARE

As shown in Figure 2.1 (p.26), depending on their skills and experience, the support required by people with learning disabilities in terms of personal hygiene and self-care can be described as lying on a continuum.

The input from the worker can therefore move from 'support' – perhaps prompting or suggesting in the case of people with mild learning disabilities – through to the provision of 'care', where individuals with profound and multiple learning disabilities require total assistance with the basic functions of daily living such as eating and drinking and the maintenance of hygiene. As recipients of this 'support' or 'care', people with learning disabilities are likely to interpret and assimilate overt and subliminal messages about their own bodies, who has access to them, what is done to them and consequently the roles played by other people in their lives. Moreover, in moving along this continuum the perceptions and feelings of staff and carers, as our research indicated (see Chapter 2), change from relatively positive associations to relatively negative ones, from liking help with social functioning to disliking help with bodily functions. Here indeed lies the challenge for developing competence and practice in intimate and personal care.

This experience is indeed an extraordinary one. The majority of the non-disabled population require intimate support as young children, and as skills and confidence develop, the need for assistance from others tends to diminish. Exceptions may be help during periods of illness or temporary incapacity, but even here formal and informal rules apply. For example, you are likely to be in special places such as a doctor's surgery or a hospital or the people doing these things to you are likely to be wearing uniforms that mark them out as different and give them social 'permission' to carry out such tasks. Generally however, the assistance that is provided is usually from parent(s) or family members. Children with learning disabilities are likely to then find themselves needing support of an intimate nature beyond the point in their lives at which their non-disabled peers are beginning to meet their own personal care needs independently (see Chapter 10). While this may be symptomatic of a developmental delay for people with mild learning disabilities, people with profound and multiple learning disabilities will require this level of support for the rest of their lives (see Chapter 9). Some individuals may even require more intrusive support – for example, as the failure to thrive necessitates the use of PEG feeding.

These experiences are likely to have significant impact on the development of self. While those providing support may have had experience of being supported themselves with intimate care while in hospital, it is unlikely that they will have experienced this on a long-term basis. In most circumstances, people with learning disabilities requiring intimate support will have done so from birth and will continue to do so. To say that empathising effectively with this life perspective is a great challenge is surely an understatement, and it is no surprise when we struggle in this endeavour. However, by confronting the more hidden or under-reported aspects of the intimate care arena we can acknowledge the potential risks involved such as sexual abuse (see Chapter 4). Indeed, on closer analysis the vulnerability of individuals receiving intimate care is overwhelming, as such vulnerability is increased in private and unregulated care settings (Lee-Treweek 1994), such as those utilised to provide intimate and personal care (see Chapter 6). Sheila Hollins (1994) has identified the points in the caring relationship where communication breaks down and the risk of abuse that results and the many inquiries into the abuse of people with learning disabilities (e.g. Cambridge 1999) identify caring interaction as the trigger or catalyst for abuse. This emphasises the importance of encouraging participation in the process of providing intimate and personal care and making a commitment to developing the communicating partnership between individual and supporter as one way of addressing the significant power imbalance (see Chapters 8, 9, 10 and 11).

DEVELOPING PERSON-CENTRED INTIMATE SUPPORT

High quality intimate and personal care is more likely to be delivered when the development of strategies begins with attempts at understanding the individual's perspective and acknowledging specific issues relating to their experience. In practical terms, this means planning support that is culturally sensitive (see Chapter 3) and cognisant of issues relating to sexuality, gender and adult protection (see Chapter 4), as well as maintaining the individual's physical health. Above all it demands the capacity to interact with the individual in ways that involve and empower them in the care interaction, helping develop a level of exchange and reciprocity generally absent in such situations, including ones that people without disabilities experience, such as meetings with consultants in hospital referrals.

Combining all of these strands is likely to be a complex task. People with learning disabilities are more likely to experience both a higher level of health problems than the general population, and be more vulnerable to health inequalities in terms of access to appropriate services (see Chapter 5). However, concentrating solely on the physical health aspects of intimate and personal care without due attention being paid to the social context within which physical health tasks are carried out risks institutionalised and depersonalised practice, which treats people as objects to be 'done to'. A participant in one of our research studies (Carnaby and Cambridge 2002) illustrated this, remarking with regret that: 'It's like working in a morgue – you get used to bodies even though you think that you wouldn't.'

While in theory person centred planning might be proposed by many as the obvious solution here (see *Valuing People* 2001), we argue that combining health and social care elements of intimate and personal care requires a commitment to moving beyond a planning system towards taking what Mansell and Bea-dle-Brown (2004, p.6) describe as 'person-centred action'. Citing Wenger and Snyder (2000) they suggest that this requires:

> a shift from a rationalist policy implementation framework, in which im-plementing is treated as a largely mechanical process, to focus on…com-munities of practice – 'groups of people informally bound together by shared expertise and a passion for a joint enterprise'. The development of such communities, with evidence of real effects in the lives of the people they serve, would be a higher priority than extent or coverage of plans.

In the context of intimate and personal care provision, 'communities' might comprise statutory providers, voluntary groups interested in disability, parents and carers, local cultural and religious leaders, advocates and self-advocates as well as professionals linked to community learning disability teams. There are also wider communities of interest and experience we can consult in achieving a more person-centred approach and in promoting person-centred action. We should seek the views of self-advocates with learning disabilities, although again acknowledging that many may not have experienced intimate and personal care directly. We should consult people with physical disabilities who rely on others for the support of their intimate and personal care and use their experiences and interpretations to guide and inform the support of intimate and personal care for people with learning disabilities who are unable to relate their experiences and preferences. People with physical disabilities may be managing their own support and be very well placed to articulate how good quality intimate and personal care might be constructed in the absence of such dialogues with people with learning disabilities themselves.

In essence, however, person-centred approaches need commitment – not just to skill teaching and the provision of opportunities for increasing independence where this is possible (see Chapter 5), but also to valuing planned *dependence* in those who are likely to require total assistance in many areas for the rest of their lives (see Chapter 9). Person-centred approaches also need commitment to the development and support of staff through open and safe debate, not shying away from the thorny and challenging issues that intimate and personal care often presents for people who receive and provide such support. Figure 12.1 provides a framework for developing such a discussion. It can help frame a review of the approaches and techniques we adopt in providing intimate and personal care, relating these to the objectives that should underpin them and the outcomes they are seeking to achieve. But it is only an aid. Most importantly we need individual and team cultures that give us permission to challenge the boundaries we have imposed by the transfer of social roles and caring into learning disability and the constraints to interaction and empathy imposed by the professional distance we have constructed between those who provide support and care and those who receive it.

ISSUES FOR ORGANISATIONS

'For collaboration to work people have to rid themselves of professional superiority and really work together, working jointly and effectively in the person's best interests' (Hutchinson 1998, p.14). This proposition for successful working across agency and professional boundaries as well as those between formal and informal care, echoes the proposals for effective trans-disciplinary working articulated in Chapter 6. Intimate and personal care is a productive area of practice for exploring the extent to which health and social care models of support for people with learning disabilities are successfully and meaningfully integrated to

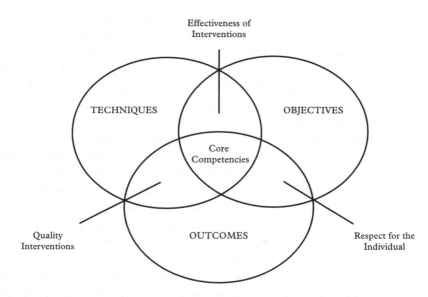

Figure 12.1 Planning intimate and personal care

create a person-centred approach. Sometimes this can be achieved through multi-disciplinary models of support, at others through the proactive co-ordination of support. Whatever solutions are adopted, however, having more person-centred teams and person-centred organisations can help achieve integrated person-centred interventions and actions (Medora and Ledger 2005; Sanderson 2003).

A repeated theme from many of the contributors is the role played by detailed policies and individualised guidelines, in as much as they should set out what needs to happen and when, and perhaps more importantly, *how* support should be offered (see Chapters 6, 8, 9, 10 and 11). Policies need to address issues relating to sexuality, gender and vulnerability (see Chapter 6) as well as being culturally sensitive (see Chapter 3), while the ways in which these considerations impact upon individual service users can be outlined in care plans and guidelines (see Chapter 6). Organisations therefore need to ensure that policies are helpful for staff trying to draw up such guidelines, and provide templates and support where needed. In addition, delivering generic training in intimate and personal care can explore both the emotional and practical 'themes' as outlined in this book, but will need to be accompanied by specific sessions where staff teams are encouraged to reflect on strategies for individual service users and how such strategies can be effectively evaluated (Cambridge and Carnaby 2000).

SUMMARY OF DEVELOPING BEST PRACTICE IN THE PROVISION OF INTIMATE AND PERSONAL CARE FOR PEOPLE WITH LEARNING DISABILITIES

Support staff need to:

- reflect regularly on their practice and participate in appropriate conversations with colleagues about how the team is providing intimate and personal care

- consult colleagues from the local community team along with parents, relatives and carers to develop a sensitive, person-centred approach.

Service managers need to:

- develop a policy for the provision of intimate and personal care and a range of templates for the drafting of individual guidelines (see Appendix 3)

- create professional space for staff to reflect on the ways in which they provide intimate and personal care and how it impacts upon them

- offer generic training about intimate and personal care, with a curriculum covering at least the following issues: adult protection, sex and sexuality, maintenance of personal hygiene including cross-infection, empathic handling, developing communication

- facilitate the formation of trans-disciplinary 'working groups' for the development of support strategies for meeting the specific intimate and personal care needs of an individual.

Service commissioners need to:

- ensure that commissioned providers are able to produce evidence of using a person-centred approach to intimate and personal care (e.g. through the production of example guidelines implemented via a clear policy)

- require service managers to limit their use of agency staff, suggesting that bank staff are used to cover leave and sickness wherever necessary and that where agency staff are needed, that they are from agencies that are aware of the service's ethos and value base around the delivery of intimate and personal care.

REFERENCES

Brechin, A. (2000) 'The challenge of caring relationships.' In A. Brechin, H. Brown and M.A. Eby (eds) *Critical Practice in Health and Social Care.* London: Sage/Open University.

Brechin, A., Brown, H. and Eby, M.A. (2000) *Critical Practice in Health and Social Care.* London: Sage/Open University.

Cambridge, P. (1999) 'The first hit: a case study of the physical abuse of people with learning disabilities and challenging behaviours in a residential service.' *Disability & Society 12*, 3, 427–453.

Cambridge, P. and Carnaby, S. (2000) *Making it Personal.* Brighton: Pavilion.

Carnaby, S. and Cambridge, P. (2002) 'Getting personal: a case study of intimate and personal care practice in services for people with profound and multiple learning disabilities.' *Journal of Intellectual Disability Research 46*, 2, 120–132.

Hollins, S. (1994) 'Relationships between perpetrators and victims of physical and sexual abuse.' In J. Harris and A. Craft (eds) *People with Learning Disabilities at Risk of Physical or Sexual Abuse.* Seminar Papers No. 4, Kidderminster: BILD.

Hutchinson, C. (1998) 'Positive health: a collective responsibility.' In P. Lacey and C. Ouvray (eds) *People with Profound and Multiple Learning Disabilities: A Collaborative Approach to Meeting Complex Needs.* London: David Fulton.

Lee-Treweek, G. (1994) 'Bedroom abuse: the hidden work in a nursing home.' *Generations Review 4*, 1, 2–4.

Mansell, J. and Beadle-Brown (2004) 'Person centred planning or person-centred action? Policy and practice in intellectual disability services.' *Journal of Applied Research in Intellectual Disabilities 17*, 1–10.

Medora, H. and Ledger, S. (2005) 'Implementing and reviewing PCP: links with care management, clinical support and commissioning.' In P. Cambridge and S. Carnaby (eds) *Person Centred Planning and Care Management for People with Learning Disabilities.* London: Jessica Kingsley Publishers.

Sanderson, H. (2003) 'Implementing person centred planning by developing person-centred teams.' *Journal of Integrated Care 11*, 3, 18–25.

Wenger, E.C. and Snyder, W. M. (2000) 'Communities of practice: the organisational frontier.' *Harvard Business Review 78*, 1, 139–145.

Staff Structured Interview – Supporting Adults with Learning Disabilities and/or Physical Disabilities with Personal and Intimate Care

This questionnaire is designed to find out about staff perceptions of providing intimate and personal care to adults with learning disabilities and adults with physical disabilities who have high support needs. The information will be used to identify where staff feel they need support in this difficult area of their work. It will also help to establish ways in which training could be offered to improve the quality of the care provided to service users.

A. INTRODUCTION

1. Name and sex.

2. What tasks would you include as personal care?

3. Does your agency have policies or guidelines on personal/intimate care?

4. If yes, what do these guidelines state/recommend?

5. What do you think about these guidelines?

6. What happens in practice and why?

B. EXPERIENCE WITH PERSONAL CARE

1. Work experience/background with people with learning disabilities.

2. Experience of providing personal/intimate care (task and to whom – refer to individual sheets at end of interview).

3. Current responsibilities for providing personal/intimate care (task and to whom).

C. TRAINING

1. Any formal training for working with people with learning disabilities (social work/NVQ/nursing).

2. Any in-house training in this service (course/coverage).

3. Any training related to personal/intimate care.

D. FEELINGS

1. What are your feelings (likes/dislikes) about providing personal/ intimate care?

2. How do personal/intimate care tasks affect your job satisfaction?

3. To what extent do you like or dislike providing personal/intimate care tasks?

4. How would you rate different intimate care tasks?
    Please circle the rating that best applies for you:
    1= like a lot, 2 = like a bit, 3 = don't mind, 4 = dislike a bit, 5 = dislike a lot

Dressing and undressing (underwear)	1	2	3	4	5
Helping someone use the toilet	1	2	3	4	5
Changing continence pads (faeces)	1	2	3	4	5
Changing continence pads (urine)	1	2	3	4	5
Bathing/showering	1	2	3	4	5
Washing intimate parts of body	1	2	3	4	5
Changing sanitary towels or tampons	1	2	3	4	5
Enemas	1	2	3	4	5
Manual evacuation	1	2	3	4	5
Pessaries	1	2	3	4	5

5. How would you rate different personal care tasks?
    Please circle the rating that best applies for you:
    1= like a lot, 2 = like a bit, 3 = don't mind, 4 = dislike a bit, 5 = dislike a lot

Shaving	1	2	3	4	5
Skin care/applying external medication	1	2	3	4	5
Feeding	1	2	3	4	5
Hair care	1	2	3	4	5
Brushing teeth	1	2	3	4	5

Applying deodorant	1 2 3 4 5
Dressing and undressing (clothing)	1 2 3 4 5
Washing non-intimate body parts	1 2 3 4 5
Prompting to go to the toilet	1 2 3 4 5

6. How would you rate different tasks associated with clearing up body fluids? Please circle the rating that best applies for you:

   1= like a lot, 2 = like a bit, 3 = don't mind, 4 = dislike a bit, 5 = dislike a lot

Changing soiled laundry	1 2 3 4 5
Cleaning up vomit	1 2 3 4 5
Cleaning up faeces	1 2 3 4 5
Cleaning up urine	1 2 3 4 5
Cleaning up blood	1 2 3 4 5

E. THE VIEWS OF OTHERS

1. What do your family and friends think about you providing intimate care for others?

2. What intimate care tasks have you undertaken for your relatives or children?

3. How do you think society views/values intimate care work?

4. What do your work colleagues think about personal care?

F. TRAINING AND SUPPORT NEEDS

1. How well do you think you perform intimate care tasks for the people you support?

2. What help, resources or support would you like?

3. What training in what areas do you feel you would benefit from?

4. What personal qualities and skills do you think someone needs to provide quality personal care?

Staff Questionnaire – Supporting Children with Learning Disabilities and/or Physical Disabilities with Personal and Intimate Care

This questionnaire is designed to find out about staff perceptions of providing intimate and personal care to children with learning disabilities and children with physical disabilities who have high support needs. The information will be used to identify where staff feel they need support in this difficult area of their work. It will also help to establish ways in which training could be offered to improve the quality of the care provided to service users.

Please answer each question as fully as you can. You need not give your name, and all responses will be treated confidentially.

Gender M/F (please circle).

Your work setting.

Please describe the needs of the children you support.

A. INTRODUCTION

1. In your work, which tasks would you describe as intimate or personal care?

2. Does the organisation employing you have policies or guidelines on providing personal/intimate care?

3. If yes, what do these guidelines state/recommend?

© Steven Carnaby/Paul Cambridge, Tizard Centre, University of Kent 2006

4. What do you think about the guidelines? (e.g. are they adequate...are they clear enough? How could they be improved?)

5. What happens in practice and why?

B. YOUR EXPERIENCE IN PROVIDING PERSONAL AND INTIMATE CARE

1. Please describe your work experience/background.

2. Please describe the nature of personal and intimate care that you have provided for children with learning disabilities or children with physical disabilities.

3. What are your current responsibilities in providing personal and intimate care for children with learning disabilities or children with physical disabilities?

C. YOUR TRAINING BACKGROUND

1. Have you had any formal training in working with children with learning disabilities or children with physical disabilities (e.g. social work qualification/NVQ/nursing qualification)?

2. Please describe any in-house training that you have received during your time in this service (i.e. the course topic and its coverage).

3. Have you received any training *specifically* related to personal/intimate care? If yes, please describe the nature of the training.

D. YOUR FEELINGS ABOUT PROVIDING PERSONAL INTIMATE CARE TO CHILDREN

1. What are your feelings (likes/dislikes) about providing personal/intimate care to children? Please be as honest as you can.

2. How do personal/intimate care tasks affect your job satisfaction? (e.g. do you find such work rewarding …would you rather not be required to provide personal care?… etc.)

3. To what extent do you get satisfaction from providing personal/intimate care?

4. Please rate the following intimate care tasks in terms of the reward you gain from providing support in this way.

    Please circle the rating that best applies for you:

    1 = great satisfaction, 2 = some satisfaction, 3 = no clear feelings either way, 4 = difficult to get any satisfaction, 5 = no satisfaction at all

Helping a child to dress or undress (underwear)	1	2	3	4	5
Helping a child to use the toilet	1	2	3	4	5
Changing continence pads soiled with faeces	1	2	3	4	5
Changing wet continence pads	1	2	3	4	5
Supporting a child to have a bath or shower	1	2	3	4	5
Washing intimate parts of the child's body	1	2	3	4	5

Changing sanitary towels or tampons	1 2 3 4 5
Administering enemas	1 2 3 4 5

5. Please rate the following intimate care tasks in terms of the reward you gain from providing support in this way.

Please circle the rating that best applies for you:

1 = great satisfaction, 2 = some satisfaction, 3 = no clear feelings either way, 4 = difficult to get any satisfaction, 5 = no satisfaction at all

Providing skin care/applying external medication	1 2 3 4 5
Providing total support with eating	1 2 3 4 5
Providing hair care	1 2 3 4 5
Helping a child to brush their teeth	1 2 3 4 5
Supporting the child to dress or undress (outer clothing)	1 2 3 4 5
Washing a child's non-intimate body parts (e.g. hands or face)	1 2 3 4 5
Prompting a child to go to the toilet	1 2 3 4 5

6. How would you rate different tasks associated with clearing up body fluids?

Please circle the rating that best applies for you:

1= like a lot, 2 = like a bit, 3 = don't mind, 4 = dislike a bit, 5 = dislike a lot

Changing soiled laundry	1 2 3 4 5
Cleaning up vomit	1 2 3 4 5
Cleaning up faeces	1 2 3 4 5
Cleaning up urine	1 2 3 4 5
Cleaning up blood	1 2 3 4 5

E. THE VIEWS OF OTHERS

1. What do your family and friends think about you providing intimate care for children?

2. What intimate care tasks have you undertaken for your relatives or children?

3. How do you think society views/values intimate care work?

4. What do your work colleagues think about intimate and personal care?

F. YOUR TRAINING AND SUPPORT NEEDS AS A PROVIDER OF INTIMATE AND PERSONAL CARE

1. How well do you think you perform intimate care tasks for the children you support?

2. What help, resources or support would you need to help improve the ways in which you provide intimate and personal care?

3. Describe any training you feel would be of benefit – what topics would it cover, how would the training be delivered (e.g. lectures/on-the-job feedback/workshops/discussion) and who is best placed to deliver such training?

4. What personal qualities and skills do you think someone needs to provide quality personal and intimate care to children with learning disabilities or children with physical disabilities?

Thank you for completing this questionnaire.

Individual Client Record for Intimate and Personal Care

Client's name:

Worker's name:

What are this person's intimate and personal care needs? (please list)

What do you do in practice to support this person when meeting each of these needs? (in detail)

How do you rate these different tasks? (please refer to ratings on main interview schedule)

How do you/did you decide the ways in which you give support? (prompt)
1. General and individual guidelines.

2. Relatives' views/advice.

3. Input from other services/professionals.

4. Informal views of colleagues.

How do you involve/communicate with the service user when undertaking personal care?

Does this person have any unmet intimate and/or personal care needs? If so, how could these needs be met?

Sandwich-Making Activity

Long-term goal

For J to be able to prepare a sandwich using sliced meat, cheese or a spread when he so desires.

Reasons for activity

J often wakes in the night and is hungry. In the past he has sought to make snacks but in doing so he is placing himself, his co-tenant and any sleep-in staff at risk from fire and/or explosion. Due to the risks involved in his using the cooker unsupervised whilst people are asleep, it is felt that it is more appropriate to teach him how to make a snack using alternative means. The means considered appropriate are that he be able to make himself a sandwich and that he be able to use the microwave oven. This teaching plan relates to his being able to make a sandwich.

Present skills

J has good fine motor skills and is able to cut unsliced bread safely. However, he does not cut it to an appropriate or uniform thickness. To avoid the difficulties inherent with slicing bread, we will for the time being use sliced bread, which is stored in the bread bin.

J is able to spread bread with butter/margarine and uses an appropriate amount of such spread.

J is able to express a choice for the food he desires and would be able to select appropriate fillings for a sandwich from a choice of fillings stored in the refrigerator.

J is able to attend to his personal hygiene, but frequently neglects to wash his hands having used the toilet and prior to preparing food. This presents a hygiene problem in so far as his failure to wash his hands may result in his having food poisoning.

J will make an attempt at clearing debris from work surfaces after he has made a snack, but requires prompting to do so.

J will make an attempt to wash up utensils after he has used them, but only if prompted.

Reinforcers

J enjoys food of his choice and the sandwich will act as a natural reinforcer in his making the sandwiches. He will require social praise in order to reinforce his cleaning up after himself. As he is unlikely to wash up and clear away after himself after he has had the sandwich, it is important that he undertakes the activity as set out below in order that eating the sandwich acts as a reinforcer for the whole task. Social reinforcers – for example, praise – may also need to be used.

Place of sessions

In the kitchen at home.

Time of activity

Once in the evening at supper time (approximately 20.30).

Materials and preparation

Ask J 'Would you like a sandwich?'

There will need to be bread, butter and a selection of sandwich fillings in the house prior to J undertaking this activity. It is therefore the responsibility of staff to ascertain that there are these items prior to asking J if he would like a sandwich.

The work surface should be cleared either by staff or by J or his co-tenant (with appropriate support) prior to John being asked to undertake the activity.

Baseline assessment: sandwich-making

Week commencing _____

NB: This is a baseline recording that should be completed for one week. The stages will then be reviewed and modified accordingly. Staff should initial when they have supported J in completing the task. If the task is not completed, for example, because J doesn't want anything to eat, please note this.

Sandwich-making activity progress report

Stage completed without prompt = /; Stage completed with verbal prompt = vp; Stage completed with gestural prompt = gp; Stage completed with physical prompt = pp; Stage not achieved = x

Stage	Mon	Tue	Wed	Thur	Fri	Sat	Sun
Handwashing:							
Runs a mixture of hot and cold water into the bowl							
Immerses his hands ensuring they are wet							
Applies soap from the dispenser located on the windowsill to his palms							
Rubs the soap into his hands, both front and rear and between his fingers							
Immerses his hands in the bowl and rinses the soap from them							
Empties the water from the bowl							
Dries his hands with the hand towel located at the side of the work unit							
Sandwich preparation:							
Gets a chopping board from the cupboard and places it on the work surface							
Collects the items he needs to undertake the task, namely, bread, butter, filling, a knife and a side plate							
Takes 2 or 4 slices of bread from the packet							
Spreads butter/margarine onto one side of each slice of bread							
Applies a filling to the sandwich, e.g. slices of meat or cheese, or spreads sandwich spread etc. onto the buttered side of one or two slices of bread (depending on the number of slices initially chosen)							

Sandwich-making activity progress report *continued*

Stage	Mon	Tue	Wed	Thur	Fri	Sat	Sun
Places the buttered bread without filling on top of the bread with the filling, thus creating a sandwich							
Uses the knife to cut the sandwich in two							
Places the sandwich on a side plate, and sets it aside until he has cleaned up							
Cleaning up:							
Puts items he has finished with away, e.g. bread, spreads, etc.							
Places all the utensils he has used in the bowl							
Puts one squirt of washing up liquid in the bowl and then runs water into the bowl at an appropriate temperature until the items are covered with soapy water							
Washes the utensils and places them on the draining board							
Wrings out the dishcloth and uses it to wipe the work surface on which he prepared his sandwich							
Takes his sandwich to the table or chair and eats his sandwich							
Takes his plate to the sink area and washes the plate prior to placing it on the draining board							
Rinses the cloth in the bowl of soapy water, wrings it out and places it at the side of the sink prior to emptying the water from the bowl							
Takes a tea towel from the side of the unit and dries the utensils, prior to putting them away							

Staff signature

Tooth Cleaning Teaching Programme
for_____

Notes

This programme is aimed at enabling _____ to achieve greater in-dependence in personal hygiene and improve appearance and self-esteem.

The programme is to commence on: _____

The programme is to be evaluated on: _____

It should be undertaken at appropriate times, that is, after breakfast, lunch and prior to their retiring for the night.

The programme should commence with the client being given the instruction 'X, clean your teeth'.

Recording achievement

Stage completed without prompt = /; Stage completed with verbal prompt = vp; Stage completed with gestural prompt = gp; Stage completed with physical prompt = pp; Stage not achieved = x

Tooth cleaning programme progress report

Date	Day 1			Day 2			Day 3			Day 4			Day 5		
Stages of tooth cleaning	a.m.	Lunch	p.m.	a.m.	Lunch	p.m.	a.m.	Lunch	p.m.	a.m.	Lunch	p.m.	a.m.	Lunch	p.m.
Goes to bathroom															
Collects flannel, toothbrush, paste and tumbler, if not situated next to the basin															
Stands by basin															
Turns cold tap on															
Wets toothbrush															
Turns tap off															
Undoes paste															
Squeezes pea-sized amount of paste onto brush															
Puts paste down															
Puts toothbrush in mouth															

Tooth cleaning programme progress report *continued*

Stages of tooth cleaning	Day 1 a.m.	Day 1 Lunch	Day 1 p.m.	Day 2 a.m.	Day 2 Lunch	Day 2 p.m.	Day 3 a.m.	Day 3 Lunch	Day 3 p.m.	Day 4 a.m.	Day 4 Lunch	Day 4 p.m.	Day 5 a.m.	Day 5 Lunch	Day 5 p.m.
Turns toothbrush on															
Cleans tops of lower teeth on left side of mouth with a backwards and forwards motion															
Cleans tops of lower teeth on right side of mouth with a backwards and forwards motion															
Cleans tops of upper teeth on left side of mouth with a backwards and forwards motion															
Cleans tops of upper teeth on right side of mouth with a backwards and forwards motion															
Cleans inside of lower teeth on left side of mouth with an up and down (flicking) motion															
Cleans inside of lower teeth on right side of mouth with an up and down (flicking) motion															
Cleans inside of upper teeth on left side of mouth with an up and down (flicking) motion															

Tooth cleaning programme progress report *continued*

Stages of tooth cleaning	Day 1			Day 2			Day 3			Day 4			Day 5		
	a.m.	Lunch	p.m.	a.m.	Lunch	p.m.	a.m.	Lunch	p.m.	a.m.	Lunch	p.m.	a.m.	Lunch	p.m.
Cleans inside of upper teeth on right side of mouth with an up and down (flicking) motion															
Puts teeth together															
Cleans outside of teeth, top and bottom on left side of mouth with an up and down motion															
Cleans outside of teeth, top and bottom on right side of mouth with an up and down motion															
Cleans outside of front teeth with an up and down motion															
Opens mouth															
Cleans inside of front upper teeth with a backwards and forwards motion															

Tooth cleaning programme progress report *continued*

Stages of tooth cleaning	Day 1 a.m.	Day 1 Lunch	Day 1 p.m.	Day 2 a.m.	Day 2 Lunch	Day 2 p.m.	Day 3 a.m.	Day 3 Lunch	Day 3 p.m.	Day 4 a.m.	Day 4 Lunch	Day 4 p.m.	Day 5 a.m.	Day 5 Lunch	Day 5 p.m.
Cleans inside of front lower teeth with a backwards and forwards motion															
Turns toothbrush off															
Turns tap on															
Rinses brush under tap															
Puts brush on charger															
Fills tumbler with water															
Turns tap off															
Rinses mouth with water from beaker															
Turns tap on															
Rinses face (with or without flannel)															

Tooth cleaning programme progress report *continued*

Stages of tooth cleaning	Day 1			Day 2			Day 3			Day 4			Day 5		
	a.m.	Lunch	p.m.	a.m.	Lunch	p.m.	a.m.	Lunch	p.m.	a.m.	Lunch	p.m.	a.m.	Lunch	p.m.
Turns tap off															
Dries face															
Returns brush, paste, beaker, flannel etc. to their normal resting place															

The Contributors

Paul Cambridge is a Senior Lecturer at the Tizard Centre at the University of Kent, teaching an MA course in the Management of Community Care and a BA course in Health and Social Care Practice. He also undertakes development work with services and individuals using services. His research has included a Department of Health funded study on the long-term outcomes and costs of care in the community for people with learning disabilities and mental health problems, care management and micro-organisation, sexuality and HIV, intimate and personal care, gender and caring roles and cross-national work on learning disability in Europe. He has published widely on these subjects in the academic and professional literature and has also developed a wide range of educational and staff training resources in learning disability. Paul also co-edits the *Tizard Learning Disability Review*.

Steven Carnaby is a clinical psychologist with Westminster Learning Disability Partnership and Honorary Lecturer in Learning Disability at the Tizard Centre, University of Kent. Steven's background is in the direct support of people with learning disabilities, working in both residential and day services. His main clinical interests are work with people with severe and profound disabilities, and his current research interests include intimate and personal care for people with complex needs, transition for young people leaving special school and the use of Intensive Interaction in supporting people with profound disabilities. He is Editor of *Clinical Psychology and People with Learning Disabilities* (published by the BPS Faculty for Learning Disabilities), Joint Editor of *Tizard Learning Disability Review*, and principal author of the *Learning Disability Awards Framework* materials developed by the Foundation for People with Learning Disabilities, the Tizard Centre and Pavilion Publishing.

Eleni Hatzidimitriadou is Lecturer in Community Psychology at the European Centre for the Study of Migration and Social Care, School of Social Policy, Sociology and Social Research, University of Kent. Her main research interests are self-help/mutual aid for disadvantaged groups, community support in old age, and alternative mental health service models for migrant populations. Her recent work is focused on settlement experiences of older refugees, transitory roles of older carers, and community resilience of migrants. Prior to her university post, she worked as a cognitive-behaviour therapist and mental health researcher in Greece and England.

Neil James is Senior Lecturer at the Unit for Development in Intellectual Disability, School of Care Sciences, University of Glamorgan, and he undertakes teaching on pre- and post-registration nursing courses. His main areas of interest and teaching are positive behavioural management, epilepsy, mental health needs of people with a learning disability, staff support, medication and side effects, experimental research and autism.

Angela Mallett has worked with children and young people with severe and profound and multiple learning difficulties for the past 26 years and at present is Deputy Head Teacher of the Shepherd School in Nottingham. Angela has vast experience of working with pupils with PMLD and for many years has provided training on relevant curricula such as sex and relationship education. In addition to teaching Angela uses dynamic psychotherapy and she has worked as an OFSTED inspector for special schools.

Michelle McCarthy is Senior Lecturer in Learning Disability at the Tizard Centre, University of Kent. She has a social work background and has worked with people with learning disabilities in a variety of residential and field settings. Before taking up her current post, she was team leader of a specialist sex education team, providing a service to people with learning disabilities and staff. She has an interest in all matters relating to the sexuality of people with learning disabilities, but has a particular interest in working with women with learning disabilities on issues of sexual abuse, sexual and reproductive health. She has previously authored several journal articles on these subjects, and authored the book *Sexuality and Women with Learning Disabilities*, also published by Jessica Kingsley Publishers.

Alisoun Milne is Senior Lecturer in Social Gerontology at the Tizard Centre, the School of Social Policy, Sociology and Social Research, University of Kent. Her key research interests are older people with mental health problems, older carers (particularly dementia carers), and preventive services. Recent work has focused on GP diagnosis of dementia, spouse carers, carers of people in care homes, and Black and Asian dementia caregivers. Prior to working at the Tizard Centre she was a Research Fellow at the Personal Social Services Research Unit; she has a background in social work.

Robina Shah is a psychologist, research fellow and trainer. She has been working with children, young people and families for 15 years. During this time she has written many publications, the most notable being *The Silent Minority* and *Sharing the News*, which describe the experiences of parents finding out about their child's disability. Robina was appointed to the Valuing People Support Team at the Department of Health in 2002 as their specialist adviser on cultural diversity and learning disabilities. She is also involved in various public services, and is a magistrate and Chairman of Stockport Acute NHS Foundation Trust.

Paul Wheeler first started working with men and women with learning disabilities in 1984. He has worked in a variety of settings, including health service, private and voluntary sector. He is a registered nurse for people with learning disabilities, and has a background in law and socio-legal studies. Paul is currently employed as a lecturer at the Unit for Development in Intellectual Disability, School of Care Sciences, University of Glamorgan. Paul's current research interests are in relation to legal aspects of care provision, social policy, sexuality and men and women with learning disabilities, forensic services and person centred planning.

Subject Index

Author Index